IN OUR OWN IMAGE

THE STORY OF
AUSTRALIAN ART

THIRD EDITION

For my family, and particularly JoAnne who encouraged my artistic pursuits

IN OUR OWN IMAGE

THE STORY OF AUSTRALIAN ART

THIRD EDITION

DONALD WILLIAMS

BEd (Art and Crafts)
GradDipAppSci (Museum Studies)

McGRAW-HILL BOOK COMPANY Sydney
New York   San Francisco   Auckland   Bogotá
Caracas   Lisbon   London   Madrid   Mexico City   Milan
Montreal   New Delhi   San Juan
Singapore   Tokyo   Toronto

Front cover
ANGELA BRENNAN (b. 1960)

The Familiar Is Not Necessarily the Known, 1994
Oil on canvas, 152 x 183 cm

Collection of the artist
Photograph courtesy of Niagara Galleries, Richmond

Contents page
For details of pictures, see pages 105 and 170.

First published 1987
Reprinted 1988 (twice), 1989
Second edition 1990
Reprinted 1991, 1993
Third edition 1995

National Library of Australia
Cataloguing-in-Publication data:

Williams, Donald (Donald Sidney).
In our own image.

3rd ed.
Includes index.
ISBN 0 07 470194 0.

1. Art—Australia—History. 2. Art, Australian—
History. I. Title.

709.94

Produced in Australia by McGraw-Hill Book Company Australia Pty Limited
    4 Barcoo Street, Roseville, NSW 2069
Sponsoring Editor: Karina Woolrich
Production Editors: Valerie Marlborough and Sybil Kesteven
Designer: Wing Ping Tong

Typeset in Australia by Post Typesetters, Brisbane
Printed in Hong Kong by Dah Hua Printing Press Co., Ltd

Contents

Introduction

In Our Own Image: The Story of Australian Art, Third Edition, fulfils the need for a textbook outlining the development of Australian painting, sculpture and architecture from colonisation through to the present day. It gives an introduction to Aboriginal art, both traditional and contemporary. The book aims to explain how and why certain movements came into being, and in the course of doing so makes reference to world art, particularly European and American.

The book was written largely because I felt that the teaching of Australian art in schools has often been neglected. The inclusion of a brief social history at the beginning of each chapter serves to reinforce material discussed in Australian history and other areas of the school curriculum, as do the chronological lists of Australian and world events. These can be an aid for students wishing to continue research within a given time period.

In order to get students to respond and seek out art in their local environment, for this third edition I have included sculpture and architecture maps of Australian capital cities (Appendix Three). Although they are not exhaustive, the maps identify a selection of both historical and contemporary work within the city centres. Teachers can use these maps to devise a suitable city walk for their students.

There are also twelve interviews with artists and architects (Chapter Thirteen). They serve to give an insight into the motivation and practice of a range of artists working with different materials. It is hoped that the conversations will help to break down the mystique surrounding the artist.

Activities are included at the end of each chapter. These vary in degree of difficulty and include comparative essay topics, discussion themes, practical activities and comprehension-type questions. It is hoped that these exercises will promote in the students some degree of critical awareness and discrimination and, at the same time, heighten their powers of observation. On working through the book the student will develop a much clearer understanding of our culture, both past and present.

I am sure that *In Our Own Image,* Third Edition, will be read and enjoyed by all teachers and students of Australian art.

Acknowledgments

There have been many people who have assisted with this project, from its beginnings as lesson plans, right through to its present state as a text. Without the gracious support and assistance of many people, including my students, colleagues and particularly my friends, who kept visiting me, this book would have been a most arduous task.

For ideas and reading the manuscript I thank Christine Baines, John Hannaford, Joe Pellegrino and Suzanne Davies who was a great source of inspiration for the final chapter. Ron Ramsey also requires special thanks for his research and writing of Chapter One. The assistance of the Aboriginal Education Board is also greatly appreciated.

Thanks are also owed to the state, regional and commercial galleries listed in the captions and the following people for their ongoing dedication to this project: Vicki Varvaressos, Frank Watters, Tony Pryor, Gus Dall'Ava, Norman Day, Roger Wood, Susan Norrie, Lyn Moore, Clive Murray-White, Hilarie Mais, Angela Brennan, James Gleeson, Peter Atkins, Audrey Dadswell, Frank and Margel Hinder, Mark Hughes, architect Charles Salter, Fulvia Mantelli and Simon Trollope.

Special thanks are owed to Jon Rendell for his patience, but particularly for his superb photography.

CHAPTER ONE

Art of the Australian Aborigine

Introduction

Australian Aborigines—the inhabitants of the continent for at least forty thousand years—are known as one of the world's oldest and most continuous cultures. Their culture, as anthropological work over the last century has revealed, is a complex, subtle and rich way of life.

It seems that the Aborigines originally came from South-East Asia, entering the continent from the north. At that time the continent of Australia included Tasmania and what is now New Guinea. Over many thousands of years they adapted to the wide range of environments and climatic conditions in Australia. The people of the colder climates of southern Victoria and Tasmania (the last areas to be settled by the Aborigines) tended to be short and thickset, which would help to conserve body heat; while at the other extreme, in the hot central deserts, the typical build was tall and lean.

The Aboriginal culture was nomadic: possessions were usually simple, ingenious and multifunctional and kept to a minimum. Life was sustained by hunting and gathering rather than by cultivating crops. Their movements about the country were not random or aimless wanderings in search of food; the Aborigines undertook regular seasonal moves over particular areas to exploit certain resources and to participate in ceremonial gatherings with other groups.

Their nomadic way of life provided them with a healthy diet. In some areas, such as coastal Arnhem Land, subsistence living required the equivalent of approximately three days work a week. This would then allow time for other pursuits.

In Aboriginal culture, art is an integral part of economic, social and religious life. In terms of language the words 'art' and 'artist' often do not exist. 'Art' for the Australian Aborigine is a part of existence.

It is by the acquisition of knowledge, not material possessions, that one attains status in Aboriginal culture. As Australian Aborigines gather knowledge and understanding of rituals and traditional life they gain status within their clan. Elder members are much respected for their knowledge, which includes the many sacred designs and paintings integral to important ceremonies. In this way art becomes a statement of a person's earthly existence.

The main source of inspiration for most traditional Aboriginal artists is a secret ritual life. Painting and other artforms are a means of practising the rites and rules of one's faith, the Dreaming, adherence to which is as important as an individual's earthly existence.

Since at least the 1930s the English words 'Dreaming', 'the Dreaming' or 'the Dreamtime' have been used in the context of the Australian Aboriginal mythological period to describe the spiritual, natural and moral order of life and beyond. The term 'Dreaming', while used widely by Aborigines, has various native translations according to location: alcheringa (Aranda), bugari (Kardjei), djugutba (Western Desert) and wongar (Murrigin).

It relates to the period from the genesis of the universe to a time beyond living memory. The term does not refer to the state of dreams or unrealilty but rather to a state of reality beyond the commonplace. The supply of animal and vegetable food was ensured through religious and magical rites, with art being a visual expression of these.

All peoples throughout the ages have displayed a desire to decorate utilitarian and sacred objects, and the Australian Aborigines are no exception. Evidence of their art can be found today: carvings on rocks; cave paintings; painted, carved and incised weapons; burnt designs on wooden objects; painting on sculptured forms such as bark; and, more recently, acrylic paint on canvas and prepared board.

An estimated 500 to 600 tribal groups of between 100 and 1000 people existed in Australia before European settlement. Each tribe occupied its own territory which could be recognised by the natural landmarks of rivers, mountain ranges or deserts. There were probably about 300 distinct Aboriginal dialects, and in a country as large as Australia there was much regional variation in their art. Some examples are:

- *South-eastern Australia*: Possum cloaks, worn for protection from the cold, had designs cut into the skin; these designs were then painted with red ochre.

- *Eastern Australia*: Decoration was highly ornate, particularly the boomerang decoration found in western New South Wales and central Queensland.

- *North-east Queensland*: Turtle and kingfish were important food sources and featured as decorative ritual elements.

- *Cape York and Torres Strait Islands*: Headdresses and sculpture were elaborate.

- *Central Australia, Northern Territory and east Kimberleys*: Curvilinear and circular elements, concentric circles, and so on were used.

- *Arnhem Land*: Decoration was lavish.

- *Bathurst and Melville Islands*: Significant carved burial poles and sculptured forms were used, plus patterned ochres.

Aboriginal bark painting

Bark painting was established well before the arrival of Europeans in Australia. Early European observers reported that Aboriginal people painted the insides of their bark shelters. In a number of early bark paintings there is evidence of faded or removed images being overpainted as in rock shelters. Due to the materials available and their nomadic existence, paintings lasted only a short time. Bark paintings in museums and art galleries might be fifty or even one hundred years old, but in Aboriginal society they would probably have lasted at most a few years.

Today some Aborigines still paint on bark. In those groups in the tropical north, Arnhem Land, the Gulf of Carpentaria and adjacent off-shore islands, bark painting is flourishing and playing an increasingly important role in Aboriginal culture.

DICK TETNJAN
Man Hunting a Kangaroo
National Museum of Australia,
courtesy of Australian Institute
of Aboriginal Studies

To prepare bark for painting, two shallow slits or rings some distance apart are cut around the trunk of the eucalyptus tree. This is usually done during the wet season as the running sap makes it easier to pry off the bark. The bark sheet is then singed to remove loose bark and help flatten it. It may also be weighed down with rocks or sand to make it lie flat. It is scraped clean and an 'undercoat' of pigment is applied, often with a feather or twig (the end of which is chewed and frayed). This can then be rubbed over with fixative, such as orchid juice (more often today this has been replaced with PVA), to provide a firm and smooth surface. The outline of the main designs, including borders within which details will be added, are then drawn. The next step is to add more details. Finally, repetitive and decorative elements such as crosshatching and dotting are painted. The pigments used are mainly red and yellow ochres, kaolin and charcoal—all are natural solids which are crushed, ground to a powder and mixed with water and a fixative. Many bark painters, particularly since the 1950s, attach supporting rods to the top and bottom ends of the bark to prevent warping of the surface.

Tribal elders paint sacred subjects but anyone may paint non-ritual ones. The sacred paintings are done on a ceremonial ground and are shown to selected members of the group, but paintings which portray major ancestral beings may be seen only by ceremonial leaders.

In north-east Arnhem Land bark paintings portray remarkable composition; the whole surface of the bark is covered in great detail. Ancestral and spirit beings, totemic animals, plants, clouds, waves, rain and other natural features of the land, sea and sky associated with the mythology and daily activities of the people are depicted. Designs can be symmetrically balanced, many divided into halves or quarters, and are often framed in a border of crossed lines.

In western Arnhem Land it is interesting to compare bark with rock painting. The latter depicts figures elongated and spread out whereas in bark paintings figures appear compressed. Similarly with kangaroos, in rock art their tails are extended whereas in bark painting they are frequently depicted with tails drawn tightly to the body.

Western Arnhem Land artists seem to prefer to paint single figures. Subjects include ancestral beings, mimi and other spirits of the bush and caves, the Rainbow Serpent and animals as totems for hunting and fishing magic. Men and women also paint to cause illness or death in connection with love magic.

The most remarkable feature of the art of this area is its so-called 'x-ray painting'. The spinal columns and internal organs are painted as well as the external features of animals and human figures. The range of subjects and manner of depicting them in x-ray style is limited; birds, fish and animals (but seldom people) are drawn in side elevation and reptiles in plan. The x-ray artists show little movement in their work, unlike the mimi artists who paint expressive subjects such as people in action— running, fighting and throwing spears.

In the past in Central Australia, artists painted on irregular surfaces such as pieces of bark, rock walls, implements, posts and the human body—very few of these were flat or regular surfaces. The new art movement of the Western Desert acrylic painters has now added rectangular canvases and artist's boards to these older media. Right-angled corners and straight sides have suddenly applied new pressures to ancient designs.

Western Desert acrylic painters

The MacDonnell Ranges, which cross the lower Northern Territory for some 800 kilometres, are a commanding presence. They are the homeland of the Aranda people. Images of this country are widely known through the landscape watercolours of Albert Namatjira and his relatives—mostly Aranda people based at the Hermannsburg Mission (founded in 1877 as a Lutheran church mission), west of Alice Springs.

The settlement of Papunya, 170 kilometres north-west of Hermannsburg and 260 kilometres west of Alice Springs, lies on the edge of the Western Desert—country

OPPOSITE:

East Kimberley and Western Desert area of the Northern Territory

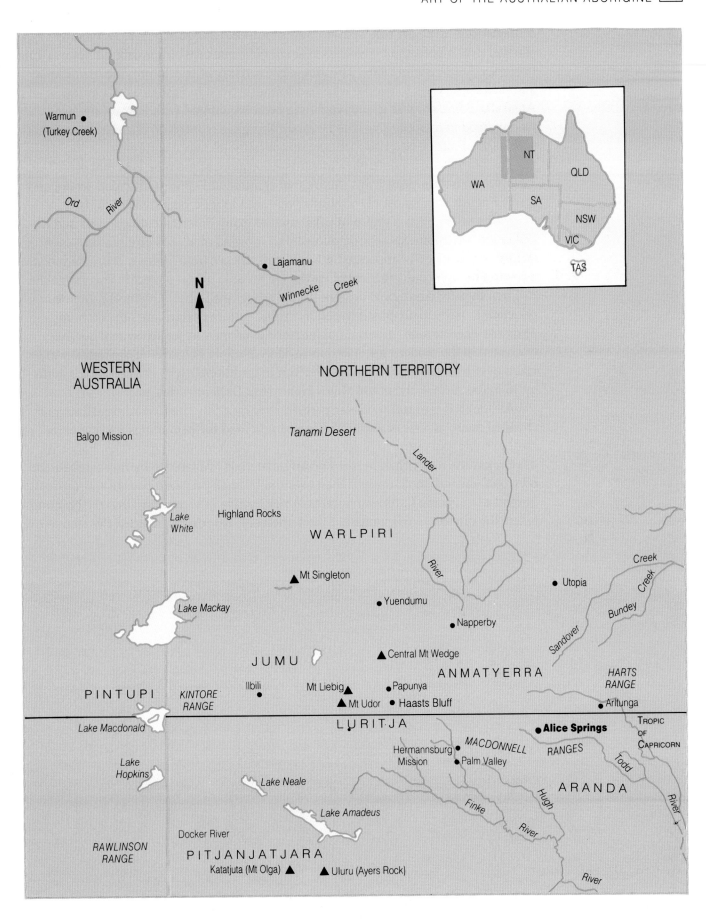

characterised by desert oak, spinifex and sandhills. Established in 1959, Papunya is situated near a bore and between two small hills, one of which is called Papunya Tula (a Honey Ant Dreaming site). The aim of the settlement was to provide educational and welfare services to people who had formerly lived in vast areas of Central Australia. Some of these groups had long been acquainted with European ways, having lived at missions (such as Hermannsburg) or worked on cattle stations; others, such as the Pintupi, had had virtually no contact with non-Aborigines.

The official Australian policy towards Aborigines at the time was that of assimilation to European ways. Aboriginal children at Papunya attended school and learnt English while most of the adults were seen to lack 'employable' skills.

It was in 1971 that a group of tribal men of many different backgrounds and Dreaming environments set in motion an art movement at the Papunya settlement. Geoff Bardon, a newly appointed art and craft teacher from Sydney, attempted to steer a course through conflicting tribal views. He set up a mural project to encourage the children to paint Aboriginal designs on the school walls. Initially the children were reluctant to participate, possibly because tribal culture designs are not common property. Then several important older Aboriginal men in the settlement became interested in the modern art materials used by Bardon. Before long the mural was taken over by these men, who completed it in traditional style. Painted on a 3 metre by 10 metre surface, the mural was a Honey Ant Dreaming design.

Although this mural was later painted over by a tidy-minded administration, it changed many aspects of Papunya life and provided the beginnings for one of the most exciting and impressive contemporary art movements in Australia. Following this project the men began to paint on any materials available to them—cardboard, plywood, tin and linoleum, and then eventually small prepared boards and canvas. Instead of imposing European notions of perspective or suggesting that the paintings reflect the physical environment of the settlement, Bardon encouraged the men to use

CHARLIE TJAPANGATI
(PINTUPI TRIBE) (b. c. 1942)
Tingari Dreaming, 1986
Acrylic on canvas,
90.5 x 182 x 2 cm
Private Collection

Photographer: Brenton McGeachie

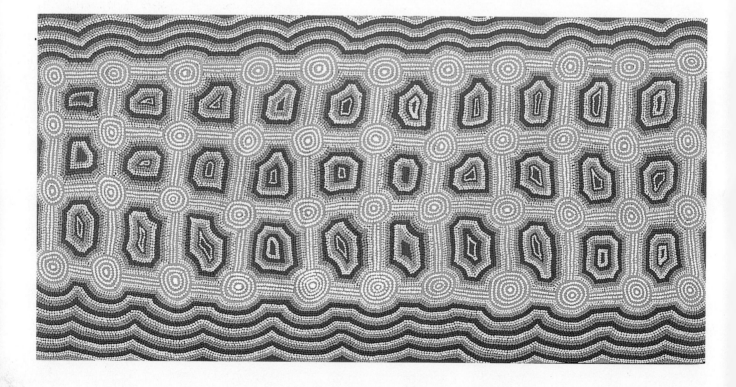

the existing system of desert culture symbols to depict their Dreamings and links with the country.

Because they began painting again, a number of senior men were effectively restored to their traditional roles as teachers, no longer mere bystanders in an educational process conceived by Europeans. Michael Nelson Jakamarra, a Warlpiri painter living at Papunya, comments:

> You gotta canvas, paint, and brush ready. Well, first you gotta ask your father and *kurdungurlu* [a person who inherits sacred designs and Dreaming]. [They'll say] 'You do that Dreamin' there, which is belonging to your grandfather and father.' They'll give you a clue, they'll show you a drawing on the ground first. You've got it in your brain now. You know it because you've seen your father [in a ceremony] with that painting on his body and one on the ground. You'll see it, then you'll know it . . .[1]

When supplies of hardboard and canvas became available, the rectangular formats had to be dealt with. The Papunya Tula artists adapted their designs quickly, working to a variety of dimensions and with new acrylic media. Between July 1971 and August 1972, over 620 paintings were recorded as having been produced.

Dotted motifs and backgrounds have become the hallmark of the Western Desert acrylic movement. Derived from the dotting of ochre pigment on the human body during ceremonies and rituals, they now form the background of paintings.

A small number of symbols form the basic visual language of central Australian artists: such as circles, lines and dots. Other shapes vary but often have developed very logically, for example the 'U' shape (which usually signifies human presence) is an abstraction of the trace left by a person sitting cross-legged on the ground. Following are some of the more common symbols and their meanings:

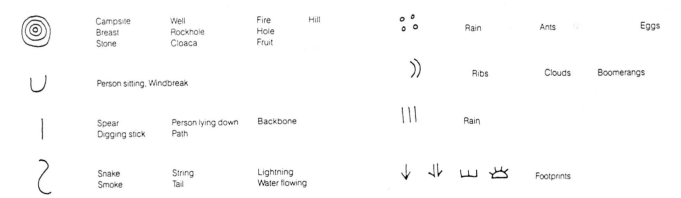

Campsite Breast Stone	Well Rockhole Cloaca	Fire Hole Fruit	Hill		Rain	Ants	Eggs
					Ribs	Clouds	Boomerangs
Person sitting, Windbreak							
Spear Digging stick	Person lying down Path	Backbone			Rain		
Snake Smoke	String Tail	Lightning Water flowing			Footprints		

Some common symbols of Western Desert painting
After N. Peterson, 'Art of the Desert' in *Aboriginal Australia*, Australian Gallery Directors Council, Sydney, 1981, p. 46, Table 1, Fig. 1

These symbols are essentially a form of calligraphy. This is particularly so in the case of sand paintings where designs are used for storytelling. When asked about their paintings artists usually respond that the painting means or is 'my country', that is, it is a depiction of the painter's territory. The ways in which particular terrain and stretches of the country are represented in paintings vary. Many paintings seem as though they are viewed from the air—a plan view. This may be due to careful observation of the ground—looking down upon a landscape and checking for particular details, rather than viewing the landscape from the side as Europeans tend to do.

---

[1] Sutton, Peter (ed.), *Dreamings: The Art of Aboriginal Australia*, Viking/Penguin Books, Ringwood, 1988, p. 2.

Even though there is a limited number of graphic symbols used, it would be wrong to assume that all Western Desert paintings are similar. Close inspection reveals a wide and complex variation in structure, colour and composition. Many paintings consist of four basic colours—yellow, red/brown, white and black—mixed to endless variations. This has been partly due to the colours provided by art advisers and partly as a response to what painters think non-Aborigines expect to see in an Aboriginal painting.

At Papunya in the early days of painting, artists used whatever colours were available; however, Aboriginal leaders moved to restrict the number of colours available to white, black, red/brown and yellow. But more recently this has changed, as has the number of women now painting, especially among the Warlpiri at Yuendumu, a settlement 120 kilometres north of Papunya.

Large paintings often require a number of painters to actually execute the design. These works may then be accredited to only one painter—the person who supervised the painters, or the initiator who claims rights to his or her ritual designs.

BARNEY DANIELS
TJUNGURRAYI
Chair with Desert Snake and Lizard Dreaming
Collection: Australian Bicentennial Exhibition, 1988

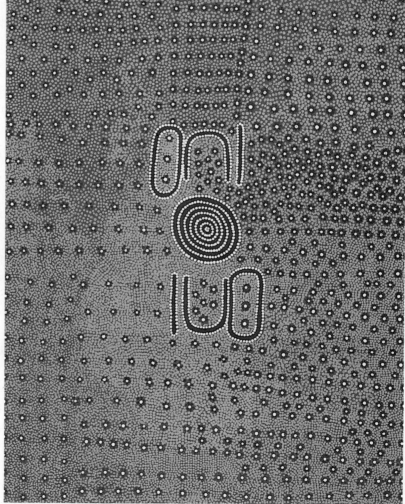

RIGHT:

TURKEY TOLSON
TJUPURRULA (PINTUPI TRIBE) (b. c. 1945)
Aboriginal Women's Dreaming, 1981
Synthetic polymer paint on canvas, 160 x 126 cm

Reproduced under a licence granted by the Aboriginal Artists Agency, Sydney

It is important to note that to Aboriginal eyes, it is the design that is most important and not the object it decorates. For example, the same design might be painted on a person's body during a ceremony, on the walls of a wet season shelter, on a painting made for sale, on a bark or log coffin, on a piece of modern furniture or on a pair of sneakers. It is the design—not the object itself—that has continuity.

Chair with Desert Snake and Lizard Dreaming by **Barney Daniels Tjungurrayi** is a Desert Snake Dreaming which takes place at a site west of Haasts Bluff, approximately 250 kilometres west of Alice Springs. People, depicted by 'U' shapes, are looking for lizards but are unsuccessful. They see a snake which they catch and eat. The rungs of the chair represent the music sticks and nulla nullas used in corroborees. The varied colours of the legs depict the surrounding countryside—sandhills, grass and flowers.

Since the late 1970s and the enactment of land rights legislation, Aborigines from the remoter areas of Australia have been leaving the centralised settlements to set up smaller, more homogeneous communities in traditional homelands. The Pintupi left the Papunya settlement between 1972 and 1980 and moved west, establishing residential communities at Yayayi, New Bore, Mt Liebig and Kintore in Central Australia and at Kiwirrkura in Western Australia. Most of the Pintupi acrylic painters now work from these communities.

Acrylic paintings have had a noticeable cultural, social and economic impact on Western Desert Aboriginal communities as well as a discernible influence on non-Aboriginal artists. Although artists such as Margaret Preston (see Chapter Eight) have been influenced by traditional elements and motifs from Aboriginal art in the past, the recent developments of the Western Desert acrylic painting movement are proving to have a great impact on the work of many contemporary Australian artists and designers. Even the Sydney Olympic symbol, designer Michael Bryce explains, includes a reference to Aboriginal dot designs:

> Working with Aboriginal artist Ron Hurley, Bryce said, 'It had to be Sydney, it had to be somehow Australia ... I just put a photograph of the Opera House on the desk and put a piece of tracing paper over it ... and drew the Opera House sail in thick black pen then put Tippex dots in white.' The dots Hurley explained were representative of Aboriginal desert art and the sails took on a rainbow serpent feel as well.
>
> *Australian magazine*, January 1994

As well known as the Sydney 2000 bid logo is our national airline Qantas, which has also been recently influenced by Aboriginal art and culture. Aboriginal art has taken to the skies of the world in the form of a painted Qantas Airways 747-400 (jumbo jet), appropriately named *Wunala Dreaming*. It is a marriage of modern aviation technology to ancient Aboriginal mythology and culture. In contrast to the Qantas logo, leaping kangaroos, painted in the traditional x-ray style, wrap themselves around the wide fuselage. Roundels, dots and journey lines also follow the shape of the aircraft to portray a dazzling, highly colourful and unusual piece of art. The colours were specifically chosen to express the fleeting romantic colours of the central Australian landscape: red for the ochre of the soil, blues or violets for the mountain ranges in the distance and greens for the lush new growth after seasonal rains.

While the images were designed by Ros and John Moriarty of Balarinji Design in Adelaide, the actual dreaming and concept come from northern and Central Australia, specifically from the Yanyuwa people of the Gulf of Carpentaria. The Moriartys explain:

> In dreamtime journeys, spirit ancestors in the form of kangaroos (Wunala) made tracks from camps to waterholes, leading people to water and food. Today, as they have for centuries, Aboriginal people re-enact such journeys through song and dance corroborees. These ensure the procreation of all living things in the continuing harmony of nature's seasons.[2]

The designs were digitally created on a computer and enlarged 100 times. The enlarged designs were then made into stencils and traced onto the body of the aircraft—again a marriage of art, technology and human labour. The jet required 800 litres of paint and it took just under two weeks painting around the clock to complete the job. It is clearly the largest piece of contemporary Aboriginal art to travel the world!

Qantas Airways 747-400, painted with an Aboriginal design known as *Wunala Dreaming*

Just as the art market has become increasingly informed, so too has Aboriginal Western Desert painting continued to develop. There has been a tendency for many artists to go beyond the 'dot and circle' paintings of the 1970s and 1980s. The bold designs of Ronnie Tjampitjinpa and restrained almost minimal paintings of *Spear Straightening Ceremony* by **Turkey Tolson Tjupurrula** are recent examples of the extraordinary development of Western Desert painting over the past two decades. In *Spear Straightening Ceremony*, Tolson's linear painting describes a traditional ceremony that took place prior to a battle. He has been working with this series and has made many similar works since 1990.

---

[2] Qantas Airways, 'Airtime, News and Views from Qantas', in *The Australian Way*, David Syme, Melbourne, October 1994, p. 8.

TURKEY TOLSON
TJUPURRULA (PINTUPI
TRIBE) (b. 1942)

Spear Straightening Ceremony,
1993 Acrylic on canvas,
61 x 91.5 cm

Private Collection, Canberra

Photographer: Brenton McGeachie

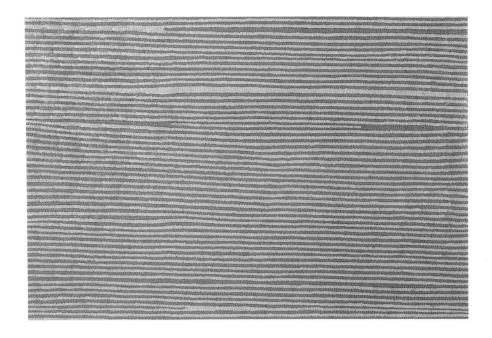

Utopia

In and around Utopia in the eastern part of Central Australia artistic traditions are similar to those of their Western Desert neighbours, despite differences in languages and social structure.

Land taken over by pastoral leases or stations in the 1920s was returned to the Aborigines in 1979. Instead of establishing a central town or settlement on what had been the Utopia cattle station, the Anmatyerre and Alyawarre people preferred to live in small outstations or camps close to their ancestral country.

At the time of the move back to their country in 1977 the women of the community were introduced, through education programs, to woodblock printing, tie-dyeing of fabrics and later that year to batik. In 1978 the Utopia Women's Batik Group was formed and decorative batiks based on ceremonial designs were produced and exhibited.

An important leader of the women's ceremonies, **Emily Kame Kngwarreye (born c. 1916)** who participated in the original Women's Batik Group, emerged as one of the senior artists from Utopia. Taking up painting on canvas in her seventies, a lifetime of creating images meant an exciting transition to this new medium. Her batik designs consist of organic forms covering the entire surface of the silk.

In her paintings Emily appears to start with a linear design, at times resembling branches or ribs and sometimes dividing the surface into smaller bordered sections. Onto this base she lays fields of colour and dots based on plants, seeds and body painting. The sharpness of her brushwork varies greatly—from earlier works with very clearly defined marks often overlayed on top of each other, to later works where brushstrokes are larger, much looser and colours merge.

In 1993 Emily Kngwarreye was awarded a Creative Arts Fellowship by Prime Minister Paul Keating. Other artists from Utopia include Ada Bird Petyarre, Sandra Holmes Kemarre, Mavis Holmes Petyarre, Lindsay Bird Mpetyarre and Lilly Sandover Kngwarreye.

The Kimberley region

In the central and northern areas of the Kimberley region of Western Australia, the most powerful visual expression of Aboriginal culture is rock art. Painted images abound on rock shelters and cave walls with two ancestor images predominating: the Wandjina and Ungud/Galeru (Rainbow Serpent). More recently these figures have been painted on barks and canvas.

Unlike Rainbow Serpents, which are known throughout most of Aboriginal Australia as powerful Dreamtime figures associated with the landscape, the Wandjina are unique to the Kimberley region. 'Wandjina' is a term for a group of ancestral beings who came out of the sea and the sky. They bring with them the rains, determine the weather, and maintain the fertility of land and vegetation. They have shaped the features of the landscape and left their images (some up to 6 metres long) in ochres and white clay on the cave and rock walls of the region.

Characteristic features of the Wandjina are white faces and bodies, and round black eyes with radiating eyelashes, and although the nose is indicated they are mouthless. Various reasons are given for the absence of mouths—the result of tightly closed lips following the first bolt of lightning, lips sealed by the Rainbow Serpent or the belief that if there were mouths continuous rainstorms would result. The head of the Wandjina is usually surrounded by a halo, possibly to represent hair, and clouds, often with radiating lines. These lines have been interpreted as feathers or lightning. It is common to see 'big mobs' of Wandjina painted together.

Part of the continuum of Kimberley art associated with the Wandjina is a group of Aboriginal artists who have settled to the east of the Kimberley, around Warmun (Turkey Creek) 200 kilometres south of Kununurra. This group, which has associations with other parts of the country, particularly the Northern Territory as well as the huge Kimberley region itself, is gaining much critical acclaim and international attention.

The most renowned artist of Turkey Creek is **Rover Thomas** who was born in 1926 on the edge of the Gibson Desert many kilometres to the south. He lived a traditional life until the age of ten when he moved to Billiluna Station in the Kimberley. There he soon became a stockman and travelled widely over the region, gaining an intimate knowledge of the landscape and also learning much of the local oral history.

In the early 1970s, with the introduction of equal wages for Aboriginal workers, many people were expelled from station properties and became fringe dwellers on the outskirts of towns. Early in 1975 Rover came to live with the Aboriginal community at Warmun. An important dream had a profound effect on Thomas, and it resulted in his painting with a relative Paddy Jambinji.

Thomas has lived through a tumultuous period for Aboriginal people, particularly in the Kimberley. Events such as Cyclone Tracy and the building of the Ord River scheme have had an enormous impact on the region and have also been the subjects of paintings by Rover Thomas.

His distinctive style of painting uses natural pigments and gums to depict ceremonies, stories and geographical features, sometimes in plan view, sometimes side on and sometimes both simultaneously. His colour scheme relates to the land— yellow, red and brown ochres, black and white. Simple and bold design, Thomas's paintings are restrained, without the layers of decoration and diverse colour schemes artists of other regions often employ. Rover Thomas said:

> Before, no nothing. When that house bin put up in Turkey Creek, me and Jambinji bin start off. We drawing all the way. We bin know something now. I'm all over now. We bin sending little bit by little bit. And so gardiya (white people) he like me. I don't know what for.
>
> Rover Thomas

In 1990 Rover Thomas and Trevor Nickolls were selected to represent Australia at the 44th Venice Biennale in Italy.

LILY KAREDADA
(b. c. 1937)
Wandjina, c. 1993
Ochre on paper bark,
107.5 x 49.5 cm
Trollope Collection, Melbourne

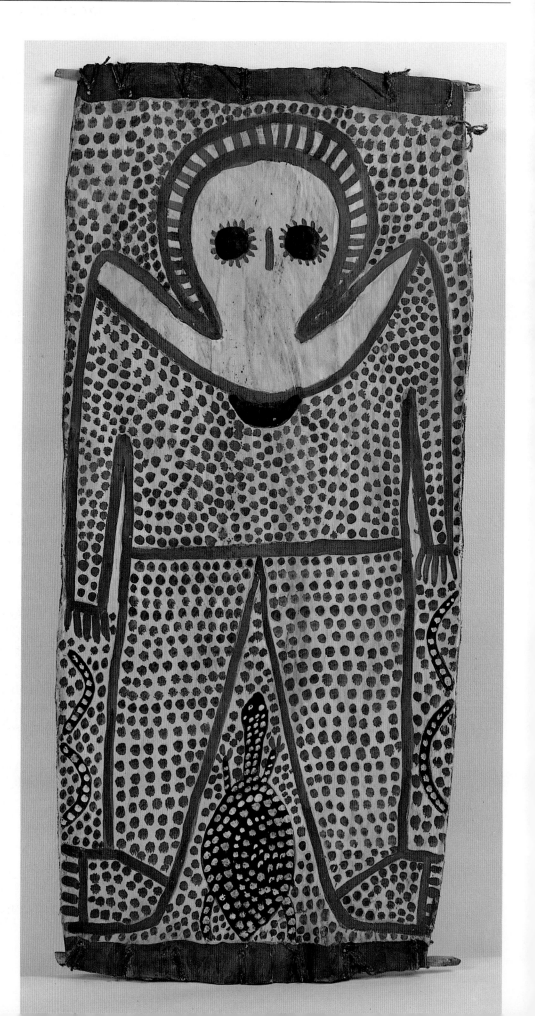

Rover Thomas painting at Kununurra

Photographer: Donald Williams

ROVER THOMAS
(KUKATJA WANGKAJUNGA
TRIBE) (b. 1926)

Canning Stock Route Well 33
(Rover's birthplace),1992
Natural pigment on canvas,
40.5 x 50.5 x 2 cm

Private Collection, Canberra

Photographer: Brenton McGeachie

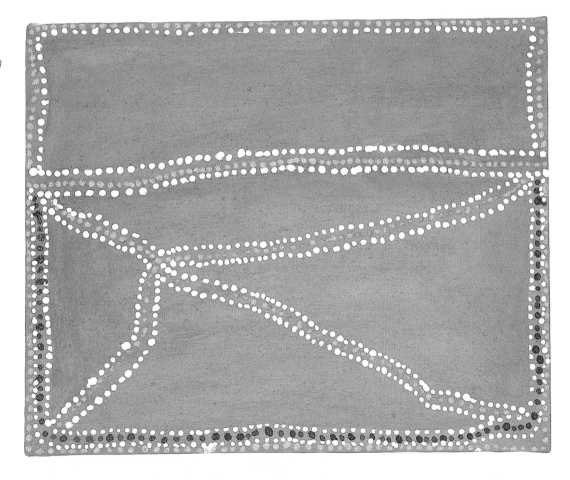

The paintings by artists from the Turkey Creek community display some of the elements of the art of the desert, particularly lines of dots to describe and outline shapes, and also a plan view of the landscape. However, the depiction of the features of the environment created by ancestors is emphasised rather than the narration of ancestral events, as in desert painting. Other Warmun artists include Queenie McKenzie, Jack Britten, Hector Jandamy and Henry Wambiny.

Urban Aboriginal/non-traditional artists

Important works of art have also been produced by Aboriginal artists not resident in traditional communities but in the many regional towns and capital cities throughout Australia. This is not a recent phenomenon—Aboriginal artists such as William Barak and Tommy McRae were commissioned by European settlers in the mid-nineteenth century to produce drawings using ink, pencil, paper and board. Their drawings provide fascinating commentaries on nineteenth-century life in a rapidly changing Australia. In the 1930s watercolour landscape painting in the European style was introduced by Rex Battarbee, a non-Aboriginal artist, to Aboriginal people near Alice Springs. Albert Namatjira, a student of Battarbee, mentioned earlier in this chapter, was the first Aboriginal artist to command wide critical attention throughout Australia as an artist in his own right.

During the 1960s and 1970s several artists such as Trevor Nickolls, Harold Thomas (designer of the Aboriginal flag in 1971) and Thancoupie were undertaking tertiary art studies in Adelaide and Sydney. By the late 1970s and early 1980s these pioneering artists had been joined by other art school graduates such as Fiona Foley, Lin Onus, Raymond Meeks and Tracey Moffatt. (See also Chapter Twelve.)

Aboriginal art, once admired solely for its anthropological value has now developed and diversified to become one of the strongest aesthetic forces in contemporary Australian art.

ACTIVITIES

Because we now assume paint comes naturally from tubes, try making some of your own.

1. Dig some earth in your backyard. How many colours do you get? The Australian Aborigines collected various colours from one site and took them to another site to use so as to vary the colours on their palette.

2. Grind the sample earth to a powder. (Use a mortar and pestle but if these are not available try grinding it between two flat rocks.)

3. Add water to some of the earth and try painting with it. Leave it to dry.

4. Mix some of the powdered earth with egg, and paint.

5. Try mixing earth with wax and / or honey.

6. Think of an animal that you have come in contact with—your dog, cat, canary, horse, and so on. From what you know of x-ray paintings, draw or paint an animal showing both the external and internal features.

7. Note how Western Desert acrylic painters use dots to cover their canvas or board. Refer to the paintings of John Russell, Grace Cossington Smith, Ralph Balson and Fred Williams in this textbook and discuss how they apply paint.

8. Find a book with a painting by Georges Seurat, a French impressionist painter who also used dots to create patterns and moods in his paintings. Now find a painting, photograph, advertisement or symbol for a product and change it from *blocks* of colour to *dots* of colour. (Western Desert painters often use cotton buds with the cotton removed as sticks for their dotting.)

9. Refer to the table of symbols used by Western Desert acrylic painters in their work (see page 7). Create a simple set of symbols that is relevant to your daily life for your own use. Draw a map of your route from home to school using these newly invented symbols. Paint or draw them in a dotted fashion and limit yourself to four colours (you may mix any tone or combination of the four colours).

10. Using the table of symbols on page 7, look at *Aboriginal Women's Dreaming* by Turkey Tolson Tjupurrula on page 8 and translate or interpret the symbols.

11. Think of a story or instruction given to you by your parents, grandparents or an elderly friend or relative. Try to depict it in graphic form. Simplify and abstract it if necessary, or use your newly developed set of symbols.

12. Look through magazines and try to find an example of a contemporary non-Aboriginal artist, fashion designer, jeweller—an artist in any field—who has been influenced by the work of Western Desert acrylic painters.

	AUSTRALIAN EVENTS	GENERAL EVENTS	ARTISTIC EVENTS	
1770	**1770** Cook drops anchor at Botany Bay.	**1770** Beethoven is born.		**Australian artists** Port Jackson Painter John Eyre Joseph Lycett Thomas Watling
1780			**1785** Stubbs: *The Reapers*.	
	1788 The First Fleet arrives, led by Captain Arthur Phillip.			
1790	**1790** *Lady Juliana* arrives with more convicts and few supplies. **1794** John Macarthur sets up. his farm at Parramatta. **1798** European population is about 5000.	**1790** The first wristwatch is designed in Switzerland. **1791** Mozart dies at the age of thirty-five. **1793** Queen Marie Antoinette is guillotined in France.	**1793** David: *Death of Marat*. **1794** Blake: *God Creating the Universe*. **1799** Goya: *Los Caprichos* series.	
1800	**1804** In order to discourage the French from making territorial claims, Captain David Collins settles Hobart Town. From this time, Aborigines are systematically killed or driven out of Van Diemen's Land.	**1800s** The Industrial Revolution is occurring in Europe. **1804** Napoleon is crowned emperor of France. **1805** Battle of Trafalgar is fought.	**1808** Goya: *The Third of May*.	**Architecture** Wattle and daub houses Elizabeth Farm House Experiment Farm Cottage
1810	**1810** Lieutenant Colonel Lachlan Macquarie arrives to replace Phillip as governor of New South Wales. **1813** Motivated by the need for more land for grazing, Blaxland, Lawson and Wentworth cross the Blue Mountains. **1817** First bank, Bank of New South Wales, is established.	**1811** King George III becomes hopelessly insane. **1815** Battle of Waterloo is fought. **1816** Lord Elgin sells his 'marbles' (Parthenon statues) to the British Museum.	**1814** Ingres: *Odalisque*. **1819** Jefferson: Rotunda at University of Virginia. Completed in 1826. Géricault: *The Raft of the Medusa*.	
1820				
1830				

CHAPTER TWO

The Penal Colony 1788–1819

Painting and the role of the artist

As far back as 1770, when Cook sailed *Endeavour* into Botany Bay, the Australian landscape was considered unusual. The crew and other members of the ship's company had never seen land quite like this; the weird animals, plants and sparse vegetation were great curiosities. On a visit to shore for exploration and documentation of flora and fauna, one of the lieutenants described a strange animal he saw. He said, 'It was about as large as a one-gallon [4.5 litre] keg, as black as the devil with wings and two horns on its head.' It was a flying-fox. The other animal that aroused their curiosity was described by one of Cook's men as a quadruped resembling a large rat. This creature did not run, it hopped. It was later explained to the men, with the help of the Aborigines, that this animal was called a kangaroo. With the help of a couple of greyhounds that were on board ship, a kangaroo was captured and stuffed, and then sent back to England and painted by the artist George Stubbs (1724–1806). To the European explorers the country was full of exotic curiosities; these were documented after the arrival of Captain Arthur Phillip and the First Fleet.[1]

In the early days of colonisation the artist's primary role—which was of the utmost importance—was basically to document, in paint and pencil, details of the new land. These documents were required by the Governor, the official government records in London and the inquisitive British public who had heard about the new land. Many hundreds of illustrations and watercolours of Australian Aborigines and of flora and fauna found their way back to England. These documents were the only pictorial evidence the British had of Australia's land, inhabitants and vegetation.

---

[1] Arthur Phillip arrived in 1788 with his crew and 778 convicts, which included 192 women and 187 children.

The Australian landscape presented many new problems to the English artists. The initial response was to try to express the strange quality of the landscape. To the European eye it was lacking in both freshness and greenness. The light was too harsh, the trees and bushes too sparse, and the land generally monotonous and dry. Most of the artists found it very difficult to comprehend so many new animals and plants. The trained artists who arrived after the First Fleet also found the landscape alien. They had been trained in Britain and Europe and they had never had to paint a land so unlike their own. Consequently, their paintings were, in part, colonial expressions of English landscape painting.

Among the convicts transported to the colony in 1788 and 1790 were a number whose talents extended to drawing and amateur drafting. Governor Phillip was aware of the interest that Sir Joseph Banks had in Australian flora and many drawings were sent back to him in England. One of the earliest convict artists was referred to as the 'Port Jackson Painter'. His real name has never been known.

The **Port Jackson Painter** made about 250 watercolour sketches, which are held in the collection of the British Museum of Natural History. The Port Jackson Painter's drawings consisted of maps, coastal profiles, and illustrations of plants and Aborigines. The Aborigines were shown in their indigenous state: hunting, fishing and generally going about their daily routine. These drawings were of most interest in Britain as the Aborigine was viewed with great curiosity there. Educated European society had only read about such people and were interested to learn more. It was believed, largely by the educated class, that the natives were heroic and noble because of their close affiliation with nature and the land. For this reason it was not unusual for the Aborigine to be represented in the manner of a classical Greek god, that is, standing in the classical pose wielding a spear. Hence the title given to the native was that of the 'Noble Savage'.[2]

The Port Jackson Painter was by no means a professional painter—as his crude drawing style shows. Although he did have a keen eye for detail and a sense of humour, his works are valuable only as social documents. His sense of humour can be seen in the work *The Hunted Rushcutter*, c. 1790. The painting shows a rather plump European gentleman being chased across the fields by three Aborigines wielding spears.

One of the first professionally trained artists to arrive in the colony was **Thomas Watling (1762–?)**. Born in Scotland, he was transported to the colony for forgery. He found his new home most unappealing. He disliked the climate, and the land and the natives. Watling believed that he and his fellow convicts were in a land that did not seem to want them.

He spent his time making drawings of birds and native plants, and topographical views of the landscape for government officials. Trained as a landscape painter in Britain, Watling had been accustomed to painting the European scene. In Australia he felt completely confused. The landscape and climate around Sydney Cove depressed him. It was bushy, flat and dry. In letters home to England he refers to 'the air, the sky, the land [as] objects entirely different from all that a Briton has been accustomed to see before'.

---

[2] The concept of the 'Noble Savage' stemmed from the writings of Jean-Jacques Rousseau (1712–78), a French philosopher and writer, Rousseau, with some other contemporary writers, believed that the Noble Savage was a man, uncorrupted by civilisation, who symbolised the innate goodness of nature.

PORT JACKSON PAINTER
The Hunted Rushcutter,
c. 1790
Watercolour, 16 x 30 cm
By courtesy of the British
Museum (Natural History)

Of the climate he said,

In the warmer season, the thunder very frequently rolls tremendous, accompanied by a scorching wind, so intolerable as almost to obstruct respiration … I have felt one hour as intensely warm as if immediately under the line, when the next has made me shiver with cold …[3]

Although Watling's paintings were scenes of local areas, they tended to be painted in the mood of the European landscape. The tall sparse eucalypts became broad, bushy, green elms and seemed not to be very Australian at all. This was to pose a problem for some of the early colonial painters. The painters were not able to reconcile what they were seeing with what they were taught. It proved to be most frustrating. Watling sought to combine topographical and landscape painting. It was work in this style that was sent back to London to show the government officials the growth of the new colony.

Watling's painting *Sydney Cove*, 1794, is almost a classically English landscape painting. The very dark foliage in the foreground and the framing of the painting with large trees is English in tradition. This style of painting tended to be very popular with early convict artists who were trained in Britain.

In the new colony artists were employed as draughtsmen, whose main task was to make topographical drawings of the new towns. The most popular topographical artists were also convicts. Their names were **Joseph Lycett (1774 – c. 1825)** and **John Eyre (1771–1812)**. Unlike Watling, these men were not concerned with producing beautiful views of Australia; rather, their concern purely was to represent the growth of the colony.

Eyre produced many finely detailed drawings which depicted houses, roads and wharves in tight and balanced compositions. There was little room for touches of

[3] Smith, B., *Documents on Art and Taste in Australia: The Colonial Period, 1770–1914*, Oxford University Press, Melbourne, 1975, p. 11.

decorative painting. The drawings were made into engravings and later hand-coloured. Eyre's watercolour *View of Sydney from the West Side of the Cove*, 1806, was typical of the topographical style. You can trace the streets and gardens throughout the painting.

During 1819 and 1821 Lycett was employed by Governor Lachlan Macquarie to make drawings of views of New South Wales and Van Diemen's Land. So, with his sketchbooks and equipment, Lycett travelled throughout these areas, drawing and painting the landscape. On his return to England in 1822 Lycett actually published these drawings, which appeared monthly under the title *Views of Australia: 1824–1825*.

The *Views* were advertised in June 1824 as 'absolute facsimiles of scenes and places having been taken from nature on the spot by Mr Lycett, who resided more than ten years in the country ...' The advertisement went on to say:

> In the compass of twelve Monthly Parts, the first of which will appear on the 1st July, will be contained twenty-four Views of Scenes in New South Wales, and twenty-four of Scenes in Van Diemen's Land, including the principal Settlements of each Colony, with their Public Buildings; and also the Mountains, Plains, Forests, Rivers, Lakes, and, in short, every object which meets the eye of a spectator of the actual scenes, whether they be such as the rude hand of Nature formed, or such as the arts of civilization have fabricated for the use of social man.[4]

His drawings depicted the rapid progress made with the expansion of the colony. This may have been Macquarie's motive in employing Lycett to make the drawings.

---

[4] Smith, B., *Documents on Art and Taste in Australia: The Colonial Period, 1770–1914*, Oxford University Press, Melbourne, 1975, p. 28.

THOMAS WATLING (1762–?)
Sydney Cove, 1794
Oil on canvas,
91.5 x 129.5 cm
Dixson Galleries, State
Library of New South Wales

JOHN EYRE (1771–1812)
*View of Sydney from the
West Side of the Cove*, 1806
34.3 x 64.8 cm
Dixson Galleries, State Library
of New South Wales

Architecture

In the oppressive heat of a summer's day on 26 January 1788, the building of
Australia commenced. As mentioned earlier, the first impressions of the new land sent
waves of horror through the convicts and officers. The convicts were set to work with
English tools, which proved to be nearly worthless against the Australian trees. The
very tall eucalypts, or gum trees, were so hard to cut that more often than not the
tools broke, or became so blunt that they were useless. Despite these initial problems,
marquees and tents were set up rapidly and the business of administering the colony
began.

The officers searched convict lists and found that as well as twelve carpenters
there were also sixteen ships' carpenters, these being the only skilled builders
available. So, with a minimum of skilled labour, a few tough, hard-wearing tools, and
only inferior materials to work with, temporary, single-roomed dwellings were
constructed.

Houses constructed at this time were rather primitive and, owing to the poor
resources and tools, lasted only a couple of years at the most. Early houses were
constructed from poles of tall gum trees; the walls were made from a combination of
branches mixed with mud, cow hair and dung. It was usually the walls that gave way
after a couple of years, especially with the heavy rains in the Sydney area. In the
following years the houses became more sturdy and, with the importation from
England of iron, glass and canvas, houses proved more durable.

The discovery of brick-making clay gave a tremendous boost to building
production. A brickmaker too was found, and employed to fulfil this important task.
Owing to the scarcity of quality bricks, tiles and stone, such materials were reserved
for official works. Within a year of European settlement Sydney's buildings were
being made from brick and roofed with clay tiles. But there were many complications,

one of the most serious being the shortage of lime. Lime was used as mortar to bind the bricks together, thus ensuring stability, but unfortunately little lime could be found locally. In an attempt to rectify this problem hundreds of shells were collected from the beaches and slowly burnt. This time-consuming activity produced only small quantities of lime. Another method of making mortar was to mix grass with the clay and bricks but heavy rain tended to wash this out. To combat this, walls were increased to an extraordinary thickness and consequently had to be kept rather short to minimise the possibility of collapse.

To the west, approximately 22 kilometres up the harbour, an area rich in soil and timber was discovered and rapidly established as a second town. In July 1790, Lieutenant William Dawes, Australia's earliest town planner, drew up the first plans. This site was to be later named Parramatta. It was here in 1794 that Captain John Macarthur settled in his farmhouse overlooking the Parramatta River. Called Elizabeth Farm, it was named after his wife. The farmhouse was a single-storey rectangle measuring 68 by 18 feet [20 by 5 metres]. The walls were made of brick and the roof was covered with shingles cut from local trees, and the house included many windows. A verandah, built as an external passage rather than as a protective covering from the heat and weather, ran along the east side of the house to give access to the rooms at either end. Elizabeth Farm was the prototype for all farmhouses in New South Wales.

Also built around this time, possibly earlier, was Experiment Farm Cottage. Designed for James Ruse (1760–1837), an ex-convict, it was established to give him a place where he could work the land. It was rectangular and built out of stone, covered with a stucco finish and punctuated by four pairs of French louvred doors. The French windows were used to take in the panoramic views of the pastoral landscape. Shingles were used to cover both the roof and wide protective verandah. Although there is no substantial proof, the cottage has been dated by local historians to 1798.

Elizabeth Farm, c. 1794
Historic Houses Trust of New
South Wales

The 1790s saw improved building standards, techniques and tools. Footings were made from locally quarried stone and floorboards replaced trampled earth and clay-packed floors. Ceilings were constructed to act as a form of insulation; internal walls were sealed, and then plastered with grass and reinforced with hair and mud. Cow dung was added to avoid the likelihood of cracking. After this tedious process the

Experiment Farm Cottage,
c. 1798

Photographer: Jon Rendell

wall was finally given a coat of paint. Doors and windows were eventually spanned by wooden lintels, which supported the weight of the overhead brickwork.

The mud-brick home still had problems with stability, a problem that was overcome by the development of a timber-framed design. Weatherboards imported from Singapore were placed on to a timber frame that was held together with iron bolts. The inside was panelled with brick and mud to aid insulation. Other improvements included sliding glazed windows, shutters, raised floors and cellars.

ACTIVITIES

1. Why were the Aborigines given the title 'Noble Savages'?

2. From your own research, find a reproduction of a classical Greek figure and compare the representation of the Greek figure with that of the Aborigine in the reproduction on page 21.

3. Watling's work is similar to the English landscape painting tradition, particularly the work of Richard Wilson. Find one of Wilson's paintings or a painting by one of his contemporaries and discuss the similarities and differences in their work. Take note of composition, colour and the general 'mood' of the work.

4. What were the major problems experienced by the English artists painting the Australian landscape?

5. Look at *View of Sydney from the West Side of the Cove* (page 23). Trace the streets. Explain what you can see.

6. How did the early builders overcome the shortage of lime? Explain why lime was necessary.

7. Make a drawing in your book of either a wattle and daub house or Elizabeth Farm. Briefly describe its construction.

8. Collect materials suitable for the construction of a primitive wattle and daub house. With the help of your teacher construct the house in miniature.

	AUSTRALIAN EVENTS	GENERAL EVENTS	ARTISTIC EVENTS	
1820	**1821** Macquarie's term as governor finishes. **1824** The British government declares New South Wales no longer a penitentiary but a British colony. Hume and Hovell explore south-eastern Australia. **1828** Sturt explores rivers, discovering the Darling River. **1829** Perth is established on the Swan River by Captain James Stirling.	**1821** Napoleon dies at the age of fifty-two. **1822** Egyptian hieroglyphics of the Rosetta Stone are deciphered by Champollion. **1827** Beethoven dies of pneumonia.		**Australian artists** John Glover Conrad Martens Augustus Earle Benjamin Law
1830	**1830** Sturt discovers the Murray River. **1835** Melbourne is settled by John Batman. **1836** The site of Adelaide is chosen by Colonel Light. Captain John Hindmarsh becomes first governor of South Australia. **1839** Caroline Chisholm works in Sydney.	**1839** Daguerre invents photography and the result is the daguerrotype.	**1830** Delacroix: *Liberty Leading the People.* **1834** Daumier: *Rue Transonain.* **1836** Barry and Pugin, architects, design the Houses of Parliament, London. Finished c. 1860. Constable: *Stoke by Nayland.*	
1840	**1840** Transportation of convicts to New South Wales ceases. **1848** New South Wales establishes state schools.	**1846** The first sewing machine is patented in the United States. **1848** Gold is discovered in California.	**1844** Turner: *Rain, Steam and Speed.* **1849** Courbet: *The Stone Breakers.*	
1850	**1850** Wool becomes a leading export industry.	**1850** The Taiping Rebellion begins in China.	**1850** Paxton: The Crystal Palace is built in London. Courbet: *A Burial at Ornans.*	**Architects and architecture** Francis Greenway Edmund Blacket Georgian Primitive Gothic Revival
1860				

CHAPTER THREE

The Colonial Period 1819–50

Painting

One of the earliest painters to attempt to capture the true qualities of the Australian landscape was the English artist **John Glover (1767–1849)**. Before his arrival in Van Diemen's Land he was a well-established English artist with a fine record of exhibition prizes. The new colonies, and especially Van Diemen's Land, had received a lot of publicity from the English press, which made them seem an exotic faraway paradise. Glover and his family were among many thousands who emigrated.

The Glover family arrived at Hobart Town in 1831 and obtained a land grant in north-eastern Van Diemen's Land. The family settled and built their homestead, called Patterdale Farm. It was on this property that Glover painted many of his landscapes.

Glover found the Australian bush interesting and unique, certainly a contrast to the English countryside. One of his initial observations was that no matter how numerous the trees, they never prevented you from looking through them to see the whole country. This was unlike European landscapes where trees tended to block the distant horizon. He realised the different qualities of the foliage and, in his painting, attempted to capture this effect.

One of the best known of Glover's paintings is *The River Nile, Van Diemen's Land from Mr Glover's Farm*, 1837. Despite some problems with proportion it is a beautifully topographical and picturesque painting. The gum trees appear long and spindly, almost rubbery in shape. Glover's traditional European training can be seen in the way he has composed the trees that frame the work. He has also been careful to show the distant landscape through the sparse gum trees.

This work also shows the Aborigines bathing in the translucent waters of the Nile River. It is an idyllic scene in both its portrayal of the landscape and of the Aborigines as 'Noble Savages'. In spite of the idealisation of the Aborigines as 'Noble Savages',

JOHN GLOVER
(1767–1849)

*The River Nile, Van
Diemen's Land from Mr
Glover's Farm*, 1837
Oil on canvas,
76.2 x 114.3 cm

National Gallery of Victoria
Felton Bequest 1956

this quaint notion played no part in their preservation. Although there were frequent representations of Aborigines as peaceful people, they were still slaughtered relentlessly by European settlers.

In colonial paintings of this time it was not uncommon to show the Aborigines gathering food and apparently enjoying such daily activities. Although this may once have been an accurate description of their lifestyle, it is unlikely the painters ever saw them enjoying such a peaceful, carefree life. By the time these painters arrived in Van Diemen's Land, most of the Aborigines had either died or gone into hiding. The Aborigines appeared in works largely to complement the natural Australian landscape. Paintings which included exotic subject matter of this type tended to sell extremely well back in England. Although Glover and other artists were fully aware of what was happening to the Aborigines, they still preferred to paint them enjoying the beautiful Arcadia as in *The River Nile*.

Another English artist from this period who worked in New South Wales, particularly in the Sydney Cove area, was **Conrad Martens (1801–78)**. With his family, he travelled extensively throughout New South Wales and finally settled in Sydney.

Although much of his work was produced for wealthy landowners and patrons, his real passion was for painting Sydney Harbour. His work was initially topographic but it later developed into powerful atmospheric landscapes. His watercolour *View of Sydney from Rose Bay*, 1836, is a superb portrayal of Sydney at sunset. The sky is a wash of crimson and gold, while the foreground displays a range of cool blues and greys. The reflection of the brilliant sun on foliage and rocks is highlighted with the application of daubs of pure white, giving an almost glowing effect. Overlooking the harbour is a grand colonial mansion, an obvious sign of colonial growth and expansion. In the middleground, an Aborigine portrayed as a 'Noble Savage' is shown in silhouette spearing fish, while in the foreground, Aboriginal women are shown preparing a fire.

CONRAD MARTENS
(1801–78)
View of Sydney from Rose Bay, 1836
Watercolour, 45.1 x 64.8 cm
National Gallery of Victoria
Felton Bequest 1950

Martens was influenced by the English romantic painters, in particular Turner. The influence is quite strong, especially in works where Martens portrays large areas of light, atmosphere and mood. *View of Sydney from Rose Bay* is a classic example of Martens's passion for depicting light; in fact Martens believed (as did Turner) that light was the most dramatic element in nature.

Martens was the first artist to actively concern himself with the promotion of art in the colony. He constantly referred to Australia as a 'cultural backwater' and tried to change this situation by giving lectures and holding demonstrations on watercolour painting technique. Martens hoped that this sort of activity would lead to an 'improved' society.

Martens's enthusiasm was well received. A patronage system was established by squatters, affluent merchants and government officials. Their desire for a painter to capture portraits of the leading members of colonial society on canvas was answered by the arrival in 1825 of the English artist **Augustus Earle (1793–1838)**.

Earle was an established and well-respected painter who had exhibited at the Royal Academy, London. One of the largest landowners in New South Wales at this time was Captain John Piper, who commissioned Earle to paint his portrait. Piper owned a rather grand yet pretentious homestead which he named Henrietta Villa. It is this property which is visible in the background of the portrait.

Captain Piper was one of the first to have his portrait painted by Earle. The large work shows Piper beside a gum tree, wearing his uniform and standing in a pose reminiscent of Napoleon. The painting of the figure appears almost too flat, like a cut-out, but the slick tonal modelling on the face tends to compensate for this. The landscape in the background shows the size of his property and his villa. Earle remained in Australia for only three years. It is said he found the local scene too depressing and in some ways primitive. He left Australia in 1828 to pursue his artistic career in Europe.

RIGHT:

AUGUSTUS EARLE
(1793–1838)
Captain John Piper, c. 1826
Oil on canvas,
191.5 x 111 cm
Mitchell Library, State Library
of New South Wales

FAR RIGHT:

BENJAMIN LAW (1807–90)
Truganini, 1836
Clay
Museum of Victoria

Sculpture

The earliest forms of sculpture in the colonies were executed in Van Diemen's Land. These were portrait busts, and architectural decorations attached to newly constructed, neo-classical buildings. The artist who sculpted the busts was an Englishman named **Benjamin Law (1807–90)**.

Law arrived at Hobart Town with his wife in 1834 and commenced business as a sculptor of busts. His models were the local Aborigines who were almost extinct by this time. Law sculpted the busts out of clay and then made plaster casts, which were later hand-painted. He offered the busts for sale at four guineas each. Of the thirty plaster casts he made, only a few survive. Law realised the difficulty in making a living this way and so he opened a general store, which he found more financially rewarding and reliable.

Australians have been hesitant to accept the value of sculpture and the role of the sculptor. Sculpting has been generally seen as falling into two areas: the first, the architect-sculptor who designs public monuments to stand on street corners, in parks and in front of office buildings; the second, the private sculptor who works purely as a means of personal expression with the aim of selling the work. Whichever form it takes, sculpture depends for its growth on the existence of a suitably interested, motivated and affluent group of people to act as patrons. Unfortunately, early colonial Australia was in no position to offer support on such a scale to any sculptor.

Civil architecture

The standard of architecture improved rapidly in the colony with the importation of improved tools, materials and skilled labour. Sydney saw the arrival of a very self-confident, aggressive and competent architect named **Francis Howard Greenway (1777–1837)**. Born into a family of architects and being well versed in art and culture, Greenway became invaluable to colonial Sydney.

Transported to Australia for forging bank notes, his talents were quickly utilised and he became the government architect. Greenway was given his ticket-of-leave by Governor Macquarie, who had been impressed by his design for the Macquarie lighthouse, and set up business as an architect in George Street, Sydney. In late 1816 he was appointed civil architect and assistant engineer with the job of planning, designing and erecting all government buildings.

Greenway's dedication to his work was evident to all those who worked with him. He was intolerant of incompetent builders and contractors, and refused to pay for slipshod work. In six years his energy and tenacity produced a large number of buildings, ranging from lighthouses to churches and schools. He also initiated plans for a sewerage system, fortifications and many bridges.

One of Greenway's finest buildings is Hyde Park Barracks. Built between 1817 and 1819, it is a particularly well-proportioned, three-storey sandstone building. Once completed, it became the jewel of the city. The main building's facade comprises four brick pilasters, running up to the gable at which is located a clock with gold leaf numerals. The belltower which called convicts to order, the ventilation shaft and a row of chimneys all sit on the shingle roof. The clock still runs on its original mechanism and only gains thirty seconds a week. Around the ground floor of the building run arches in which windows and doors are placed. Above the front door is located a decorative fanlight, a Georgian feature. Hyde Park Barracks became the subject of a painting by the Sydney artist Sali Herman (*The Law Courts*, 1946).

One device Greenway used to protect the foundations of his buildings was that of the extended eaves. The rains in Sydney were so heavy that the constant dripping of water from the roof led to the rotting of bricks and mortar. To alleviate this problem, Greenway extended his eaves so that water fell away from the foundations. Although the introduction of cement mortar and roof gutters made extended eaves superfluous, the device is still used today as decoration and protection from the sun.

Greenway's architecture reflects a strict control of form, decoration and proportion. Although classical in its foundation, the expression was English, but to this Greenway added his personal touch with Australian adaptations.

Domestic architecture

Apart from the grand mansions built for such people as Captain John Piper, houses for the not so wealthy tended to be modest but functional. The first pioneering home was a simple and basic design called the Georgian Primitive or Colonial Georgian. It was derived from the grand stately Georgian homes of England but interpreted on a much smaller scale. Another influence was the bungalows that were built in colonial India.

Compared to the earlier wattle and daub house, this style was sturdier and more refined. The Colonial Georgian house was built out of stone and handmade bricks and usually had a verandah running along the front. Hand-blown glass was used in the windows and a limited range of paint was available. Imported cast iron and steel was used partly in the structure of the house but more usually as decoration.

Features of the Colonial Georgian style, 1788–1850, are:

- symmetrical arrangement
- windows often comprising twelve small panes
- painted walls
- fanlight over door
- four-panelled door
- kitchen usually at the rear of the house, semidetached
- imported flat iron tiles, shingles or slate on a steeply pitched roof

For the wealthy, who wanted to emulate the British aristocracy and landed gentry, a much grander style of Georgian house was developed. This style was known as Regency. Common throughout the years 1820–50, it was a combination of all the Georgian styles. There was not a great deal of decoration and details but architects of Regency buildings were very conscious of proportion and scale. Some wealthy members of colonial society had a penchant for ostentatious decoration in their houses and gardens: the grounds of one grand mansion displayed over four hundred spotted deer imported from India.

Captain John Piper's residence, Henrietta Villa, was a Regency house. At the time it was a significant work as it was one of the first examples of classical architecture built in Australia. Although from the front the building appeared symmetrical, it was an 'L' shape with a verandah running around it. The most novel feature of the mansion was the ballroom, which was capped by two domes. The painter Joseph Lycett remembered the wonderful balls that were held there. He claimed they would have put a society ball in London to shame. In 1824 Lycett described the villa as the most superb residence in the colony:

> The interior of the villa is fitted up in a style that combines elegance and comfort. The principal apartments are a spacious dining room, a banqueting room and a drawing room: all finished in the most tasteful manner. This naval villa may be considered the most superb residence in the colony, having cost, according to general report, at least ten thousand pounds.

Features of the Georgian Regency style, 1820–50, are:

- design by architect
- occasionally with two storeys

OPPOSITE

FRANCIS GREENWAY
(1777–1837)
Hyde Park Barracks,
1817–19

Photographer: Jon Rendell

- symmetrical arrangement
- large windows
- stylistic classical details such as columns
- occasionally with bay windows
- formal entrance porch
- verandah

JOSEPH LYCETT (1774–
c. 1825)
*Captain Piper's Villa at Eliza
Point*, 1824
Mitchell Library, State Library
of New South Wales

ACTIVITIES

1. Glover noticed something odd about the Australian countryside. What was it? Why did he find it so unusual?

2. Take a careful look at Glover's *The River Nile*, (page 28) and decide if you like it. Explain fully why, or why not. Use the Guide in Appendix One to help you (page 265).

3. Compare a work by the English painter, Turner, with a watercolour by Conrad Martens. Can you find any similarities? Look at composition, colour, light and mood.

4. Why do you think the depiction of Aborigines was an important element in colonial paintings by Martens and Glover?

5. Why did sculpture take so long to be established?

6. In what way could Law's busts be of great value to Australian historians?

7. Make a drawing of one of Greenway's buildings. Mark the following architectural elements:
   - fanlight
   - gable
   - pilaster

8. Make a detailed drawing of either a Colonial Georgian house or a Regency house. Note all the architectural features.

9. On the verandah of Henrietta Villa there were supporting Doric columns. Make a careful drawing of a Doric column. Are there any on buildings in your local area?

	AUSTRALIAN EVENTS	GENERAL EVENTS	ARTISTIC EVENTS	
1850	**1850** University of Sydney, Australia's first university, is founded.			**Australian artists** S.T. Gill Eugène von Guérard Nicholas Chevalier Louis Buvelot William Strutt John Simpson Mackennal Charles Summers
	1851 Edward Hargraves discovers gold.			
	1854 The crisis of the Eureka Stockade, Ballarat, occurs.	**1854** Florence Nightingale takes charge of nursing during the Crimean War.		
	1856 Parliaments in Victoria, New South Wales, South Australia and Tasmania open.	**1856** The Treaty of Paris ends the Crimean War.		
		1859 Charles Darwin publishes *The Origin of Species*.		
1860	**1860** Burke and Wills set off to explore Australia's centre.	**1861** The American Civil War breaks out.	**1862** Daumier: *The Third-Class Carriage*.	
	1862 Rail connections between Melbourne, Ballarat and Bendigo are completed.	**1864** Louis Pasteur invents the technique of pasteurisation.	**1863** Manet: *Olympia*.	
	1864 The first sugar is produced commercially in Queensland.	**1865** Abraham Lincoln, United States President, is assassinated.		
	1865 The first Arnott's biscuit is eaten.	**1867** Russia sells Alaska to the United States for US $7.2 million in gold.		
		1869 The Suez Canal opens.		
1870	**1872** Laws are passed in Victoria that schools are to be compulsory and free.	**1870** The Franco-Prussian War begins.	**1871** Whistler: *Arrangement in Black and Gray: The Artist's Mother*.	
	1874 The Art Gallery of New South Wales is established in Sydney.			
	1878 Reward of £100 offered for Ned Kelly.	**1876** Alexander Graham Bell invents the telephone.	**1876** Rodin: *The Bronze Age* (S). Renoir: *Le Moulin de la Galette*.	
	1879 The National Gallery of South Australia is established in Adelaide.	**1879** Thomas Edison invents the light bulb.		
1880	**1880** Ned Kelly is hanged in Melbourne.			**Architects and architecture** Joseph Reed Edmund Blacket
	1885 Cable trams run in Melbourne.			Victorian architecture Italianate style
1890				

CHAPTER FOUR

Eureka 1850–80

Social and economic background

The discovery of gold in 1851 in New South Wales and Victoria led to many changes in Australia's economic, social and cultural life. The most obvious change was of a financial nature. Building activity boomed and towns grew into cities. These became centres of culture and thriving businesses.

Initially the excitement created by 'gold fever' slowed life down in the cities. The arrival of thousands of Europeans, hoping to strike it rich on the goldfields, turned Melbourne and Geelong into virtual ghost towns. Thousands of people, carrying only a few personal possessions, and perhaps with a cart and a dog, took to the dusty roads bound for the goldfields.

Life on the goldfields was, for the most part, unpleasant, tedious and extremely overcrowded. On the Bendigo goldfields, the mostly male population reached 40 000. With everyone wanting to make their fortune one way or another, food, medical supplies, doctors and general goods tended to be outrageously overpriced. Gradually people became disheartened by the crowded tent cities. As the prospect of finding gold diminished quite significantly, slowly people packed up and headed for home, rarely with anything to show for their months of misery but empty pockets and poor health.

By late 1851 news of the gold rush had spread to Europe, encouraging families to migrate. Of the artists who arrived and travelled to the goldfields, most ended up depending on their art for survival. Despite the interest and excitement created by the gold rush, most of the artists chose to depict the unique qualities of the landscape.

Painting

Of the few artists who drew upon the experiences of the goldfields, the most popular was the Englishman **Samuel Thomas Gill (1818–80)**. His work remains as a fine social document of colonial life, and also depicts views of the growing cities and their people. Gill arrived in South Australia in 1839 and later travelled to the Victorian goldfields in the hope of making his fortune. After prospecting for a few months and experiencing the climate and harsh conditions of the goldfields, he turned his attention to illustrating what he saw around him. In pen and ink, and watercolour, he made hundreds of sketches of a wide range of subjects: Sunday morning church services; panning for gold; striking it rich; and even scenes of the unlucky prospector drowning his sorrows with a glass or two of ale. Although he was not a brilliant drawer his works were instantly popular and admired by all.

The handcoloured lithograph, *The New Rush*, 1863, shows the arrival of the prospectors at the goldfields. Men, with their possessions strapped to their backs, and with dogs and horses in tow, are arriving to try their luck. Although some of the figures appear a little rigid, the work still conveys what it must have been like on the goldfields.

Gill was a sensitive man who always chose to represent the prospector or the working man with dignity and charm. He was the first artist to depict the early attitudes of Australian life.

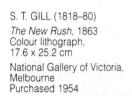

S. T. GILL (1818–80)
The New Rush, 1863
Colour lithograph,
17.6 x 25.2 cm
National Gallery of Victoria, Melbourne
Purchased 1954

After the initial excitement of the goldfields had died down, Gill left Ballarat and returned to Melbourne. He continued to work on his drawings, depicting scenes around the new growing city. He became depressed later on in his life and eventually turned to alcohol. In 1880 the drunken Gill collapsed dead on the steps of the Melbourne Post Office. Throughout his working life Gill completed more than 1500 works and his art remains as popular today as it was in the gold rush period.

Another painter who spent time on the goldfields but responded differently to what he saw was the Viennese-born **Eugène von Guérard (1812–1901)**. He heard of the gold rush while in Europe and decided, like thousands of others, to come to Australia to try his luck. He arrived in Geelong in January 1852 and immediately left

EUGÈNE VON GUÉRARD
(1812–1901)

*Ferntree Gully in the
Dandenong Ranges*, 1857
Oil on canvas, 92 x 138 cm

Collection: National Gallery
of Australia, Canberra
Gift of Joseph Brown

for Ballarat. After a year on the goldfields, enduring such curiosities as scorpions sharing his bed, large black ants, persistent bush flies and the threat of robbery by bushrangers, he packed up his tent and returned to Melbourne.

He was a very traditional painter who had been trained in the great academies of Europe. He was the son of a court painter to Emperor Franz I of Austria. His aim, while in Australia, was to seek out those unique parts of the land and capture them in paint. Although he made a few sketches on the goldfields, the great bulk of his work is of large panoramic landscapes. He was a very polished painter who was concerned with depicting every visible leaf, tree and rock with extraordinary accuracy.

Von Guérard was constantly in awe of the unique flora and fauna of this new land. He regularly battled with the horrors of the Australian bush—such as snakes and flies—to seek out new and exciting subject matter. He travelled extensively throughout Gippsland and central Victoria. His work was extremely popular in the western district of Victoria where the wealthy pastoralists employed him to paint scenes of their properties and homesteads. One of these journeys took him to the Dandenong Ranges near Melbourne where he painted the lush, green Ferntree Gully. The work entitled *Ferntree Gully in the Dandenong Ranges*, 1857, is a fine example of his style. It shows the lush ferny vegetation in the gully with the typical gum tree bushscape visible on the ranges in the background.

Von Guérard painted the gully and its surrounding vegetation and rocks with detailed accuracy. Even the carefully placed lyrebird, displaying its tail, is painted with great care. His attempts to display the Australian landscape were hampered by his attention to detail, a legacy of his traditional European training. Like many other

NICHOLAS CHEVALIER
(1828–1902)

The Buffalo Ranges, 1864
Oil on canvas,
132.4 x 183.2 cm

National Gallery of Victoria,
Melbourne
Purchased 1864

European painters, he found the differences in the landscape hard to accommodate in his art. In his other paintings, von Guérard's Victorian hills resemble European alps and the unique Australian light seems wrong: even the gum trees appear too green and lush. Despite this, von Guérard's paintings are still magnificent panoramas of Australian, and especially Victorian, landscape. In 1870 he took the position of curator and master of the newly established National Gallery of Victoria.

The British believed that, especially in such a newly established city as Melbourne, art was required to set the tone in society—to add a touch of sophistication. A writer at this time, Joseph Moore, reflected on the state of the arts in Australia in 1857:

> … here are we—upwards of half-a-million civilized men,—living in a glorious land, in an age of Art-Revival, and yet the time has not arrived for our cultivation of the Beautiful![1]

Moore's lectures and essays emphasised the need to establish art schools and urged the need for increased patronage of artists.

English colonial settlers became patrons to artists and it was not long before the desire for a State collection of art arose. The National Gallery of Victoria was endowed with its first State collection in the 1860s.

---

[1] Smith, B., *Documents on Art and Taste in Australia: The Colonial Period, 1770–1914*, Oxford University Press, Melbourne, 1975, p. 149.

The pioneer in the landscape was a popular subject during the 1850s and remained so until the end of the century. Swiss-born **Nicholas Chevalier (1828–1902)** dealt with this theme. Chevalier was an architect and a painter whose works had been accepted by the Royal Academy in London. Chevalier encountered similar problems to von Guérard, especially with his work *The Buffalo Ranges*, 1864. This work was the first purchase by von Guérard for the newly opened National Gallery. Despite its imperfect execution, with areas of conflicting light and tone, the work became instantly popular. Its charm lay in its topical and sentimental subject matter depicting the pioneering family complete with a small dog, as a symbol of domesticity. A criticism levelled at the work was the fact that the mountains could have been the Swiss Alps. It was essentially a European expression of an Australian landscape.

Chevalier continued to paint both landscapes and, to a small degree, portraits. His work was noticed by the visiting Duke of Edinburgh who became Chevalier's patron. The royal patronage was held in high esteem and Chevalier left on a world tour painting scenes on the way, the results of which were exhibited in London in 1871.

The desire to seek out and romanticise the unique aspects of the Australian landscape came to an end with the arrival of the middle-aged painter **Louis Buvelot (1814–88)**. Buvelot, already an established European painter, arrived from Europe via Brazil (where he had lived for eighteen years as a painter, lithographer and photographer).

Buvelot was familiar with the technique of *plein air* painting (the French term, 'in the open-air', meaning the technique of painting the whole picture out of doors), and was the first European painter in Australia to work directly from nature. Von Guérard and Chevalier had both worked in their studios largely from preliminary drawings,

LOUIS BUVELOT (1814–88)

Yarra Valley, Melbourne, 1866
Oil on canvas,
57.2 x 71.1 cm

National Gallery of Victoria,
Melbourne
Felton Bequest 1934

LOUIS BUVELOT (1814–88)
Survey Paddock, 1871
Oil on canvas,
25.4 x 35.5 cm
National Gallery of Victoria, Melbourne
Presented by Mr John H. Connell 1914

and laboured over their paintings, at times losing the freshness and spontaneity for which they aimed. Buvelot painted peaceful domestic views of cattle grazing on the fringe of growing, prospering cities, as seen in *Yarra Valley, Melbourne,* 1866. This shows the growth, expansion and urbanisation of Melbourne that came with the gold rushes.

Although some of Buvelot's landscapes—such as *Survey Paddock*, 1871, with its gum tree like a windswept European oak—are reminiscent of European fields, he did manage to capture some features unique to the Australian landscape. He was the first painter of the Australian landscape to analyse its colours and attempt to capture the quality of the Australian light. The *plein air* manner in which he worked would no doubt have contributed to this. It is for these reasons that Buvelot must be viewed as the painter who bridged the gap between academic colonial landscape painting and *plein air* painting, the latter being intrinsic to the art of the later Heidelberg School painters.

Buvelot has often been described as the father of Australian landscape painting and it is for the above reasons that this is true. Although in some of his work references are made to European painting, his practice of *plein air* and his use of colour and light set the foundations for one of his students, Tom Roberts, together with his friends, to give Australian painting true direction.

During the colonial period, painters had an enormous supply of subjects to draw upon—from the expeditions of explorers to the unique animals in the landscape.

William Strutt (1825–1915) was one painter who saw his role as that of a documenter of the history and hardships that befell early pioneers and explorers in the colony, such as natural disasters and hold-ups by bushrangers. The son of a painter, Strutt arrived in Australia in 1850 and settled in Victoria for eleven years.

During the period 1862–64 Strutt worked on his most ambitious painting, *Black Thursday, 1851*. The work depicts the tragedy of bushfire very graphically. Although Strutt relied mainly upon his preliminary drawings, a great deal of other material for the painting came from his diary. Strutt wrote of the eeriness he felt at seeing Melbourne streets and grasslands taken over by hundreds of thousands of flies and grasshoppers. He went on to write about the intense heat:

> … The heat had become so terrific quite early in the day that one felt almost unable to move. At the breakfast table the butter in the butter dish was melted into oil, and bread when just cut turned to rusk. The meat on the table became nearly black, as if burnt before the fire, a few minutes after being cut. Everything felt hot to the touch, even the window panes in the shade …
>
> … The sun looked red all day, almost as blood, and the sky the colour of mahogany.[2]

The Australian heat was unlike anything Strutt had ever experienced before!

Long and rectangular, *Black Thursday* vividly depicts the tragedy, misery and chaos that the pioneers experienced. It was reported that the fire swept across the state from The Grampians to Mt Otway where temperatures rose to 117° Fahrenheit [47° Celsius]. In the painting one is confronted by the charred remains of dead animals and birds, about to be trampled by fleeing families and livestock. Although the subject matter is unpleasant, Strutt's superb drawing and technique cannot be denied. In terms of the emotion the work evokes, it stands alongside European

WILLIAM STRUTT
(1825–1915)
Black Thursday, 1851
(Detail), 1862–64
Oil on canvas,
106.7 x 774.7 cm
La Trobe Collection, State
Library of Victoria

[2] Smith, B., *Documents on Art and Taste in Australia: The Colonial Period, 1977–1914*, Oxford University Press, Melbourne, 1975, p. 131.

paintings depicting similar natural disasters, such as *The Raft of the Medusa*, 1819, by Géricault.

Once completed, Strutt's work was displayed in Australia and at the Royal Academy in London where the response was one of great curiosity, interest and admiration. The painting was later purchased by the State Government of Victoria and now hangs in the State Library, Melbourne.

Sculpture

The call for a museum was finally answered when the National Gallery of Victoria opened in Melbourne in 1861. The inaugural exhibition contained, along with other things, a collection of classical Greek, Roman and modern sculpture. Although the classical pieces were only plaster copies, such sculptures had never been seen by young Australians in the colony and the show proved very successful. These sculptures were the only examples of work to which sculptors could aspire. It remained so for decades. Despite the lack of interest in three-dimensional work there was a handful of sculptors who managed to make an income and contribute to the cultural life of the late colonial period.

With the building boom of the 1880s, grand European-style buildings rose rapidly out of the dirt streets. The affluence of the time can be seen in the highly decorative mouldings plastered onto the facades of buildings. This decoration was added largely to show off the wealth and prosperity that Melbourne was enjoying. One sculptor who contributed to this style of decoration was **John Simpson Mackennal (1832–1901).**

Owing to the general lack of interest in sculpture and few commissions, Mackennal was employed essentially as an architectural sculptor, his job being to sculpt decorations and figures for the new buildings. He produced a number of pieces, including farm animals for the lunette above the entrance to the Victoria Market; figures above the Hotel Windsor; and stone figures for the Law Courts building, all in Melbourne.

Although painting commissions were plentiful, the same could not be said for sculpture. The first sculpture commission came from the Victorian Government and it was given to an Englishman, **Charles Summers (1825–78).** Trained in Europe with a solid grounding in casting techniques and the history of art, Summers was well qualified for the job. After a brief and unsuccessful stint on the Victorian goldfields he,

BELOW:

JOHN SIMPSON MACKENNAL (1832–1901)

Figures, Queen Victoria Market, Melbourne

Photographer: Jon Rendell

BELOW RIGHT:

JOHN SIMPSON MACKENNAL (1832–1901)

Figures, Hotel Windsor, Melbourne, c. 1883–7

Photographer: Jon Rendell

CHARLES SUMMERS
(1825–78)
Burke and Wills, 1865
Bronze, height 4 m
City Square, Melbourne

Photographer: Jon Rendell

like many others, returned to Melbourne disheartened and broke. Initially he worked on the construction of Melbourne's Parliament House and then on a commission which was to depict the explorers Burke and Wills, who had recently perished tragically in Central Australia. It was the Victorian Government's way of posthumously honouring the courage and achievements of the two explorers and their party.

Summer's sculpture of *Burke and Wills*, 1865, is 13 feet [4 metres] in height and depicts the men in relaxed poses. The sculpting of the figures was heavily influenced by Michelangelo's figure of *Guiliano de' Medici*, c. 1530 (in the Medici Chapel, Florence). The standing figure of Burke may have been influenced by the classical

Greek figure of *Apollo Belvedere*, c. fourth century BC. It is quite likely that Summers would have seen these works while travelling through Europe. Burke and Wills are shown surveying the landscape and documenting the vast continent which they undertook to explore.

Owing to the lack of skilled craftsmen and metal foundries in Melbourne, Summers cast the work himself. The process was an incredible feat, which, when completed, was unveiled in 1865 by the Governor, Lord Darling, in the presence of 90 000 Victorians.

Summers's persistence in casting the bronze himself in Melbourne and not in Europe set an important precedent in the development of late colonial sculpture. Although he was encouraging the growth of sculpture and paving the way for others, unfortunately would-be-sculptors were still forced to travel overseas to learn their craft. The following decades in Australia's history saw a steady stream of art students departing for Europe.

Civil architecture

The gold rush had turned Victoria into a bustling and thriving colony. During the 1860s Victoria experienced the peak of its building boom—there were up to 170 buildings springing up each month. The benefits of the European Industrial Revolution, coupled with the importation of building materials such as coloured glass and decorative cast iron, enabled Australia's building industry to forge ahead in new directions.

Neo-classicism, directly from Europe, had taken its place as the predominant building style for public buildings. This style was actually a return to the principles of Greek and Roman architecture and was very popular. Buildings in this style started to fill Melbourne's and Sydney's dusty streets. One of Melbourne's grandest examples of this boom period can be seen in the State Library and Museum. Designed in the new exotic style, it dominated Melbourne's Swanston Street and heightened the importance of education (Melbourne University opened in 1853) and, of course, became a well-respected landmark.

The Victorian State Library (1854–1913) was designed by **Joseph Reed (1823–90)**. This grand building, with its portico of Corinthian columns, was very ambitious for such a new city. Buildings in such styles as this instilled in people a sense of pride in their city, and also reminded them of the England most had left behind. The library design boasted the incorporation of the then largest concrete reinforced dome in the world. It was intended to be placed on top of the reading room. It was not added until 1912 by Reed's successors, Bates, Peebles and Smart. Reed's work was much appreciated and respected. It was not long before he was in great demand to design other buildings. His other constructions, all in the similar neo-classical style, included the Geelong (1853) and Melbourne Town Halls (1867–70), the Melbourne Trades Hall and Ripponlea homestead. His other grand and extravagant design was for the Melbourne Exhibition Building.

The arrival of international exhibitions from overseas in the late 1870s sparked new enthusiasm into the commercial centres of both Sydney and Melbourne. The blockbuster exhibition of 1880 opened with a great deal of pomp and ceremony. There were guards of honour, processions of trade unions, fire trucks and nine brass bands

ABOVE:

JOSEPH REED (1823–90)
*The State Library,
Melbourne*, 1854–1913
Photographer: Jon Rendell

ABOVE RIGHT:

JOSEPH REED (1823–90)
*Exhibition Building,
Melbourne*, 1880
Photographer: Jon Rendell

whose music filtered throughout Melbourne's Carlton Gardens. The exhibition, open for seven months, introduced to the people of Melbourne many new machines and other inventions. Housed in Reed's grand building, it contained displays which continuously impressed Melburnians. The exhibition introduced the latest in world fashion.

The Exhibition Building was a large brick and wooden construction which was covered with stucco, resembling a wedding cake. With its towering octagonal dome (influenced by the Renaissance architect Brunelleschi and his Florence Cathedral), it typified the spirit of the age. Today this building is still used to house various exhibits and commercial shows. Reed's architecture turned Melbourne into a lively city of refinement and culture. Another grand piece of Victoriana is the Treasury building, Melbourne, 1857–62. In its day it was Melbourne's most elegant building. Built to house the gold collected from local mining towns, it was made of bluestone and Bacchus Marsh sandstone.

Other neo-classical 'Victorian' buildings are:

- Parliament House, Melbourne, 1856–92 (Knight and Kerr)
- Customs House, Melbourne, 1858–70 (Knight, Kemp and Kerr)
- Queensland National Bank, Queen Street, Brisbane, 1887 (Stanley)
- Treasury buildings, Adelaide, 1860 (Hamilton)
- Town Hall, Launceston, 1864 (Mills)
- Town Hall, Sydney, 1868–88 (Wilson Tower by T. and E. Bradbridge)

Domestic architecture

These 'gold' years in Victoria saw the scarcity of housing reaching desperation point. Thousands upon thousands of people continued to arrive in the colony daily. Hobsons

Bay was bulging at the sides with ships anchored anywhere they could find room. At this stage Melbourne was largely a 'canvas town' with settlers pitching their tents along the Yarra or wherever they could find space. When the gold boom collapsed in 1870, people returned to Melbourne from the goldfields, and this put added strain on the already crowded and cramped conditions.

Owing to the inadequacy of public transport in the big cities there was very little suburban expansion. With the need to accommodate many families in inner city areas, houses had to be plentiful and, at the same time, not take up too much land. It was from these requirements that the Victorian terrace house came into being. These two-storeyed or sometimes three-storeyed homes were mostly replicas of English terraces, even down to the decoration on the iron fences. They were built out of bluestone or brick and displayed ornate decorative facades. Balconies tended to be decorated with beautiful iron lace, and fences too, made from iron, displayed exotic Greek motif designs. Windows were larger, and often imported coloured glass was used to highlight the terrace's facade.

During this period there were two variations of the Victorian style. These were English Gothic, or Gothic Revival, and British-Italian known in Australia as Italianate. These styles were both products of the new ideas and imported materials that were flowing into the country.

The Gothic Revival style was essentially influenced by the English Gothic churches and cathedrals of the thirteenth and fourteenth centuries. It was introduced into Australia in 1842 by the English architect **Edmund Blacket (1817–83)**. The Gothic Revival style was extremely popular in England. In fact Pugin and Barry (architects of the Houses of Parliament) had built many churches throughout the English countryside, using as their inspiration the great Gothic cathedrals.

Although Gothic Revival was mainly a church style, its features were nevertheless applied quite successfully to office buildings, universities, schools and houses. It was

Gothic Revival house, East Melbourne, 1861

Photographer: Jon Rendell

a particularly romantic and nostalgic style which kept alive the memory of 'mother' England.

Features of the Gothic Revival style, 1845–90, are:

- pitched roofs, similar to those on a church
- carved wooden fretwork and bargeboards
- tall chimneys with chimney pots
- arched windows
- chimneys often placed at the front of the house

One of the most unusual buildings to contain Gothic Revival features is the Perth Town Hall, 1867–70, designed by the English immigrant Richard Jewell (1810–91). It is a unique building, reminiscent of a European castle with its towers and turrets. Openings at ground level are in the form of arches while openings on the clocktower are Gothic in decoration and style. The building remains as one of Perth's earliest signs of a flourishing city.

The Italianate style was, for the most part, exotic and the most decorative style seen in Australia until this period. Although borrowed from Britain, it originated with the Italian Renaissance buildings with their tall towers, porticos and mouldings. This style had a definite charm of its own and was very popular in Melbourne.

Features of the Italianate style, 1850–80, are:

- patterned brickwork
- imported slate roofs
- classical moulding around windows and doors

Italianate style house, Hawthorn, Victoria

Photographer: Jon Rendell

- ornamental tower-like chunky chimneys
- mosaic tiles or marble porch floors
- coloured floors
- four-panelled doors
- iron lace

The late colonial period was one of the most affluent, exciting and prosperous periods in Australia's history. Extravagant forms of behaviour such as wiping down hotel benches with champagne and lighting cigars with banknotes have never been repeated. These were the manifestations of success which filtered throughout the social, cultural and commercial centres of colonial Australia.

ACTIVITIES

1. Do you think it is valid to say that von Guérard rarely achieved a depiction of a truly Australian scene? Explain with particular reference to a reproduction in this or any other book.

2. Using specific European works from the Romantic school can you draw any similarities with the work of the 'gold' artists? Explain. Look at colour, style, subject matter and composition.

3. Find out what a lithograph is. Explain the process.

4. If you were painting a picture of a typical Australian landscape what aspects would you include? Why? Paint your favourite landscape.

5. Find out all you can about the Barbizon school. How does it relate to the painting of Buvelot?

6. Look for a reproduction of Michelangelo's *Guiliano de' Medici*, c. 1530. Draw comparisons between it and Summers's figure of Wills in *Burke and Wills* (page 45).

7. In your city or town are there any Classical or Neo-classical buildings? Which ones are they and have they been restored?

8. In Chapter Three you made a drawing of a Doric column. Now list and draw carefully the remaining two types of columns. Make a list of buildings around your area which feature these columns.

	AUSTRALIAN EVENTS	GENERAL EVENTS	ARTISTIC EVENTS	
1880	**1880** The *Bulletin* magazine is founded. The Salvation Army is established in Adelaide. **1883** The railway crosses the Murray River at Albury–Wodonga, and joins New South Wales and Victoria by rail. **1886** Finishing an 18-day strike, Victorian wharf labourers are granted an 8-hour day.	**1884** The Home Life Insurance Building, the first skyscraper, is built in Chicago. **1887** Celluloid photographic film is invented in the United States. **1888** George Eastman invents the first simple, inexpensive camera. Thomas Edison invents the movie camera.	**1886** Seurat: *Sunday Afternoon on the Island of La Grand Jatte*. **1889** Van Gogh: *A Starry Night*. Eiffel: The Eiffel Tower is built in Paris.	**Australian artists** Tom Roberts Jane Sutherland Frederick McCubbin Charles Conder Arthur Streeton Thomas Woolner Bertram Mackennal
1890	**1890** After more than three decades of prosperity, Australia suffers a depression. **1891** Queen Victoria Museum is opened in Tasmania. **1892** Gold rush at Kalgoorlie, Western Australia **1895** 'Waltzing Matilda' is sung for the first time.	**1895** X-ray technique is developed in Germany for use in medicine. Marconi invents the radio in Italy. **1899** The Boer War breaks out.	**1892** Toulouse-Lautrec: *At the Moulin Rouge*. Cézanne: *The Card Players*. **1893** Munch: *The Scream*. **1897** Rousseau: *The Sleeping Gypsy*. **1898** Rodin: *Monument to Balzac* (S). **1899** Monet starts his *Water Lilies* series.	
1900	**1900** The New South Wales government is the first to supply public housing in The Rocks, Sydney.	**1900** The first escalator is installed at the Paris Exposition.		
1910				**Architecture** 'Boom' style architecture

CHAPTER FIVE

The Search for an Identity 1880–1901

Social and economic background

The years from 1885 until Federation in 1901 saw massive social and economic improvements in Australia. General communication and rail links became much more widespread and helped to bring the country together. The population was still increasing and 60 per cent of all Australians were native born. But it was also a period which saw droughts, the collapse of the money markets, an economic depression and the rise of trade unions.

Culturally there was a quickening of nationalist sentiment in all areas of the arts. Such writers as Henry Lawson and Banjo Paterson wrote romantically of the outback and the shearer, and created the notion of the bushman as the true Australian.

The *Bulletin* magazine was founded in 1880. It sought to unify Australians through its down-to-earth approach. It was a radical weekly: anti-English and anti-royalist, the *Bulletin* was the most popular magazine on the newsstands. It became the bible of the bushman and boasted a weekly circulation of 80 000 copies.

This notion of the bush ethos comes through in part of one of Lawson's poems, 'The City Bushman', where he says:

Though the bush has been romantic and is nice to sing about,
There's a lot of patriot fervour that the land could do without—
Sort of British workman nonsense that shall perish in the scorn
Of the drover who is driven and the shearer who is shorn
Of the struggling western farmers who have little time for rest,
Facing ruin on selections in the sheep-infested West
Driving songs are very pretty, but they call for little thanks
From the people of a country in possession of the banks.[1]

---

[1] Lawson, Henry, *Collected Verse Vol. I 1885–1900*, Angus & Robertson, Sydney, 1967.

Although this is only part of the poem, the idea of the struggling bushman working hard to support his country appears to come through loud and strong. This was the flavour of Australian nationalism and it filtered through into other areas of literature.

Painting

The group of painters led by Tom Roberts and known as the Heidelberg School wanted to paint views of national life and the landscapes. In their quest to do so they made the break from traditional academic English painting. They aimed at developing an all-Australian school of landscape painting. **Tom Roberts (1856–1931)** was a student under Louis Buvelot at the Gallery School. Late in 1881 he travelled overseas to look at the European landscape and art. In 1883, in Europe, Roberts embarked on a walking tour of Spain with three other Australians, one of whom, John Peter Russell (see Chapter Seven), later became closely associated with the French Impressionist movement. While travelling through Spain, the group met two young artists fresh from art school in Paris. These artists introduced Roberts to the technique of *plein air* painting. *Plein air* was the technique similar to that which the French Impressionists used. It meant painting the whole picture out of doors, capturing the light and colour as spontaneously and accurately as possible. Buvelot had been doing similar things in Australia but this radical technique really became popular on Roberts's return to Australia in 1885.

Although Roberts was not entirely responsible for introducing *plein air* into Australia, he certainly developed it, consistently put it into practice and stressed its importance. On his arrival home, he found the atmosphere a little too rigid and suspicious to accept this new import; particularly unreceptive were the teachers at the Gallery School and critics such as James Smith. Similarly, the French Impressionists were experiencing trouble having their work understood in Paris.

In 1885 Roberts, with his friends Fred McCubbin, Louis Abrahams and Jane Sutherland camped at Box Hill just outside Melbourne where they painted the sunlit and twilight landscapes for days on end. The group also went on weekend trips to Eaglemont. In order to capture the unity of light and colour they painted the works quickly and completely out of doors. They focused on entire views rather than on detail. Previously painters would only sketch outside and complete the finished product in the studio. In order to quickly apply the paint, Roberts introduced the other painters to the broad brush, which made the job infinitely easier.

The following year, McCubbin and Roberts rented a cottage near Mentone on Port Phillip Bay, Melbourne. It was while painting here that they met Arthur Streeton, who was sitting out on the rocks painting the sea. From this time onward they developed a long and supportive friendship.

During this period at Mentone Roberts painted his masterpiece *Mentone*, 1887. It is a painting partly influenced by French Impressionism. The scene of ordinary people enjoying their leisure time on the beach or in the park is typical Impressionist subject matter. The rich and thickly applied paint surface is built up with different brushstrokes. The solid, ochre cliffs have their paint applied in vertical strokes contrasting with the sea which is approached in a broad horizontal manner.

Robert's other seaside painting was *The Sunny South*, c. 1887. The work shows three naked youths enjoying the great outdoor life, swimming and sunbaking, a popular Australian pastime. Unfortunately the work stirred Victorian morals. Such behaviour, as well as being an act worthy of prosecution was certainly unsuitable as subject matter. Although the nude in the landscape was a common theme in European art it certainly was not acceptable in Australia. Previously paintings depicting nudity were those of Aborigines enjoying nature. By all accounts *The Sunny South* appears to be the first Australian painting of its kind to show white Australians at leisure.

TOM ROBERTS
(1856–1931)

Mentone, 1887
Oil on canvas (mounted on board), 50.8 x 76.5 cm

National Gallery of Victoria, Melbourne
Purchased with the assistance of a special grant from the Government of Victoria, 1979

In 1888 Roberts went to Sydney where he met the Sydney artistic set made up of artists and critics and in particular the young bohemian, **Charles Conder (1868–1909)**. Conder had only just arrived in Sydney from Europe where he had mixed with the art societies of Paris and London. He had been a friend of Toulouse-Lautrec, the American artist Whistler and the English writer Oscar Wilde. Roberts and Conder spent so much time discussing the merits of French Impressionism and *plein air* that they made several sketching trips together around Sydney. They both painted scenes at Coogee in 1888. Roberts invited Conder to return with him to Melbourne where he was readily accepted into the group with McCubbin and Streeton.

In his never-ending quest to convert the art establishment into accepting *plein air* painting, Roberts organised another camp and follow-up exhibition. He collected wooden cigar box lids measuring 9 by 5 inches [23 by 13 centimetres] which were used to paint on. The group went out near Heidelberg and made rapid impressions of the landscape. The paint was applied thickly, broadly and hastily with the intention of capturing that fleeting moment. When the works were finished they were framed and exhibited at Buxton's Gallery, Swanston Street, Melbourne, in August 1889. The intention of the group was made clear with an essay displayed in the catalogue, the cover of which was designed by Conder. The introduction states:

An Effect is only momentary: so an impressionist tries to find his place. Two half-hours are never alike, and he who tries to paint a sunset on two successive evenings, must be more or less painting from memory. So, in these works, it has been the object of the artists to render faithfully, and thus obtain first records of effects widely differing, and often of very fleeting character.

Despite this introduction the critics were outraged. The critic of the *Argus*, James Smith, wrote in August 1889:

The modern impressionist asks you to see pictures in splashes of colour, in slap-dash brush work … Of the 180 exhibits catalogued on the present occasion, something like four-fifths are a pain to the eye. Some of them look like faded pictures seen through several mediums of thick gauze; other suggest that a paint-pot has been upset over a panel nine inches by five; others resemble the first essays of a small boy, who has just been apprenticed to a house-painter; …

The review concluded that:

'Impressionism is a craze of such ephemeral character as to be unworthy of serious attention.'[2]

TOM ROBERTS
(1856–1931)

Holiday Sketch at Coogee,
1888
Oil on canvas,
40.3 x 55.9 cm

Art Gallery of New South Wales
Purchased 1954

Roberts responded to this criticism by arguing that the group could paint landscapes in the tradition and style of earlier painters and thus work in acceptable mediocrity, or they could make a serious attempt to work towards a distinctive school of Australian landscape painting.

It must also be kept in mind that not all of the painters involved in the painting camps were exclusively landscape artists. Roberts had also established himself as a fashionable society portrait painter who had a wide clientele. It was in the late 1890s

[2] Smith, B., *Documents on Art and Taste in Australia: The Colonial Period, 1770–1914*, Oxford University Press, Melbourne, 1975, pp. 203–4.

that Roberts's subject matter changed to dealing with life in the bush and the outback, that is, nationalist themes.

Poets such as Lawson and Banjo Paterson (who visited Roberts's studio) wrote on similar themes to some of Roberts's paintings, such as *The Golden Fleece*, 1894, and *Shearing the Rams*, 1890. These works specifically aimed to show the dignity and honour of hard work and pastoral labour, idealising the shearer. Until the depression of the 1890s, wool had been Australia's major industry. Of *Shearing the Rams* Roberts said:

> … I had there the best expression of my subject, a subject noble enough and worthy enough if I could express the meaning and spirit—of strong masculine labour, the patience of the animals whose year's growth is being stripped from them for man's use, and the great human interest of the whole scene.[3]

Work and labour was also a popular theme with the European Realist painters such as Courbet, Millet and later the Dutchman, van Gogh. Contemporary French writers around the 1850s frequently wrote of the peasant who worked the land. They believed that peasants were not only the most numerous part of the nation, but also the strongest and the healthiest. The notion of the honourable worker on the land was not unique to Australia. Although modified, its roots lay firmly entrenched in European art.

TOM ROBERTS
(1856–1931)

Shearing the Rams, 1890
Oil on canvas (lined on to board), 121.9 x 182.6 cm

National Gallery of Victoria, Melbourne
Felton Bequest 1932

[3] *Argus*, 4 July 1890.

At the time, paintings showing labour and work were viewed with little respect. Wealthy art patrons and critics believed that the subject matter was totally inappropriate for a gallery or wall. People simply did not want to see men sweating their life out in a smelly, steamy shearing-shed.

Jane Sutherland (1855–1928) was born in Scotland and arrived in Australia in 1870. She enrolled in the National Gallery school in Melbourne between 1872 and 1885 where her talent rapidly earned the respect of the other students. She shared the Grosvenor Chambers Studio at 9 Collins Street with Tom Roberts, and participated in many of the painting excursions to outer Melbourne.

As mentioned previously, images of men at work were popular themes both in art and literature during this time. Jane Sutherland produced pictures that dealt with themes similar to the images explored by Roberts and McCubbin of men working the land. In *The Mushroom Gatherers*, c. 1895, Sutherland shows a rare view of women working outdoors. While they are not shown in the same heroic and glamorised way as the men in *Shearing the Rams* or *The Pioneer*, they do show the role played by women in early Australian life, subjects often ignored by their male colleagues.

The women in this landscape are not involved in chopping trees or burning off but are involved in another form of land work, one that is less intrusive and destructive. One woman is collecting the mushrooms from the soil while the other holds them in her apron. Sutherland's painting of the landscape is consistent with work of this time: long panoramic vistas saturated with light and atmosphere.

JANE SUTHERLAND
(1855–1928)
The Mushroom Gatherers,
c. 1895.
Oil on canvas, 41.3 x 99 cm
National Gallery of Victoria,
Melbourne
Gift of Dr Margaret Sutherland
1972

Frederick McCubbin (1855–1917) was a painter of the bush and dealt directly with such themes as isolation, pioneering and the struggle against the elements. After leaving Heidelberg, he started to paint the agonies and hardships experienced by the early settlers in the bush. The swaggie who has lost all his money panning for gold is shown sitting by a campfire in *Down on His Luck*, 1889. *On the Wallaby Track*, 1896, brought home the tragedy of the economic depression and unemployment with the depiction of a man and his family literally on the wallaby track (moving from place to place in search of work). This work displays many of the characteristics of French Impressionism, especially in its application of paint—the flecks and daubs across the

ABOVE:

FREDERICK McCUBBIN
(1855–1917)

On the Wallaby Track, 1896
Oil on canvas,
122 x 223.5 cm

Art Gallery of New South Wales
Purchased 1897

RIGHT:

FREDERICK McCUBBIN
(1855–1917)

The Pioneer, 1904
Oil on canvas (triptych),
223.5 x 86 cm; 224.7 x
122.5 cm; 223.5 x 85.7 cm

National Gallery of Victoria,
Melbourne
Felton Bequest 1906

canvas representing foliage and grass. By far his most popular work seems to be the triptych of *The Pioneer*, 1904. It was painted near McCubbin's home at Mount Macedon and deals with the life of a pioneer in three stages. The first panel shows the pioneering couple making a fire while contemplating their new life. The second panel shows the clearing of the land and the woman holding a new baby. The third panel, a decade or two later, shows a bushman discovering a grave with a city in the background; just whose grave is open to interpretation. The National Gallery of Victoria finally purchased the painting and, with the money, McCubbin travelled to Europe.

Arthur Streeton (1867–1943) was the artist who said that Australia was the land of the 'blue and gold' and many of his works seem to reflect this belief. He was concerned with dealing with the light, heat and sun on the landscape and because of this most of his landscapes tend to be very high in key. He loved the Australian landscape, its vastness and depth. In letters he wrote to his friend Roberts he appears to be almost in awe of the land. He speaks passionately of the 'gums looking like thousands of bronzy ants coming over the gentle rise'. Dusk he wrote as being 'a mellow liquid full flood of twilight'. Such passages also became titles to his paintings such as *The Purple Noon's Transparent Might*, 1896, and *Still Glides the Stream, and Shall Forever Glide*, 1890.

Streeton preferred to paint in a long horizontal format but in order to achieve a different effect he would use a strong, thin, vertical board to represent a typically horizontal subject like a seascape. Although slightly unorthodox they are powerful

ARTHUR STREETON
(1867–1943)

The Purple Noon's
Transparent Might, 1896
Oil on canvas,
121.8 x 122 cm

National Gallery of Victoria,
Melbourne
Purchased 1896

ARTHUR STREETON
(1867–1943)

Near Heidelberg, 1890
Oil on canvas, 53.5 x 43 cm

National Gallery of Victoria,
Melbourne
Felton Bequest 1943,
reproduced by courtesy of
Mrs M. H. Streeton

and confident works. Streeton loved manipulating paint and he was a master of the flat brush. In paintings such as *Near Heidelberg*, 1890, the thin brushwork is most evident. He applied paint aggressively. For large areas such as pastures or skies he used the flat brush technique, which he had copied from Roberts. To depict trees, people or branches, Streeton used the flat-edged tip of the brush.

A long-respected master of Australian art, his landscapes were mostly well received. In 1918 he was posted to France to take up a position as official war artist. In his later years he painted around Sydney and the Hawkesbury. For his contribution to Australian art, he was knighted in 1937. He died in Melbourne in 1943.

The Heidelberg group of painters established themselves as serious artists who, in their own way, were concerned about the direction of Australian art. In an effort to break away from the English conservatism they applied their newly acquired techniques of *plein air* and maintained an interest in impressionist and realist art. In their attempt to develop a distinctive school of landscape painting, they attracted quite a significant amount of condemnation. This unpleasant fate is, however, common to all innovators and it is only with the passing of time that the public can objectively look at and accept new work.

Sculpture

The advances created by the discovery of an Australian school of painting unfortunately did not have much influence on the practising sculptors of this period. The sculptures that had been created up to this point had been very diverse in style and very broad in influence, and, unlike painting, appeared to lack any real direction. The other problem associated with the rise of sculpture was that often materials were scarce, and those imported from Europe were often damaged by the sea journey. The English sculptor Thomas Woolner actually stated that the imported plaster of Paris he used was ruined by the sea air and he was forced to make his own by grinding and drying out gypsum. He also made his own modelling tools from wood, and the clay he used was dug from river beds and worked into a suitable consistency. Despite these setbacks some fine sculpture was created during these years, the most notable by **Thomas Woolner (1825–92)** and Bertram Mackennal (1863–1931).

Woolner arrived in Melbourne to make his fortune on the goldfields. Being unsuccessful there he made money by sculpting portrait medallions of the local government officials. His biggest job was a commission by the New South Wales Government to make a statue of the navigator Captain James Cook.

The 3-metre high bronze sculpture was cast in London and shows Cook as the proud navigator that he was—discovering land, telescope in one hand, the other raised in a sign of excitement. Woolner stated that his idea when designing the work was to fill Cook with wonder and delight in the moment of discovering the new land. The work was finally unveiled in Hyde Park, Sydney, in 1879. It was reported that there were between 90 000 and 100 000 people present.

Another sculptor to make a considerable contribution to Australian art was **Bertram Mackennal**. Unlike other artists from this time who drew upon their local environment and history for stimulus, Mackennal looked towards Europe, or more specifically Greek mythology. For his work of 1893, Mackennal used the mythical figure of Circe who had the power to turn men into swine. She is depicted as a very beautiful woman with her arms extended in front of her and her fingers outstretched. She stands nude with an almost evil and powerful glare in her eye while snakes writhe through her hair, somewhat reminiscent of Medusa. The work was placed on a pedestal which has a relief of naked entangled bodies. These figures created a stir when first exhibited at the Royal Academy, London, in 1894. It was later requested by the officials that, in order to preserve moral standards, the base should be covered with cloth.

Mackennal enjoyed popular success and also the support of many famous and influential people, one of whom was the Australian singer Dame Nellie Melba. In 1899, at her request, Mackennal sculpted a very beautiful but traditional marble bust of her. The delicately and sensitively carved work was enthusiastically purchased by the National Gallery of Victoria for its collection.

The sculptures being created during this period were still very much in the European tradition. Sculptors had to be flexible enough to meet the demands of the public they were working for, largely the English cultured minority. Unlike painting, sculpture had to wait a little longer for its independence from European influences.

ABOVE:

THOMAS WOOLNER
(1825–92)
Captain Cook, 1874–79
Bronze, height 3 m
Hyde Park, Sydney
Photographer: Jon Rendell

ABOVE RIGHT:

BERTRAM MACKENNAL
(1863–1931)
Circe, 1893
Bronze, height 2.1 m
National Gallery of Victoria,
Melbourne
Felton Bequest 1910

Civil architecture

With the ever-increasing population and the availability of money from the gold rush days, not surprisingly the building industry started to boom. Named after this explosion, 'Boom' style spanned two decades from about 1870. It was a highly decorative style in which an attempt was made to show the wealth and prosperity that Australia was enjoying.

Both Melbourne and Sydney boast superb examples of High Victorian or Boom architecture. Sydney's Queen Victoria building, designed in 1893–98 by George McRae, is a most decorative and grand construction. When first completed it housed fruit and vegetable stalls in the basement and shops on the ground floor, while upstairs it comprised a banquet hall, concert hall, lending library and artists' studios. Designed with many extravagant copper cupolas and domes including one large central dome, it was a symbol of the increasing sophistication and style of the city. The facade of the building displays rows of pilasters and a decorative row of relief carving. The building has been thoroughly restored to its original grandeur.

The architect William Pitt designed Melbourne's equivalent to Sydney's Queen Victoria building. Known as the Rialto, it is situated in Collins Street. Designed as office buildings in 1890, it is one of the city's outstanding examples of the architecture from this period. Although the style of the Rialto is Gothic Revival, its eccentric and imaginative combination of multicoloured brickwork, marble columns, turrets and decorative friezes reflects the ostentation and wealth that was characteristic of the Boom period. The building was under threat of demolition for years but was given a reprieve when its facade was incorporated into a hotel and office block complex.

Other High Victorian (Boom) buildings are:

- Medley Hall Drummond Street, Carlton, 1892–93 (Walter Law)
- The Lands Department building, Sydney, 1876–90 (James Barnet)
- Edmund Wright House, 59 King William Street, Adelaide, 1867–77 (Wright and Tayler)
- His Majesty's Theatre, Perth, 1904 (William Wolff)
- Treasury Building, Brisbane, 1885–89 (J. J. Clark)
- Customs House, Rockhampton, 1900 (A. B. Brady)

BELOW:

GEORGE McRAE

Detail of Queen Victoria Building, George Street, Sydney, 1893–98

Photographer: Jon Rendell

BELOW RIGHT:

WILLIAM PITT (1855–1918)

Rialto Building, Melbourne, 1890

Photographer: Jon Rendell

Domestic architecture

As discussed earlier, the terrace house became the most sought after form of inner city accommodation. It was economical to build rows of terraces and also brought in lots of money as an investment for the people who later owned them. The Boom terrace house became much more decorative than previous terraces—an obvious sign of extravagance and wealth—and flaunted a variety of decoration both internally and externally.

During this time home owners generally became more conscious of their environment and gardens. English trees were planted at the expense of natives, which were uprooted and discarded. English gardens were much more fashionable. One most exciting and useful product, the lawn mower, came to Australia for the international exhibition of 1880. It had been invented in Britain in 1869 and by 1880 had been adapted to Australian conditions, revolutionising the gardener's weekend.

Boom style architecture continued well into the 1880s whereupon the economic collapse brought an end to such extravagant building styles. Although the terrace was not ideally suited to Australian conditions it has, today, remained a most popular form of housing. With people eager to restore them to their previous Victorian charm

Boom style house, South Melbourne

Photographer: Donald Williams

since the renovation boom of the 1960s and 1970s, terrace houses have become very expensive.

The features of High Victorian (Boom) style, c. 1870–90, are:

- heavily decorated and ornamented facades
- leadlight windows
- slate or iron roof
- lace work used extensively
- mosaic tiles used on the porches
- merging of varying styles such as Gothic and Italianate

ACTIVITIES

1. What did the Heidelberg School painters aim to do. Why?

2. Compare a work by Monet or another French impressionist with a work by any of the Heidelberg painters. How are they similar? Discuss subject matter, application of paint, colour and anything else you would like to add.

3. In relation to The 9 by 5 Impression Exhibition, what other work of art has recently caused similar controversy? Why do you think it did?

4. Research the work of Clara Southern and Jane Sutherland.

5. Compare a painting from the 'gold' period with any from the 'Heidelberg' period. What do you think are the obvious differences?

6. Using a book from your library, name a couple of the predominant European sculptors from the period 1850–1900. Can you draw any similarities with Woolner's or Mackennal's work?

7. Using either books or magazines, find examples of terrace houses (whether renovated or in their original state) and pick out their typical Victorian features. Draw a terrace house showing these features.

8. Find a High Victorian (Boom) or Neo-classical building in your city. Select a part of the building (tympanum, capital, part of facade, and so on) and make a careful, detailed tonal drawing. Make sure you know the architectural names of the section you choose.

9. Artists have often used myths and legends in their work. Research some Greek myths and produce a work based on them.

10. What was the controversy with Roberts's *The Sunny South*?

11. Using the study guide (Appendix One), review a painting in this chapter.

	AUSTRALIAN EVENTS	GENERAL EVENTS	ARTISTIC EVENTS	
1900	**1901** On 1 January, Australia becomes a Commonwealth. William Farrer releases a tougher variety of wheat called Federation. On 9 May, the first Parliament opens. Edmund Barton becomes Prime Minister. Population is about 3 773 809.		**1901** Guimard· Art Nouveau entrances to the Paris metro stations. Maillol: *Seated Woman (Méditerranee)* (S).	**Australian artists** David Davies Clara Southern Sydney Long J.J. Hilder Blamire Young Norman Lindsay Elioth Gruner Charles Douglas Richardson
1902	**1902** Melbourne is made capital of Australia, which it remains for twenty-six years. Women in New South Wales are given the vote. **1903** Alfred Deakin becomes Prime Minister.	**1903** The Wright brothers fly their first aeroplane.		
1904	**1904** George Reid becomes Prime Minister.	**1904** The Russo-Japanese War begins. **1905** Einstein publishes his theory of relativity.	**1905** First Fauvist exhibition is held in Paris. Matisse: *Woman With Hat.*	
1906	**1906** Deakin resumes office as Prime Minister. Sydney's Bondi Beach establishes the world's first lifesaving club.	**1906** Karl Nesser produces the first 'perm' in his London hairdressing salon.	**1906** Picasso: *Les Demoiselles d'Avignon.* **1907** Klimt: *The Kiss.* Bonnard: *The Artist's Studio.* Cubism is developed by Picasso and Braque.	**Architecture** Queen Anne and Federation style housing
1908	**1908** Victorian women are given the vote. Every State of the Commonwealth now acknowledges women's suffrage. The site is chosen for the new capital of Australia, Canberra.	**1908** The first radio broadcast is made in the United States. Ford develops the Model T in the United States.	**1908** Braque: *The Houses at L'Estaque.* Brancusi: *The Kiss* (S). **1909** Matisse: *Dance.* Lloyd Wright: Robie House, Chicago. Gaudi: Church of the Sagrada Familia, Barcelona. Futurism manifesto issued.	
1910		**1910** The first neon sign, invented by George Claude, flashes at the Paris motor show.		
	1911 Mawson leaves to explore Antarctica.			
1912				

CHAPTER SIX

Federation and Art Nouveau 1901–10

Social and political background

On the first day of the new year, 1 January 1901, thousands of people crammed into Sydney's Centennial Park in searing summer heat to join in the celebrations welcoming Australia's nationhood. Decorated floats, shearers, men on horseback, and superb displays paraded through Sydney's streets to thousands of applauding and cheering onlookers. In front of 7000 invited guests at the Park, Lord Hopetoun read out the congratulatory telegrams from Queen Victoria and the British Government. It was a day of celebration and festivities that were long remembered.

Despite the pomp and ceremony of the Federation festivities the beginning of the twentieth century saw many Australians regain their enthusiasm and confidence rather slowly. The early years saw a considerable degree of hardship and suffering. The long drought from the late 1890s, which sent many farmers bankrupt from their land, added to the already growing rate of unemployment that was being experienced in the cities. The 1890s depression, coupled with other worries, contributed to the loss of enthusiasm and energy that was so common during the period of nationalist inspiration of the 1880s and 1890s.

Painting

Culturally this period was a time when artists realised the importance of overseas travel to their education and their careers as successful professional artists. Tom

Roberts had demonstrated that it was indeed a valuable experience to study overseas and it did not necessarily mean the abandonment of Australian subject matter and influences. The bush had a certain mystique. It was with the melancholy of the bush that artists such as David Davies were particularly concerned. Unlike the Heidelberg School painters who preferred to show the landscape in its full sun-bleached appearance, this later group of painters' concerns lay in depicting the qualities of the landscape at dusk, the moon's reflection, romantic hazes and mysterious dark shadows.

DAVID DAVIES (1862–1935)
Moonrise, 1894
Oil on canvas,
119.8 x 150 cm

National Gallery of Victoria,
Melbourne
Purchased 1895

David Davies (1862–1935) was concerned primarily with exploring the 'soul' or spirit of the land. He travelled to Europe and studied the work of the English impressionists, and also the work of Whistler. Whistler's *Nocturne* paintings seemed to impress Davies sufficiently for him to take an interest in similar themes. Davies's *Moonrise*, 1894, was painted while he lived near Melbourne at Templestowe. Although it is simplistic in subject matter the careful and sensitive approach of its execution displays Davies's skill as a painter. Painted in browns, golds and mauves, the painting conveys the end of an extremely hot day with the heat rising from the ground. It was one of a series of nocturnal works, all of which contained a certain romantic quality which grew in popularity during this time.

CLARA SOUTHERN
(1861–1940)
Evensong, c. 1910
Oil on canvas,
54.4 x 112.2 cm
National Gallery of Victoria,
Melbourne
Purchased 1962

Born in Kyneton, Victoria, **Clara Southern (1861–1940)** went to art school with the painters of the Heidelberg School and was good friends with Jane Sutherland. Like Sutherland, Southern also painted many views of women at work, but she is particularly known for her evocative panoramic views of the landscape on the outskirts of eastern Melbourne.

Southern was not involved in the excursions to Heidelberg, but she did establish another camp of her own in the bush surrounding Warrandyte, where she lived from mid-1905. In its mood *Evensong*, c. 1910 resembles the peaceful landscapes painted by Davies and one of her teachers, Walter Withers (1854–1914), and was most probably painted near her home. The rather romantic name of the painting recalls the poetic titles given by Streeton to his works. In terms of its composition the painting is rather formal. Southern breaks the view neatly into foreground, middleground and background and modulates the tone and colour accordingly. Her choice of colour is subdued and evocative of the season and time of day. Southern's technique and brushwork was confident; scumbling the paint onto the canvas she also worked into the oil paint with the other end of the brush to suggest blowing grasses, twigs and foliage. On the right side of the picture a tree—in its winter dormancy—provides a compositional device to balance the picture. It is self-assured and recalls the romance and spirit of the Heidelberg School tradition.

The romantic and mysterious qualities of the Australian bush were developed even further in the work of painter **Sydney Long (1871–1955)**. Long transformed the Australian bush into a romantic Art Nouveau paradise where gypsies, Pans and other mythical characters frolicked peacefully. The Art Nouveau movement developed in England at the end of the nineteenth century and then later spread to Europe, America and Australia. In Britain it grew out of a reaction to previous styles of art—Gothic and Classical—which were machine-like and tight in appearance.

SYDNEY LONG
(1871–1955)

Fantasy, c. 1916–17
Oil on canvas,
127.3 x 101.6 cm

Art Gallery of New South Wales
Purchased under the terms
of the Florence Turner Blake
Bequest 1971

Craftsworkers and artists felt it was time to develop a new style which reflected the age in which they lived. Art Nouveau landscape painting had its roots in Impressionism yet aimed at keeping up with an age which was concerned with exploring new forms of expression.

Art Nouveau artists aimed at stylising nature's lines and making the straight, natural forms of nature into much more decorative, flowing, graceful and rhythmic lines. Australian Art Nouveau spread out into many forms of art and craft. Nationalistic motifs, such as natural Australian flora and fauna, were popular at this time. They were reflected in all areas of the arts and tended to be used as stylised designs. In painting, Art Nouveau not only determined the composition, it also played a large part in determining colour. More decorative colours such as soft pinks, pale mauves, ochres and pale greens tended to be favoured over the 'real' colours of the Australian bush.

SYDNEY LONG
(1871–1955)
Spirit of the Plains, 1897
Oil on canvas on wood,
62 x 131 cm

Collection: Queensland Art Gallery
Gift of William Howard Smith Esq. in memory of his grandfather Ormand Charles Smith, 1940

Sydney Long was the first Australian painter to depict the Australian bush in an Art Nouveau style. His work *Spirit of the Plains*, 1897, depicts a pipe-playing figure majestically gliding through the golden fields. Following behind is a group of stylised brolgas, their necks outstretched, gracefully moving from side to side. The silhouettes of the brolgas are sharply contrasted with the trunks of the swaying grey eucalypts in the distance. The patterns of the Australian gum trees lent themselves perfectly to Art Nouveau stylisation.

Other artists to show similar interests and influences were **Jesse Jewhurst Hilder (1881–1916)** and Blamire Young. J. J. Hilder used the medium of watercolour to its fullest capacity, that is, the quality of transparency and the dissolution of the paint into the paper which all added to the misty quality of the work. Hilder's work *The Dry Lagoon*, 1911, depicts the natural disasters of a drought. The burnt ochre colour of the ground and the orange-mauve wash in the sky all help to convey the mood of heat and dryness. Heat rising from the soil seems to be complemented by the technique of watercolour. The trees are depicted in a wavy elongated manner while parts of the foliage disappear into the horizon. Hilder's gum trees appear to waver and bend as in a mirage, a quality he liked to include in his work.

Blamire Young (1862–1935) was a watercolourist who has almost been forgotten. He travelled extensively throughout Europe, consistently drawing and painting. He returned to Australia in 1911 and later received public acclaim with a series of works based on Mount Buffalo. Generally his subject matter was wide and varied; however, some features of Art Nouveau do come through in the work *Mansion of the Grey Thrush*, c. 1925. This work depicts a woman sitting under a large, gnarled tree. The trees continue into the background at which point they become purely decorative. Silhouettes similar to the trees depicted by Long and Hilder appear frequently in Young's work.

Art Nouveau did not prove popular with many artists at the turn of the century. Consequently, it died out in painting in the mid-1920s; however, it did continue for a little while longer through the medium of illustration. Magazines, books and other assorted publications had used Art Nouveau decoration on their covers for a couple of decades. In fact, as early as 1889, Charles Conder designed a type of Art Nouveau catalogue cover for The 9 by 5 Impression Exhibition.

Although not influenced by Art Nouveau, **Norman Lindsay (1879–1969)** became an influential artist around this time. Born into a large artistic family, his talents and pursuits were rather extensive and included painting, drawing, illustrating for books and magazines, etching and poetry. He rebelled against the conventions of the day

CHARLES CONDER
(1868–1909)

*Catalogue for The 9 by 5
Impression Exhibition*

and was totally against the philosophies behind developing a national identity in art such as the Heidelberg School. He thought it was too insular. He was also annoyed at the indifference of most Australians to culture. From all the evidence it would seem that he would have settled well into bohemian Paris or London.

In his art, unlike his contemporaries, Lindsay drew his subject matter from past myths and legends and chose not to respond to local subject matter such as landscape. His work was typified by Rubensesque naked women, and 'blasphemous' subject matter which created much controversy. By the press, the conservative artistic circle and the middle class he was called a 'perverter of the young', a 'pornographer' and 'morally outrageous'. He had, if nothing else, made a name for himself so that even people who were not particularly interested in art knew of Norman Lindsay.

The drawing *Pollice Verso*, 1904, is an example of one of his controversial works. Rococo in flavour, it shows Roman warriors with their naked women in tow all gesturing thumbs down signs to the crucified Christ. It created an absolute storm of

NORMAN LINDSAY
(1879–1969)
Pollice Verso, 1904
Pen and indian ink drawing,
47.5 x 60.5 cm
National Gallery of Victoria,
Melbourne
Felton Bequest 1907

protest. When the work was exhibited in the National Gallery of Victoria in 1907 it caused such a stir that it was removed.

Although Lindsay's artistic influence on Australian painting was negligible, his exuberance and knowledge proved to be most beneficial for Australian art as a whole. During these years his art, particularly his etchings, proved to be popular with collectors.

ELIOTH GRUNER
(1882–1939)
Spring Frost, 1919
Oil on canvas,
131 x 178.7 cm
Art Gallery of New South Wales
Gift of F. G. White 1939

A contemporary and friend of Lindsay was **Elioth Gruner (1882–1939)**. Like the impressionists he was a keen observer of the effects of light on the landscape of which *Spring Frost*, 1919, is a classic example. The work explores the atmospheric conditions associated with a morning frost and in particular the transient effects of light and mist. The morning sunlight is shown creating a halo effect on the cows and fence, cutting its way through the large trees and shimmering on the frosty grass. The daubs of paint are similar to the technique used by Davies. It also shows a debt to Impressionism. Gruner continued to be a popular landscape painter throughout the 1920s and 1930s.

Sculpture

Among the earliest evidence of Art Nouveau in sculpture was Bertram Mackennal's *Circe* (see Chapter Five). Both the treatment of the snakes writhing through her hair and the entangled figures on the pedestal depict Art Nouveau curves and lines.

Most of the sculptors working in Australia at the turn of the century were, to a small degree, influenced by Art Nouveau trends. The first sculptor to make a concerted effort to develop the Art Nouveau theme in his work was **C. Douglas Richardson (1853–1932)**. After studying art for a few years in England he returned to Australia to launch a campaign to make the public more aware of art and, in particular, sculpture.

Richardson's biggest commission was the designing of a Golden Jubilee memorial for Bendigo called *The Discovery of Gold*, 1906. Carved in marble, the central figure is a woman representing the State of Victoria. She is depicted leaning over the gold

RIGHT:

C. DOUGLAS RICHARDSON
(1853–1932)

The Discovery of Gold,
1906, Bendigo
Marble

Photographer: Jon Rendell

FAR RIGHT:

C. DOUGLAS RICHARDSON
(1853–1932)

The Cloud, c. 1900
Marble, height 1.7 m

Collection: City of Ballarat
Fine Art Gallery

prospector and is about to place a nugget in his pan. The Art Nouveau treatment of the woman is evident in the flowing dress and curves of her long hair and stole.

Richardson's other work, *The Cloud*, c. 1900, was partly inspired by a poem by Shelley, the English poet (1792–1822), 'I bring fresh showers for the thirsting flowers'. The work shows a graceful figure of a woman rising up from the soil, her body partially covered with wet drapery. The beautiful curves and lines of her body serve to add to the surge of movement. She is carrying an urn full of water which she pours over the wilting flowers at her feet. When first exhibited *The Cloud* was described as one of the most graceful pieces of sculpture ever shown in Melbourne.

The Art Nouveau style in painting and sculpture was relatively short lived, tending to be much more popular in areas such as stained-glass windows, furniture design and other craft work. By 1920 there was very little trace of Art Nouveau in either painting of sculpture.

Civil architecture

Australian architecture did not reflect the same upsurge of nationalism that was evident in the other areas of the arts. Although housing styles in different States responded to climatic changes, there was certainly no 'true' Australian style as such. From the Federation period came the Queen Anne style. Spanning 1890–1910, its origins lay in the English domestic architecture of the years 1702–14 (the reigning years of Queen Anne). This style of architecture was revived in England but also spread to America and Australia where it became extremely popular. In Australia it also became known as the 'Federation' style.

Queen Anne style was in direct contrast to the previous 'Victorian' style. Stucco walls, iron lace work and slate roofs were replaced with red bricks and Art Nouveau wooden fret, trellis work, terracotta tiles and decoration. Art Nouveau decoration tended to lend itself particularly well to the wooden decoration around verandahs. The leadlight windows also displayed native designs such as gum leaves and nuts, kookaburras and possums. The ring-tailed possum, just by the nature of its curvy tail, became a very popular motif for leadlight window designs.

In the public buildings constructed during this time the Art Nouveau influence tended to be minimal and was rarely used for anything more than decoration. One of the finest examples of Australian Art Nouveau can be seen as decoration on the old South Yarra Post Office, Melbourne, 1893. The facade of the building is divided into many stucco panels, each of which is sculptured relief. The panels are decorated with native flora and fauna, such as snakes writhing through bullrushes, cockatoos, goannas, emus, gum nuts, the Sturt pea, waratah, as well as many beautifully carved figures.

Another fine example of Art Nouveau design in Melbourne is Milton House, Flinders Lane. Built in 1900–02, this Federation period building is superbly designed, with various Art Nouveau trappings which all add to its charm. The three-storeyed, red brick building boasts two highly decorative, carved balconies, one of which features a beautiful example of curved iron work that echoes the Art Nouveau patterns of the leadlight windows. Decorative terracotta tiles fill a panel between the ground and first floor. The fanlight and leadlight windows all display simple yet typical Art Nouveau patterns.

Another Art Nouveau building is the Bendigo Hotel in Johnston Street, Collingwood, Victoria.

Domestic architecture

The Queen Anne house saw a marked change in both design and mood. Most examples of Queen Anne style were particularly quaint and picturesque. Red in colour (red brick and terracotta tiles), the houses were usually detached and the desire

to create a fine lawn and garden was the order of the day. The winding pathway from gate to front door also became a popular characteristic.

Characteristics of Queen Anne style, c. 1890–1910, are:

- terracotta tiles on the roof, with false gables and frilled ridges
- terracotta ornaments often gracing roof tops in the form of kangaroos, birds and dragons
- red brick construction
- wooden trellis and lattice work, first geometric and then Art Nouveau in design
- leadlight windows
- shadowed verandah
- tall, ornamental, red brick chimneys
- irregular plan

ACTIVITIES

1. Using Australian native flora and fauna as your starting point, draw your own stylised Art Nouveau design. Keep in mind the qualities that make Art Nouveau so attractive and decorative.

2. Research the work of the European Symbolist/Art Nouveau painters. Can you see any similarities to the work of the Australian, Sydney Long? Quote specific examples in your discussion.

3. What is Rococo art?

4. Charles Richardson used a poem by Shelley for inspiration in designing *The Cloud*. Select a poem of your own choice and develop it into either a sculpture or a 2D piece of work.

5. Check in your school library for the work of the Spanish architect Gaudi (1852–1926). Describe one of his buildings. How is it different from previous forms of architecture? Give specific examples in your discussion.

6. Who was Norman Lindsay and what was his view of Australian culture?

	AUSTRALIAN EVENTS	GENERAL EVENTS	ARTISTIC EVENTS	
1910		**1911** The da Vinci painting, *Mona Lisa*, is stolen from the Louvre Museum, Paris, but is later returned.	**1911** Chagall: *I and the Village*. Picasso: *Guitar* (S).	**Australian artists** Rupert Bunny George Lambert John Longstaff Emanuel Phillips Fox Hugh Ramsay John Peter Russell Hans Heysen Margaret Baskerville Charles Web Gilbert Paul Montford
1912		**1912** The *Titanic* sinks south of Newfoundland after hitting an iceberg.	**1912** Duchamp: *Nude Descending a Staircase*. Collage is introduced. **1913** The Armory Show arrives in New York, introducing America to Post-impressionism and Modern European art. Kandinsky: *Picture with White Edge*. Boccioni: *Unique Forms of Continuity in Space* (S).	
1914	**1914** Australia enters World War I. **1915** The Anzacs land at Gallipoli. Of the 300 000 Australians who left our shores, 60 000 are killed and 120 000 injured. William Morris (Billy) Hughes becomes Prime Minister. BHP opens iron and steel mills in Newcastle.	**1914** World War I breaks out. **1915** Bombs are dropped on London by the Germans.	**1914** Bourdelle: *Dying Centaur*. (S). **1915** Malevich: Manifesto of Suprematism published. Mondrian: *Composition in Black and White*.	
1916	**1917** E.W. Holden produces the Holden car body.	**1917** The Russian Revolution begins.		
1918	**1919** William Morris (Billy) Hughes attends the peace negotiations at Versailles, France.	**1918** On 11 November at 11.00 am, the armistice is signed and World War I ends. **1919** The Treaty of Versailles, a peace treaty with Germany, is signed on 28 June.	**1918** Klee: *Gartenplan*. **1919** Duchamp: *L.H.O.O.Q.*	
1920		**1920** American women achieve the right to vote.	**1920** Matisse begins his *Odalisque* series.	
1922				

CHAPTER SEVEN

Australians Abroad 1911–20

Painting

> Australia was too young a country, it had no culture, there were no castles, no abbeys, no folk songs. There was no Bloomsbury or Montmartre or Latin Quarter of Paris, with its exciting Bohemian life—no one was interested in art or literature, it was crude, materialistic and Philistine ...[1]

This rather vicious, but no doubt accurate, quotation came from Louis Esson, an Australian playwright who was describing the state of the arts in Australia at the turn of the century. He was dissatisfied and hoped for a change in the way most Australians responded to local culture.

The first Australian artist to travel overseas and gain international recognition was Adelaide Ironside (1831–67). After departing for London in 1855 she finally settled in Rome in 1856 where she painted and, among other things, studied fresco painting. Although there were a number of artists who followed in Ironside's footsteps, the big exodus of artists took place in the 1890s.

For artists the urge to travel abroad had become stronger. If one wanted to study art seriously, then Europe was the place to go to. Conder departed permanently in 1890, Streeton was away between 1898 and 1924, Roberts followed from 1903 to 1923 and the list went on. Roberts and Streeton actually became war artists based in France.

Owing to the still casual approach towards art and artists, money for art patronage in Australia was rare. This ruined the already fragile art market. The art schools had been established a couple of decades earlier (the National Gallery School,

---

[1] Serle, G., *The Creative Spirit in Australia: A Cultural History*, Revised Edition, Heinemann, Melbourne, 1987, p. 110.

Melbourne, opened in 1870) but still the climate was not quite right for the growth of an artistic milieu. Art, and particularly painting, was thought of as a light, graceful recreation. The artist Norman Lindsay actually stated that he believed Australians to be exceptionally blasé about art and that they were not really the slightest bit interested. Most young artists were encouraged to go to Europe to further their artistic careers and to mix in a culturally rich environment.

Once in Paris, dressed in smocks, and with brushes and easels in hand, they went off to the Louvre to copy the great masters.

Tom Roberts had started the ball rolling when he went to England first in 1881; and the desire to travel to Europe to see the art of the great masters grew. One of the finest Australian artists to actually become a significant figure in France was **John Peter Russell (1858–1930)**.

Russell, unlike his contemporaries in Australia, preferred to work in the mainstream of world art, which at that time was in Europe. He went to Paris and enrolled in art school with other artists such as Toulouse-Lautrec, van Gogh and Emile Bernard, and also the sculptors Frémiet and Rodin. Russell later became great friends with van Gogh.

On one of Russell's trips to Italy he took an active interest in rural landscapes, showing the workers on the land, similar to the work of the realist artists. The work *Paysannes à Monte Cassino (Peasant Women at Monte Cassino)*, 1886, depicts peasant women engaged in conversation. It is a harmonious painting in which Russell's use of short, strong brushwork aims at giving the effect of sparkling light. The two trees on the left of the painting balance the composition while the small daubs of colour on the tree are reminiscent of the impressionist style with which he was familiar. The application of the green paint for the sky has been used to unite the painting; however, arguably, it serves only to confuse the work and upset the balance of colour.

JOHN RUSSELL
(1858–1930)

Paysannes à Monte Cassino,
1886
Oil on canvas,
50.2 x 73.2 cm

Collection: National Gallery
of Australia, Canberra

GEORGE LAMBERT
(1873–1930)

Important People, 1914–21
Oil on canvas,
134.7 x 170.3 cm

Art Gallery of New South Wales
Purchased 1930

Russell continued working in the south of France and became friendly with other artists such as Monet and the young Henri Matisse. Russell actually introduced the young Matisse to the art of colour painting, an interest Matisse keenly pursued. Owing to the great distance between Paris and Australia, Russell's work was better known in France. Later in his life he returned to Sydney where he died a relatively unknown artist.

One of the most successful expatriate artists to be recognised in Australia as well as in Europe was the flamboyant **George Washington Lambert (1873–1930)**. Lambert was one of the more colourful figures of this period. He sported a fine mop of red hair and a curly moustache, and rapidly earned the nickname 'Ginger'.

His artistic career commenced when he was an illustrator with the *Bulletin* magazine. His opportunity to travel overseas came when he won a travelling scholarship in 1900 with the painting *Across the Black Soil Plains*, 1899. When exhibited it drew instant success and praise for Lambert.

Lambert fitted into the artistic circles of London and Paris extremely well. No doubt his flamboyant and gregarious nature would have helped him. He regularly visited exhibitions and took a keen interest in the work of Edouard Manet. Some of Lambert's paintings are influenced by Manet's work. *Important People*, 1914–21, is a classic example of this. Painted while he was in Europe, the work is a most interesting piece. The young fighter was Albert Broadribb, at the time an up-and-coming boxer. The top-hatted gentleman was an art dealer and the woman was a local mother whose baby died before Lambert finished the painting. The painting is similar in many ways to the subject matter of the Impressionists and, in particular, Manet. The flattening of the figures and the background, and the way in which the clothes have

HUGH RAMSAY
(1877–1906)
The Sisters, 1904
Oil on canvas,
125.7 x 144.8 cm
Art Gallery of New South Wales
Purchased 1921

been worked over are all characteristic of Manet. The painting also deals with aspects of contemporary life and, like the French Impressionist paintings, the figures appear to be caught in a moment of time, almost like a snapshot. Lambert himself called it Botticelli without the finish.

Lambert continued to paint consistently while in Europe, engaging himself in many portrait commissions. As one of the finest and most fashionable portrait painters, he painted all the influential people and mixed in the 'correct' circles. Like Streeton and Roberts he worked for Australia as an official war artist based in Palestine. On his return to Australia he was welcomed with a grand State reception. Perhaps the artistic climate had matured after all.

By far the most talented painter to develop during the turn of the century was a young Melbourne man called **Hugh Ramsay (1877–1906)**. Born in Scotland but educated in Essendon, Victoria, Ramsay was both a talented musician and painter. After entering the National Gallery School he departed to London, coincidentally on the same boat as Lambert. The two of them struck up a long friendship.

Ramsay studied at the fashionable Paris art school called Colarossi's, which had trained many great European artists. He quickly established himself as one of the most talented and enthusiastic students. His interest in music was still strong and in order to pursue this talent and hire a piano, he cut his food rations. This rash move led to a severe illness, forcing an early return to Australia where he died a couple of years later.

Two of his most famous works are *Jeanne*, 1902, and *The Sisters*, 1904. Of the many influences Ramsay fell under while in Paris, the strongest seemed to come from the American expatriate painters Whistler and Sargent. In the portrait of his French landlady's daughter Jeanne, the Whistler influence is quite evident in the colour, mood and composition. The subtle tones of greys, greens and blues are all colours from the Whistler palette. The gaze on the little girl's face is that of patient watchfulness.

Ramsay's greatest painting by far is *The Sisters*, 1904. In this work Ramsay creates a superbly vibrant and grand portrait study. The sisters are dressed in beautiful white silk dresses which lend themselves to being painted in such an abstract way. The broad and carefully placed brushstrokes give the painting a particular excitement and energy that Ramsay had never previously achieved. Ramsay's untimely death in 1906 robbed Australian art of a superb talent.

Two other expatriate artists were Rupert Bunny and Emanuel Phillips Fox. Although they spent a large amount of time living and working overseas they made a valuable contribution to Australian art. Both artists studied together at the National

EMANUEL PHILLIPS FOX
(1865–1915)

The Arbour, 1911
Oil on canvas,
190 x 230.7 cm

National Gallery of Victoria,
Melbourne
Felton Bequest 1916

Gallery School in Melbourne, departing soon after to pursue their careers in London and Paris.

Phillips Fox (1865–1915) was born in Melbourne and proved himself to be a fine and competent painter. He travelled to Paris in 1887, sponsored by younger brothers and friends. It was the wonderful experiences that he had in Paris that led him to experiment and produce works in the style of French Impressionism.

Although he was a competent landscape painter, Fox's other interest was in portraiture. *The Arbour*, 1911, is a work which shows Fox's understanding of French Impressionism and in particular the work of Renoir. It is a beautifully sunlit painting which shows the pleasures of life—a popular French contemporary theme, particularly as pretty young children are included. The treatment of the paint is rather passionate while the brushstrokes of rich colour give us the impression that Fox really enjoyed his painting.

Fox's fellow student and good friend was **Rupert Bunny (1864–1947)**. Bunny, too, spent much time enjoying the cultural activity of turn-of-the-century Paris, and later settled in the south of France where he painted the rural landscape. These paintings did not do justice to his real talent, which was for producing grand and graceful paintings of Edwardian women.

RUPERT BUNNY
(1864–1947)

A Summer Morning, c. 1908
Oil on canvas,
223 x 180.3 cm

Art Gallery of New South Wales
Purchased 1911

A Summer Morning, c. 1908, is a typical example of this theme. In depicting the lifestyle of the privileged class, Bunny chose to show the women displaying their beautiful patterned dresses and enjoying perpetual luxury. The green shutters and pattern work are reminders of Manet's work, as is the subject matter. The application of the paint is bold, with luscious strokes of pigment particularly evident in the treatment of the women's dresses.

As with Fox's work, Bunny's subject matter was for the most part fuelled by fashionable Edwardian society and the theories of French Impressionism. Although their years of isolation from Australia led these artists to develop a style different from that of their contemporaries at home, their work still played an integral part in the development of Australian Edwardian painting. Both Fox and Bunny spent their final years painting and exhibiting in Melbourne.

One of the most prolific portrait painters of the early twentieth century was **John Longstaff (1862–1941)**. He too attended the National Gallery School. Like the other artists previously discussed, Longstaff received great encouragement and financial support to travel to Europe. On his arrival in Paris he established a long and rewarding friendship with John Peter Russell. Longstaff remained abroad for six years and during this time established himself as a well-respected and sought-after portraitist. He enjoyed commissions from the Prince and Princess of Wales, Queen Alexandra, counts and countesses, Australian prime ministers and more.

Longstaff's most reproduced portrait is of the poet *Henry Lawson*, 1900. Painted when Lawson was thirty-three, it is a traditional work in which the poet looks directly out at the viewer, his fine creative hands holding a pipe. Lawson is portrayed as one of the sophisticated elite; this is certainly in direct opposition to the man's philosophies. The paintwork is thin in some areas while the face appears to be rather laboured. An Art Nouveau influence is also evident in the lettering of Lawson's name and the year of the work.

Longstaff is also known for his huge painting of Burke and Wills. Called *The Arrival of Burke, Wills and King at the Deserted Camp at Cooper's Creek*, 1902–07, it portrays the tragic misfortune of that journey. In 1928 Longstaff became the first Australian artist to receive a knighthood for services to art.

JOHN LONGSTAFF
(1862–1941)

The Arrival of Burke, Wills and King at the Deserted Camp at Cooper's Creek, 21st April, 1861, 1902–07
Oil on canvas,
429.2 x 282 cm

National Gallery of Victoria, Melbourne
Gilbee Bequest 1907

In 1904 the German, **Hans Heysen (1877–1968)**, returned from years of study abroad to settle with his wife in the Mount Lofty Ranges near Adelaide. Like most painters from this period, his interests lay in depicting the Australian landscape, particularly in the area where he lived—Hahndorf, South Australia. The grand old eucalypts were to Heysen what the haystacks were to Monet. He painted them with great dedication and skill; every bough, piece of bark and leaf were explored. The painting *Summer*, 1909, is a typical example of Heysen's Hahndorf landscapes. Heysen opened an art school in Adelaide and spent the remainder of his life teaching and painting.

HANS HEYSEN (1877–1968)
Summer, 1909
Watercolour on paper,
56.5 x 78.4 cm

Art Gallery of New South Wales
Purchased 1909

The experience of studying overseas proved to be most valuable for both the artists concerned and Australia. Owing to the rather undeveloped state of the arts, there really was a need to travel abroad, which enabled Australian artists to improve their skills and confidence. Artists studying abroad injected a significant degree of exotica into Australian art. Australia's culture was enriched through their experiences.

Sculpture

Despite the countless difficulties confronting women artists, there were a significant number of women sculptors working in the late nineteenth and early twentieth centuries. It was from this period onwards that women artists started to play key roles in the development of Australian art.

By looking at the sculpture produced in Australia between 1890 and 1920 the improved standard of the work can be seen, due largely to the influence of artists studying overseas and then returning with their new ideas and techniques. Many sculptors, like painters, travelled overseas to improve their skills. The sculptors who contributed a great deal to the development of Australian public sculpture were Margaret Baskerville, Charles Web Gilbert and Paul Montford.

Margaret Baskerville (1861–1930) studied art with Phillips Fox, Bunny, Longstaff and Streeton. She travelled to London to study sculpture in 1904, and, as well, spent a couple of years studying in Paris where her work was favourably criticised by the French master Rodin.

MARGARET BASKERVILLE
(1861–1930)
Sir Thomas Bent, 1911–13
Nepean Highway, Brighton,
Victoria
Bronze, height 6.1 m

Photographer: Jon Rendell

Baskerville returned to Australia in 1907 full of enthusiasm, confidence and new ideas. She exhibited work at the Women's Work Exhibition held at the Exhibition Buildings, Melbourne, winning first and second prizes. Skilled and competent both in carving marble and modelling clay (clay being used as the preliminary step for bronze reproduction), she was the only professional woman sculptor practising in Australia. Her largest bronze work is that of a former Premier of Victoria, *Sir Thomas Bent*, 1911–13.

The *Argus* newspaper, at the time the work was unveiled, reported:

> It is an excellent likeness of Sir Thomas Bent. It stands 9 feet 6 inches [3 metres] high above its pedestal and was reproduced (assembled) from the sculptor's model in hammered and welded bronze plate by Mr C. W. Marriot of Melbourne. Two new principles have been introduced, therefore into this work the fact that a woman sculptor has, for the first time in Australia, given the community a portrait in bronze of a public man and the principle of welding statues with oxy-acetylene jet …[2]

The sculpture is larger than life. Reproduced in bronze, the modelling is very smooth and polished. It stands on the Nepean Highway at Brighton, Melbourne. It was a major achievement for a woman in 1913 to actually receive such acclaim and even be given the chance to prove her talent and skill. The remainder of Baskerville's life was spent making war memorials, busts and smaller marble carvings. In 1916 she became assistant and, later, wife to the sculptor Charles Douglas Richardson.

The sculptor who was initially trained as a pastrycook was **Charles Web Gilbert (1867–1925)**. He entered the National Gallery School where he remained for two and a half years. His interest in sculpture and modelling was aroused by the countless number of icing sugar flowers and decorative moulds he was making for cakes. He decided to take up sculpture full time.

In 1914 Gilbert travelled to Europe where he studied and worked for almost three years. Like a lot of other Australian artists during the war years, he was employed as official sculptor in charge of modelling for the war records section. He returned to Australia in 1920 to commence work on private commissions.

Gilbert's most famous work in Melbourne is the bronze statue of the navigator *Matthew Flinders*, 1923–25. Cast in France and completed in 1924, the work shows the explorer stepping from a boat which is being hauled with great strength up on to the beach by two of his sailors. Gilbert's knowledge of anatomy is evident in the modelling of the muscles on the sailors' arms, backs and legs. Flinders's face is also modelled with great skill and sensitivity, showing him to be a serious and proud man. The sculpture was finally unveiled in November 1925, a month after Gilbert's death.

The sculptor known mainly for his contribution of the four buttress figures on Melbourne's Shrine of Remembrance is **Paul Montford (1868–1938)**. Montford arrived in Australia a few years after World War I. As a consequence of the war there was a great demand for sculptors to undertake contracts for war memorials. Montford entered a contest to design the sculpture for the Melbourne Shrine and, out of eighty-three submissions, his design was judged to be the most appropriate. The four buttress groups, all carved directly in granite, represent Sacrifice, Justice, Peace and Goodwill, and Patriotism. A young boy leads a pair of lions drawing a chariot, which

---

[2] *Argus*, 28 October 1913.

is modelled on the prow of a ship and is summoned by a winged throne before which stands an heroic female figure.

After experiencing the enthusiasm and support given to the arts in Europe, Montford was actually rather critical of the support given to sculpture in Australia. He claimed that, through grants and scholarships, the Government should encourage sculpture schools to teach students all the basic skills. He believed it was unfortunate for Australia that all prospective sculpture students were forced to travel to Europe to gain their education.

CHARLES WEB GILBERT
(1867–1925)

Matthew Flinders, 1923–25
Flinders Street, Melbourne
Bronze, height 3.9 m

Photographer: Jon Rendell

PAUL MONTFORD
(1868–1938)

Adam Lindsay Gordon, 1933
Spring Street, Melbourne
Bronze

Photographer: Jon Rendell

Montford's other Melbourne work is the bronze statue of the poet, farmer and boxer *Adam Lindsay Gordon*, 1933. The bronze sculpture depicts Gordon sitting cross-legged in a chair, pen in hand, and with his riding apparel, riding boots and saddle under his chair. The sculpture is opposite Parliament House in Spring Street, Melbourne.

Montford, like all the sculptors from this period, continued to receive both public and private commissions. The sculpture produced tended to be rather conservative throughout these years and reinforced the attitudes of the day. This in itself was not a bad thing but the younger, up-and-coming modern artists, attempting to introduce their own ideas and work, tended to make things difficult and created much conflict. It was only after consistent subtle challenging that the break from traditional academic sculpture finally came about. An alternative approach to sculpture was to develop.

ACTIVITIES

1. Why did so many young artists feel the need to travel to Europe?

2. Find out what life would have been like in turn-of-the-century Paris or London. How would it compare with the life in Australia at that time?

3. Can you draw any similarity between Lambert's *Important People* and a Botticelli work? What do you think 'Botticelli without the polish' means?

4. Find a reproduction of Ramsay's *Jeanne* and, using the guide in Appendix One, discuss the work.

5. Compare and contrast a painting by Renoir with Fox's *The Arbour*. Discuss subject matter, colour and any other information you would like to include.

6. Write an essay, discussing the statement that 'French Impressionist painting had a large influence on the work of young Australian artists'. Give examples of artists' work. (Approximately 250 words)

7. Produce a portrait of someone in your class. You can use either clay or paint. Try to capture the person's particular characteristics and personality.

8. What form of public sculpture was common to most sculptors from this period? Why?

9. Make a list or write informatively about the process of making a bronze statue.

10. Why was Montford critical of the Government?

11. Look carefully at Longstaff's painting, *The Arrival of Burke, Wills and King* (page 89). Describe how the work makes you feel. Why?

12. While in France John Peter Russell influenced one of the twentieth century's greatest modern colour painters. Who was he?

	AUSTRALIAN EVENTS	GENERAL EVENTS	ARTISTIC EVENTS	
1915				**Australian artists** Norah Simpson Grace Cossington Smith Grace Crowley Thea Proctor Roland Wakelin Roy de Maistre Margaret Preston George Bell William Frater Arnold Shore Max Meldrum Daphne Mayo Rayner Hoff
1920	**1920–30** Registered motor cars increase tenfold. **1923** E. W. Holden starts production of cars in Woodville, South Australia. Stanley Bruce becomes Prime Minister. Sydney Harbour Bridge construction commences. Canberra is founded.	**1922** Fascist revolution occurs in Italy. Howard Carter discovers the Tomb of Tutankhamen, Egypt.	**1921** Mendelsohn: *Einstein Tower* (destroyed). Man Ray: *Gift* (S). Braque: *Still Life with Guitar.* **1924** Surrealist manifesto is written.	
1925	**1926** The first underground train runs in Sydney. **1927** Seat of government is moved from Melbourne to Canberra. **1928–33** The Great Depression occurs. **1928** Charles Kingsford Smith makes the first solo flight across the Pacific. **1929** James Scullin becomes Prime Minister	**1925** The first traffic light is installed in London. **1926** Television is invented by John Logie Baird. **1927** Lindberg makes a solo flight across the Atlantic. **1929** The Great Depression begins in the United States. Kodak invents colour film.	**1926** Grosz: *Pillars of Society.* **1928** O'Keefe: *Nightmare.* **1929** Rivera: *Workers of the Revolution* (Mexico City mural).	
1930	**1930** Unemployment reaches 19 per cent. **1931** Qantas Airways carries mail and passengers between Darwin and Sydney. Joseph Lyons becomes Prime Minister. **1932** Sydney Harbour Bridge opens. The Australian Broadcasting Commission is created.	**1930** Amy Johnson flies solo from Great Britain to Australia. **1932** Amelia Earhart becomes the first woman to fly solo across the Atlantic Ocean. **1933** Adolf Hitler is appointed German Chancellor. **1934** With the death of President Hindenburg, Hitler proclaims himself President.	**1930** Shreve, Lamb and Harmon: Empire State building. Wood: *American Gothic.* **1931** Dali: *The Persistence of Memory.* **1932** Bonnard: *Nude in a Bathroom.*	**Architects and architecture** Walter Burley Griffin Californian bungalow Tudor Spanish mission
1935	**1938** Coca-Cola is first bottled in Australia. **1939** Robert Menzies becomes Prime Minister.	**1935** The board game 'Monopoly' is invented. **1936–39** The Spanish Civil War takes place. **1937** The airship, the *Hindenburg*, bursts into flames in New Jersey, killing thirty-five people. **1939** World War II breaks out.	**1936** Oppenheim: Object—*Fur-covered Cup, Saucer and Spoon* (S). Lloyd Wright: Falling Water House, Pennsylvania. International Surrealist exhibition is held in London. **1937** Picasso: *Guernica.* **1938** Moore: *Reclining Figure* (S).	
1940			**1940** Lascaux caves are discovered in France.	

CHAPTER EIGHT

Women Artists and Modernism 1913–40

Social and political background

The 1920s was a period which ran between two significant events in Australia's history: the end of World War I and the Great Depression. Throughout the 1920s people shared great feelings of optimism. The war had finished and generally life was improving.

Australia's population rose from 5 million in 1918 to 6.5 million only five years later, due partly to a baby boom and partly to a steady rise in immigration. These immigrants, mainly from the British Empire, arrived on Australian shores to work in the expanding industries.

The early 1920s also saw the return of World War I soldiers. Streets filled with thousands of cheering people throwing streamers, waving flags and, if the opportunity came around, patting one of the soldiers on the back. The returned servicemen were treated to a real heroes' welcome.

Australians generally enjoyed a new range of entertainment. Dance halls were popular with the young. Single men and women, dressed in their best clothes, crammed into the local hall where they 'tangoed' or did the 'shake' to 'twenties music. The dance hall saw many a romance blossom.

Radio and cinema also became popular. Movies such as *The Story of the Kelly Gang* and *For the Term of His Natural Life* drew steady and enthusiastic crowds eager to be transported into this new fantasy world. Listening to radio plays was also a favourite pastime for the whole family.

The arrival of the motor car changed the way many Australians spent their leisure time. Despite the problems of motoring—bad roads, trouble with spare parts and car maintenance—it still proved popular among the more affluent families. They frequently made the journey out into the country where they would then picnic or bushwalk. The other favourite spot for car travellers was the seaside. Seaside picnics were all the rage and became more popular with the establishment of surf carnivals and lifesaving clubs.

In the 1920s, women artists started to emerge as a significant force for two reasons. The first was largely to do with the thinning out of the male population due to World War I, while the second had to do with the continuing awareness of the feminist movement of the 1880s–1890s. Up until that time women had not been involved so much in the visual arts, mainly because of their status in Victorian and Edwardian societies. With the increasing numbers of women in the workforce and the struggle for equal rights, women became more vocal; however, they still rarely found jobs in the male-dominated fields:

> Sydney had its first two policewomen in 1915, Western Australia its first woman architect in 1924. Five out of the eight doctors employed by the Victorian Education Department were women, which is fair indication that they were not accepted as general practitioners. Women in jobs like these were the exception which proved the rule about male supremacy. They were exhibition females pointed to as proof that there was no discrimination.[1]

Women's magazines of the day promoted a new lifestyle in which one could use birth control and play an active role in political issues. The 'all electric' home encouraged the invention of electrical gadgets that made housework less tedious and less time consuming. In short, it gave women more free time to pursue other interests and have some say in the direction of their lives. There were women keen to pursue an artistic pastime. The women discussed in this chapter perceived their role to be more than that of wife and mother. A few of these women devoted their entire lives to art, casting away the traditional role of housewife and mother to become professional artists. If they married they invariably had to stop painting in order to have a family. If they did not marry but instead decided to make a career out of art they were looked on as non-conformist and even eccentric.

Painting

Women were responsible for introducing modern painting into Australian art in the early twentieth century. In 1913 a new wave of enthusiasm swept into Sydney art schools with tremendous gusto. It was a totally new style of painting, which, although born in Europe, had traits that fitted well into Australian art. The artists concerned were Norah Simpson and Grace Cossington Smith.

The artist who actually imported post-impressionist painting to Sydney was **Norah Simpson (1895–1974)**. With her parents she left for England in 1911. Two years later she returned and entered art school, and then went to Paris where she was introduced to the paining of Gauguin, van Gogh and Seurat. It was the work of these Post-Impressionists that had a tremendous impact on Simpson. Before her return to

---

[1] McQueen, H., *Social Sketches of Australia, 1888–1975*, Penguin Books, Melbourne, 1978.

Sydney in 1913, she collected many reproductions and books of their work to show her fellow art students at Rubbo's Art School. These reproductions aroused much excitement at the school. Two male painters, Roy de Maistre and Roland Wakelin, appeared to be most impressed and began experimenting themselves. Simpson was not all that interested, only producing a couple of works in this style. *Studio Portrait, Chelsea*, 1915, is a very bold and colourful painting. The paint is applied thickly and in little daubs, while the subject matter is indeed European. Behind the sitter is a piece of African tribal art, which was a common theme in European art at the turn of the century. The work is also highly experimental in its use of bright colours. Simpson returned to live in London in 1915. Her influence on the Australian art scene,

NORAH SIMPSON
(1895–1974)
Studio Portrait, Chelsea, 1915
Oil on canvas, 50.8 x 40.7 cm
Art Gallery of New South Wales
Purchased 1960

although brief, was crucial. She opened a new door and injected new stimulus and energy into Australian art.

Simpson's friend at Rubbo's was a New Zealand artist, **Roland Wakelin (1887–1971).** He came to Sydney in 1912 and settled there with his family. After a brief stint in Europe where he became instantly attached to the work of Cézanne, he returned to Sydney where he painted seriously. He picked up the elements of French Impressionism and Post-Impressionism, both of which he used in some of his later paintings.

Down the Hills to Berry's Bay, 1916, was one of the first major impressionist works exhibited in Australia. Painted in small daubs of paint, it shows Sydney harbour with its sandstone buildings and bright blue water. A red steam train is seen coming out from behind a hill and this also acts as a flash of colour on the left side of the painting. The shapes in the painting are all simplified and rather formal as in Post-Impressionist painting.

ROLAND WAKELIN
(1887–1971)
Down the Hills to Berry's Bay,
1916
Oil on canvas on hardboard,
68 x 122 cm
Art Gallery of New South Wales
Purchased 1961

The other friend of Wakelin and Simpson was **Roy de Maistre (1894–1968).** Brought up in the country, he came to Sydney with the intention of combining music studies with art. He enrolled to study the violin at the Conservatorium of Music and painting at Rubbo's Art School. He later studied at Julian Ashton's Art School where he made tremendous headway, combining both music and painting.

De Maistre's enthusiasm for Simpson's imports led him to waste no time in experimenting. His work *Interior with Mother and Child*, 1916, painted in Exeter, New South Wales, shows a mother and baby sitting in a light-drenched room. The work shows fluidity and a knowledge and awareness of the impressionist technique, in that he has eliminated black from his palette and supplemented it with violet. Rich blues, violets, reds and oranges are placed throughout the painting in true impressionist manner, while the sun produces pale lemon shapes on the floor.

De Maistre was also responsible for creating the first abstract paintings ever shown in Australia. He saw some European art books on Cubism and abstraction and it was from these books that he and Wakelin produced their first 'modern' paintings. They produced paintings which combined music and art. De Maistre produced a colour-music scale—a visual instead of an aural one—making a colour the equivalent of a musical note. Because of de Maistre's interest in music he found this type of

ROY DE MAISTRE (1894–1968)
Interior with Mother and Child, Exeter, NSW, 1916
Oil on canvas on paperboard, 35 x 25 cm

Art Gallery of New South Wales
Purchased 1960

experimenting most rewarding and stimulating. Called 'synchronist',[2] the works were exhibited in August 1919. The exhibition, in spite of its new concepts and theories, was reviewed as 'elaborate and pretentious bosh'. The two painters did not persist with this style but returned to using simplified, natural forms. The work *Arrested Phrase from Beethoven's Ninth Symphony in Red Major*, 1935, is one of de Maistre's synchronist paintings.

From her childhood days, **Grace Cossington Smith (1892–1984)** had a keen interest in painting and drawing. Her parents supported her consistently throughout her early artistic pursuits. This was rare as the prospect of a woman becoming a full-time artist was socially questionable.

In 1912 she travelled with her sister to London where she enrolled in drawing classes. After this she travelled to the continent, spending quite a few months in France. This trip, unlike Simpson's trip a few years earlier, did not have all that much effect on her art. (It was on her second trip in 1948 when, like Wakelin, she 'discovered' the art of Cézanne.)

On her return in 1914 she entered Rubbo's Art School where the Post-Impressionist import was still continuing to be popular; the Post-Impressionist use of

ROY DE MAISTRE (1894–1968)
Arrested Phrase from Beethoven's Ninth Symphony in Red Major, 1935
Oil on paperboard, 72.4 x 99 cm
Collection: National Gallery of Australia, Canberra

[2] Synchronism was an art movement founded by two American artists, Stanton MacDonald-Wright and Morgan Russell, working in Paris in 1913, but Wakelin and de Maistre added the colour-music combination which slightly varied it.

colour had a great influence on her work. Cossington Smith's early work was largely figurative, relying heavily upon the events and images that surrounded her immediate environment. In fact, most of the modernist women artists chose to respond directly to local and immediate imagery. *Rushing,* c. 1922, shows a group of anonymous commuters rushing for the ferry. This is one of a number of crowd scenes, from soldiers marching in streets to racecourses, all done in the same simplified manner and all tending to contain rather subtle political content.

GRACE COSSINGTON SMITH
(1892–1984)

Rushing, c. 1922
Oil on canvas on paperboard,
65.5 x 91.3 cm

Art Gallery of New South Wales
Purchased 1967

Her later work was often centred on her immediate environment, particularly her home, the flower gardens, the intimacy of her bedroom and the domestic scene of her kitchen. Her interiors are light saturated, beautifully colourful and cheerful, and are an insight into Cossington Smith's life. *Interior with Wardrobe Mirror,* 1955, shows us her bedroom. With the help of the wardrobe door mirror we are also given a view out of the window, an interesting device. Books and other personal objects are lying about the room. Painted predominantly with broad flat brushstrokes, the work is mainly in yellows and greens; however, the red and violet mat on the floor provides an interesting contrast.

In her later life Cossington Smith consistently painted in isolation from other Sydney artists. She, de Maistre and Wakelin were actually the first Australian artists to have an exhibition of their Post-Impressionist paintings.

The first Australian woman to experiment with the European modern movement of Cubism was **Grace Crowley (1890–1979)**. She studied at Julian Ashton's Art School and later travelled to Paris in 1926 where she visited museums and galleries. She finally settled in the south of France. Although her family disapproved of her involvement with this Bohemian lifestyle, they still gave her financial support for the years she lived abroad.

GRACE COSSINGTON SMITH
(1892–1984)

Interior with Wardrobe Mirror,
1955
Oil on canvas on paperboard,
91.4 x 73.7 cm

Art Gallery of New South Wales
Purchased 1967

Her painting *Girl with Goats,* 1928, was one of the works she painted in France. it was exhibited at the famous Salon des Indépendents and received much favourable comment. Crowley's favourite work, it mainly comprises a selection of browns and warm dark reds. In the treatment of the figures the work tends to be lightly influenced by Cubism.

When Crowley returned to Australia in 1932 she opened an art school with another painter, Rah Fizelle. Their school became an extremely important venue for the study and promotion of modern painting. Unfortunately, the school closed in 1937.

GRACE CROWLEY
(1890–1979)

Girl with Goats, 1928
Oil on canvas, 54 x 72.1 cm

National Gallery of Victoria,
Melbourne
Presented by the National
Gallery Society of Victoria,
1967

Two other significant artists from this period were both extremely independent and dedicated. They were Thea Proctor and Margaret Preston. **Thea Proctor (1879–1964)** chose to patronise mostly the younger artists who, led by the nature of their new and experimental art, encountered an unfortunate wave of hostility. She went to London and studied art but, owing to lack of money, she withdrew from art school and spent her years in London doing odd jobs and painting the occasional portrait. After living in London for more than eighteen years she returned to Sydney where she practised painting and, in particular, printmaking.

Proctor's woodcuts are extremely decorative and strong in design. The linework is complementary to the images she portrayed, such as women reclining on benches ostentatiously showing off their fashionable new clothes. Superbly exotic decorative fans and flowers were also included as fashionable accessories. Her imagery was largely concerned with typical feminine activities, quite the opposite to the pursuits of Margaret Preston. The woodcut *Women with Fans*, c. 1930, is typical of Proctor's subject matter. Proctor also spent her later years teaching both painting and printmaking.

Known as 'Mad Maggie' for her persistence and energy, **Margaret Preston (1875–1963)** was born in South Australia and was first taught art in Adelaide. Later she transferred to the National Gallery School in Melbourne. Intelligent and independent, she travelled extensively throughout the world looking at museums and galleries.

Preston's art incorporated three distinct periods: the beautiful traditional colour painting of all life, 1915–28; the modern geometric phase, 1927–28, and the Aboriginal phase, which flourished in 1940–45. She consistently pushed for a national art in both

ABOVE:

THEA PROCTOR
(1879–1964)

Women with Fans, c. 1930
Woodcut, 22.0 x 22.1 cm

National Gallery of Victoria,
Melbourne
Purchased 1966

ABOVE RIGHT:

MARGARET PRESTON
(1875–1963)

Implement Blue, 1927
Oil on canvas on paperboard,
42.5 x 43 cm

Art Gallery of New South Wales
Gift of the Artist 1960

RIGHT:

MARGARET PRESTON
(1875–1963)

Protea, c. 1925
Woodcut, 24.8 x 24.5 cm

Art Gallery of South Australia,
Adelaide
David Murray Bequest Fund
1939

MARGARET PRESTON
(1875–1963)

Flying over the Shoalhaven River, 1942
Oil on canvas, 50.6 x 50.6 cm

Collection: National Gallery of Australia, Canberra

her teaching and painting, and exploited the beautiful designs and shapes of Australian flora. She used these designs in her prints, particularly woodcuts.

Protea, c. 1925, is a fine example of her interest in these native plants. Its boldness suits the medium of a woodcut and the print is strong in both design and colour.

From the geometric stage came *Implement Blue,* 1927. Preston chose to use domestic objects such as cups, glasses and a jug, and positioned them in an extremely formal way. Painted in a cool palette of blues, whites and black, it conveys Preston's acute knowledge of design and organisation.

Preston was one of the earliest Australian artists to use the images and symbols of Aboriginal art without oversimplifying them to suit Western taste. The painting *Flying over the Shoalhaven River,* 1942, is one of her first attempts at an aerial view of the landscape. The colours and marks she has used in this work have all been carefully chosen in order to be respectful to Aboriginal art and culture.

Preston was one of the very successful women artists of this period who achieved early recognition. She was able, unlike many other women in her circle, to marry and also pursue her art. She sold a great deal of her work and it was through these sales that she financed many of her overseas trips. She died in Sydney in 1963.

Melbourne Modernism

The Post-Impressionist, modern period in Melbourne dates from 1925 and it can largely be attributed to the academic painter **George Bell (1878–1966)**. He became the guiding star of the young artists interested in the Modern movement and, although not a modernist himself, he had a great understanding of the importance of this style.

In 1932, with two other artists, **William Frater (1890–1974)** and **Arnold Shore (1897–1963)**, Bell established a school specifically for teaching Modern art. Three years after establishing the school Bell travelled to Europe for the sole purpose of studying modern European art.

The school was then run by Frater and Shore, the latter another keen modernist. Although originally trained under Frederick McCubbin, Shore chose to break away and pursue his own interests. He became very impressed with the work of van Gogh and painted in a manner similar to his style. Shore painted richly coloured landscapes the modern way. His interest in, and pursuit of, Post-Impressionism created much antagonism among the older and more conservative set who felt this new style was a waste of time. Shore's *Valley*, c. 1940, is a careful study of the Australian bush. The dashing brushwork of the grassed area at the bottom of the work shows Shore's debt to van Gogh, while the painting of the sky, carefully worked with warm yellows and blue tones, is typical of the desire to unify the work.

Bell's other partner was William Frater. A student from the Glasgow Art School, Scotland, he emigrated to Australia and worked as a stained-glass craftsman. It is actually Frater who is seen as the leading Melbourne exponent of Post-Impressionist painting. *The Red Hat*, 1937, is evidence of Frater's modern technique. Flat thin areas

BELOW:

ARNOLD SHORE (1897–1963)
Valley, c. 1940
Oil on canvas, 61.8 x 44.6 cm
Collection: National Gallery of Australia, Canberra

BELOW RIGHT:

WILLIAM FRATER (1890–1974)
The Red Hat, 1937
Oil on canvas, 93 x 73.1 cm
National Gallery of Victoria, Melbourne
Felton Bequest 1943

MAX MELDRUM
(1875–1955)

Family Group, 1910–11
Oil on canvas, mounted on
board, 217.5 x 140 cm

Collection: National Gallery of
Australia, Canberra

of paint are placed on the canvas and then mixed to their desired colour. This technique is called *alla prima*. The spontaneous and aggressive brushwork gives *The Red Hat* strength, highlighted by the splashes of rich red on the hat, lips and scarf.

In order that Modern painting could progress and survive, it was decided that a society should be established. Called the Contemporary Art Society, it was formed in 1938 and gave support to younger artists whose interest lay in Modern painting. (The CAS will be further discussed in Chapter Nine.)

The Melbourne art scene was also greatly influenced by the conservative tonal painter **Max Meldrum (1875–1955)**. Born in Scotland, Meldrum came to Australia when he was fourteen and later enrolled in classes at the Gallery School. In 1895 he won a travelling scholarship, which he finally undertook in 1899. He travelled to Paris where he lived until 1913. Unlike Norah Simpson, who returned to preach the new word about Modernism, Meldrum returned to discredit it.

While in Paris, Meldrum was exposed to Cubism, Futurism and Fauvism, all of which he thought were rubbish. He loathed modern colour painting and became greatly concerned about its social effect. He believed that an excess of colour in painting brought with it a decline in moral standards; it reflected a sick, decadent civilisation. He claimed that:

> Social decadence ... brought with it a slackening interest in tone and proportion and an increasing interest in colour: modern art with its distortions and excessive interest in colour was a supreme example of social decadence.[3]

In short, Meldrum believed that painting should be a pure science of optical analysis and that the aim of the artist was to transfer on to canvas an exact illusion. He totally ignored the social and personal creative function of art.

While in Paris he studied and copied the great works of the old masters, in particular the Spanish painter Velázquez. It is the work *Family Group,* 1910–11, that relies heavily on the work of the Spanish master for its composition and colour. The painting shows Meldrum, his wife and eldest daughter, who is portrayed in a similar pose to the young blonde girl in Velázquez's painting *Las Meninas,* 1656. Meldrum also shows his face in chiaroscuro, which gives the work a touch of drama; this pose too is borrowed from Velázquez's self-portrait in *Las Meninas.*

Sculpture

The demand for sculpture in this period was not as strong; sculpture was frequently seen as a male domain. In 1925 Australia's best known woman sculptor of the time was commissioned to work on the Brisbane Town Hall. **Daphne Mayo (1895–1982)** was also affectionately known as the 'local girl sculptress'. Although this title is patronising, Mayo's work was in fact highly respected and she contributed extensively to the making of a large number of Brisbane's monuments. She had travelled throughout Europe and had proven herself to be most talented and skilful after winning the prestigious Rome Scholarship; Mayo was the first woman to receive the honour.

---

[3] Smith, B., *Australian Painting, 1788–1970,* Second Edition, Oxford University Press, Melbourne, 1971, p. 178.

DAPHNE MAYO (1895–1982)

The Progress of Civilisation,
tympanum—Brisbane Town
Hall, 1925–28
Sandstone, 9 x 16 m

A Brisbane City Council
photograph

RAYNER HOFF (1894–1937)

Sacrifice, 1931
Anzac Memorial, Hyde Park,
Sydney
Polished bronze

Photographer: Jon Rendell

Mayo's first piece of public sculpture was a traditional work which was designed for the tympanum on the Brisbane Town Hall (1925–28). Carved in sandstone, the overall length of the tympanum is 54 feet [16 metres] with the central figure being 9 feet [3 metres]. Called *The Progress of Civilisation*, the tympanum depicts the arrival of the Europeans and their influence over the land and its native people. The classically posed figures on the left are the 'natives' while on the right-hand side of tympanum are the Europeans with their livestock in tow. The draped central figure represents the State. Although she had been exposed to modern sculpture such as Cubism and Futurism, Mayo's work continued to be traditional and classical. She actually felt that getting involved with the 'avant-garde' was a cheap way of receiving notoriety.

The break, like Mayo's, from traditional, academic sculpture, came with the arrival of **Rayner Hoff (1894–1937)** in 1923. He began his career as an architecture student, travelling throughout Europe and studying such things as Renaissance and Classical sculpture. He arrived in Australia where he accepted a position as director of sculpture and drawing at the East Sydney Technical College.

Hoff's major work came from war memorial commissions, and one of his most controversial and best known pieces executed in the Art Deco style is *Sacrifice*, 1931. Part of the Anzac Memorial in Hyde Park, Sydney, the polished bronze work shows the naked corpse of a young soldier, arms outstretched, lying on a shield and sword, supported on the shoulders of three women. The women's skirts all join together to form a column. The work is designed to be viewed both from the ground and from above. This new Art Deco style created quite a fuss among traditional artists who thought it was an inappropriate style for a war memorial. Traditional styles of sculpture had held their own for such a long time that it was probably quite difficult to imagine that there could have possibly been any other. Hoff's work eased Australian sculpture out of its traditional style into styles more appropriate to the fast, modern twentieth century.

Civil architecture

The modernist style developed in Australian architecture with the aid of a young American architect, **Walter Burley Griffin (1876–1937)**. A student of Frank Lloyd Wright, Griffin came to Australia to work on the design of the nation's capital, Canberra.

Although probably best known for this work, he also contributed to modernising both Melbourne and Sydney's streetscapes. He designed homes, industrial incinerators, theatres, office buildings, as well as many other public buildings.

Australia's new capital was situated halfway between Sydney and Melbourne at Canberra. In 1911 an international competition was held for the submission of a town plan but, owing to political disagreements, it was blacklisted by British and Australian architects. One hundred and thirty-seven entries were submitted, unfortunately none from Australia. The board decided that Griffin's entry was the winner.

The design was modern and radical, and in a style never previously seen in Australian town planning. Still the board felt confident with its choice. When the submission was presented to the Government the response was one of outrage. After a great deal of arguing and plan changing, Griffin finally arrived in Sydney in 1913 to take up the position of Federal Capital Director of Design and Construction.

Despite interruptions and missing plans, files and preliminary drawings, Griffin finally completed the first stage by 1920. By this time, when all that he had been able to accomplish was the layout and construction of major roads and avenues, the position of Federal Capital Director was abolished and Griffin's employment terminated. His plans and ideas were retained, however, and in 1957 an English planner, Sir William Holford, was invited to recommend changes. In 1958 John Overall, Chief Architect of the Federal Works Department was appointed to Griffin's previous position.

Griffin and his wife moved to Melbourne where they set up an architecture business, designing buildings and houses. He made a significant impact on Melbourne with his houses, Newman College and, in Essendon, a reverberatory incinerator.

Newman College is a unique Melbourne building. Neither a modern nor a traditional building, it was essentially transitional. At first glance one could be forgiven for thinking it a medieval fortress. In fact an early critic of the building stated that 'the ground plan was more in keeping with a gaol'. Newman is a sandstone building with a rotunda from which two residential arms or wings jut out. There are enclosed courtyards which are surrounded by the heavy and squat residential wings; the small leadlight windows also help to give it a medieval or gaol-like appearance. The building fell into disrepair and was under threat of demolition until a public campaign in 1983–84 made money available for its renovation and conservation.

Griffin was also responsible for the unique task of designing about a dozen reverberatory incinerators. From an initial concept of a waste incinerator, Griffin came up with fabulously modern designs. The Essendon incinerator near the Maribyrnong River was designed in the Spanish mission style. When it was completed in 1930, it became the show piece of the area. Griffin built others in Adelaide and in Sydney.

Domestic architecture

The building industry progressed in leaps and bounds with materials in abundant supply. Wood was freely available from northern Australia and its Pacific neighbours. Steel, for use in building construction, was freely available. In 1915, the first steel was mass-produced in Newcastle and by 1920 it was used in all buildings. Concrete was another new material from America, which was beginning to be used extensively in Australian building. In fact, in 1912 the then largest concrete dome in the world was lowered on to the top of the reading room at the State Library, Melbourne. This event completed Reed's original design (see page 47).

The great move from the inner city out into suburbia became possible and popular with the popularity of 'wheels'—the car, the bus and public transport. The bus did not require any tracks or overhead wires and so it was economically viable.

Griffin's domestic architecture

With Griffin's designs in the Sydney harbourside suburb of Castlecrag, a whole new concept of modern living was introduced. He made a considerable contribution to domestic architecture by incorporating natural surroundings into his building plans and using materials which were close at hand. Griffin believed that landscape and

WALTER BURLEY GRIFFIN
(1876–1937)

*Newman College, University of
Melbourne, 1915–17*

Photographer: Jon Rendell

architecture should be in harmony with each other and that the house should not dominate the landscape. He loved the natural Australian bush and constantly aimed at using it to its fullest capacity.

The Griffin houses at Castlecrag blend into the landscape. They are squat, solid and, like the ground they rest on, made from stone. They have been constructed by the 'knitlock' system, a new design technique which was patented by Griffin—the houses comprise concrete modular underlocking tiles which slot together to form walls. Once locked together they are secured by cement-filled cavities. The flat roof, made out of concrete, is then added to the structure. Griffin loathed the high-pitched red Marseilles tile roof (from Queen Anne and Federation style), as he maintained it spoilt the landscape's colours and more importantly obliterated the superb views of surrounding harbour and landscape. Griffin also insisted on no fences or boundaries of any sort as these would destroy the natural feeling. His interest in medieval architecture was evident in his naming the streets of Castlecrag after parts of a medieval castle. 'The Citadel', 'The Scarp' and 'The Parapet' are a few such streets.

WALTER BURLEY GRIFFIN
(1876–1937)
House at Castlecrag, Sydney
Photographer: Jon Rendell

In order to suit Melbourne's geography Griffin's designs again differed. In Melbourne, Griffin built tall homes of timber. One of his Melbourne commissions was the Langi flats. Situated on the corner of Lansell and Toorak Roads, Toorak, the flats were actually refurbished in 1923 with Griffin's plans. Basically of a strong horizontal construction, the design is reminiscent of the work of Theo van Doesburg (1883–1931) and the De Stijl movement. The balcony ornamentation originated with American architect Frank Lloyd Wright (1869–1959). The superb iron gates are decorated in a geometric Art Deco design. The flats are surrounded by gum trees and other native plants and shrubs.

Griffin was one of the first modernists to work in Australia and his work established links with Frank Lloyd Wright and the Chicago School. In essence he was to the early twentieth century what Francis Greenway was to the colony a century earlier. Although his contemporary ideas such as the flat roof and the 'knitlock' system of construction were never very popular, nevertheless his impact on Australian architecture cannot be diminished or dismissed. He had a large following and his students carried on his tradition enthusiastically. Later, Griffin left Australia for India where he was employed to design, among other things, a Maharajah's palace. Unfortunately, Griffin contracted peritonitis while he was in India and died in 1937.

Some other Walter Burley Griffin works are:

- Melbourne's Capitol Theatre, 1921–24
- The Valhalla Cinema, Northcote, Victoria

WALTER BURLEY GRIFFIN
(1876–1937)
Langi Flats, Toorak, Victoria
Photographer: Jon Rendell

California bungalow 1920s–30s

The search for a type of Australian home suitable to Australian conditions culminated in the American Californian bungalow. It was marketed as being rugged and suitable for Australia's changing climate, yet sufficiently cosy. The style tended to look heavy and fortress-like, almost ignoring the natural environment, but many natural textures were used. In the interior, there was a lot of natural stained timber, while on the outside, weatherboards or cement-covered pebble mix, stone and shingles were popular.

The bungalow style was much less decorative than the Queen Anne and seemed more conscious of the climate. Deep verandahs were an important part of the design and were supported by heavy pillars which served to cut out the heat and keep the rain away from the foundations. The windows were small. Light did not seem to be an important design element; larger windows tended not to face the direct sunlight, possibly an advantage in the peak summer temperatures. In the 1930s there were variations which resulted in the departure of the heavy, light-inhibiting verandah and small windows.

The 1920s also saw the introduction of the 'all electric home'. With appliances such as electric irons, fans and radiators, people's lives became easier. Gas was still in use, and so the concept of power with the flick of a switch was very exciting. More appliances came on to the market and soon most homes had electric toasters and even stoves and refrigerators, which replaced ice chests previously used. The 'mod con' age had arrived, and with it the housewife's day became easier.

Characteristics of the Californian bungalow are:

- a garden surrounding the house
- detached garage
- projecting verandahs for sun protection, usually with massive supporting pylons
- bay windows
- lounge room facing south and east, if possible
- heavy chimney on external wall
- cement tile roof
- shingled gable ends
- green paint a favoured exterior colour

Californian bungalow style house, Glen Iris, Victoria

Photographer: Jon Rendell

Spanish mission 1930s–1940s

Established at the same time as the bungalow style was a style which came from the churches and the mission stations built by the Spanish religious orders in Mexico.

Houses in a quasi-Spanish style were built throughout California. In Australia the style was introduced by a professor at Sydney University, Leslie Wilkinson, and given the appropriate name of Spanish mission.

After the Depression had reached its peak, houses in the Spanish style became popular in Melbourne, Sydney and Brisbane. Spanish mission houses were particularly suited to the hot climate of Australia: they had verandahs and courtyards, small windows facing the sun and long, wide ones opening out onto shaded areas. These were also features of the Californian bungalow house.

Characteristics of the Spanish mission style are:

- roof of Cordoba tiles
- wide paved verandahs or terraces
- rounded arches on verandahs and occasionally on windows
- 'barley sugar' columns
- wrought iron gates and balustrading
- stucco facade which was smeared giving an effect called *pisé*
- painted with Mediterranean whites and creams
- ornately decorated lantern on porch
- heavy chimneys

Between the Depression and the war there were other developments in domestic housing, from Tudor style through to Neo-Georgian Revival—neither of which were as popular as Californian bungalow and Spanish mission. Of the Tudor style, London Court, 1936, designed by Bernard Evans, is a major tourist attraction in Perth. The Toorak Village shopping centre is one of the best examples in Melbourne.

Tudor style is characterised by:

- black-stained decorative woodwork attached to brick walls (usually white) or clinker brick
- fancy red roofs and chimneys
- clear leadlight windows

ACTIVITIES

1. From your reading of this chapter and any other material, why was it so difficult for women artists to gain recognition?

2. Make comparisons between pre-modernist work and work after 1913. What are the obvious differences? Discuss subject matter, technique, colour, and so on.

3. Try painting in the *alla prima* technique.

4. Design a lino cut. Use natural Australian subject matter similar to that of Margaret Preston.

5. How is Preston's *Flying over the Shoalhaven River* (page 107) reminiscent of Aboriginal culture? Give a detailed explanation.

6. Where else did 'new' styles of painting create a controversy? Refer to other chapters in this book for your answer.

7. From your own research, find out all you can about Art Deco.

8. Who was Frank Lloyd Wright? Name some of his buildings.

9. Find out all you can about the De Stijl movement.

10. Discuss the different aims of Burley Griffin's Sydney and Melbourne houses.

11. What was Griffin's unusual building technique design?

	AUSTRALIAN EVENTS	GENERAL EVENTS	ARTISTIC EVENTS	
1930				**Australian artists** Danila Vassilieff Josl Bergner Noel Counihan Albert Tucker Sidney Nolan Arthur Boyd John Perceval Lyndon Dadswell Clive Stephen Victor O'Connor James Gleeson Eric Wilson Paul Haefliger
1935				
1940	**1941** Australia declares war on Japan. John Curtin becomes Prime Minister. **1942** Darwin is bombed on 19 February. **1943** Arthur Streeton dies. **1944** The Liberal Party is formed.	**1940** The first bomb is dropped on London by Germany. **1941** Japan bombs Pearl Harbour. **1942** The Battle of Midway takes place. **1943** American forces arrive in New Guinea.	**1941** Hopper: *Nighthawks*. **1942** Mondrian: *Boogie Woogie Broadway* **1943** Hepworth: *Oval Sculptures* (S). **1944** Bacon: *Three Studies at the Base of a Crucifixion*.	
1945	**1945** Ben Chifley becomes Prime Minister. **1946** TAA (now Qantas Airways) begins operating between all States. The United Nations grants Australia trusteeship of New Guinea. **1949** The Snowy Mountains project commences. Robert Menzies becomes Prime Minister.	**1945** America drops atomic bombs on Hiroshima and Nagasaki. World War II ends: Germany surrenders on 7 May; Japan surrenders on 2 September. **1947** The Dead Sea Scrolls are discovered in Israel. **1948** Gandhi is assassinated. **1949** The system of apartheid is set up in South Africa.	**1945** Moore: *Family Group* (S). **1946** Rothko: *Prehistoric Memories*. **1948** Wyeth: *Christina's World*.	**Architecture** The Mercy Hospital Freemasons' Hospital The P&O style Newburn Flats, Melbourne Stanhill Flats, Melbourne Early Modern House Melbourne's Shrine of Remembrance
1950	**1951** Conscription is reintroduced. ANZUS Treaty signed.		**1950** Pollock: *Lavender Mist*.	
1955				

CHAPTER NINE

The Dark Years and the Depression 1933–50

Social and political background

Unfortunately, the hope of a prosperous future, evident in the 1920s, disappeared as quickly as it came. People's joy turned to dismay and misery as the Great Depression reached Australia in the late 1920s. Economically, Australia was in great trouble: production halved and, as a consequence, jobs were lost. Wages too were cut by between 10 and 20 per cent. With increasing unemployment many families were left penniless and out of work, in many cases evicted from their homes because they were unable to pay the rent. By 1930, unemployment was 19 per cent and in 1933 it was as high as 40 per cent. People literally wore their shoes out walking from job to job.

Inner city streets were turned into meeting places where people would line up to receive handouts. People formed queues that stretched for many blocks in order to receive food coupons, or soup from the many soup kitchens that were established by local charities and the Salvation Army.

People's entertainment declined and families had to find alternative and cheaper ways of occupying their spare time. The cinema or 'talking pictures' tended to be too expensive for a family, as were train and car trips. While many people gathered in parks to listen to singing and theatre, others stayed at home and listened to the radio, played cards, went to dances and generally made their own entertainment.

By the middle 1930s Australia's economy started to improve. This was a slow process. Eventually, around 1934, things were looking up; families were planning their futures. Jobs were becoming available, wages were rising and housing was more plentiful. The outlook was rosy until the outbreak of World War II in 1939.

With the outbreak of war, most Australians foresaw no danger to their country or wellbeing. Regarding the war as irrelevant, they were extremely hesitant to enlist; however, Australians rose to the occasion when the Japanese bombed Pearl Harbour in 1941.

Japan went from strength to strength, attacking Hong Kong, Burma, Malaya, Singapore and the Philippines, Rabaul, the Australian city of Darwin in 1942 and, later, Broome and Townsville. In 1942, Sydney became the target of a Japanese submarine attack. American troops under General Macarthur arrived in Australia to head the Pacific fight. Australia joined forces with America to finally remove all threat of invasion by the Japanese. On 6 August 1945, America dropped an atomic bomb on Hiroshima and, three days later, another on Nagasaki. On 15 August Prime Minister Chifley announced the end of the war.

Despite the terrible losses of human life, the news of the end of the war brought much excitement, celebration and, above all, renewed hope for the future. The returning soldiers were welcomed to an Australia of increasing exports, productivity, population and suburban sprawl.

During the height of the Depression parts of the inner cities became slums, where people frequently dumped their household waste into the streets, thus creating a public health hazard. Hygiene was a serious problem in these areas and public health suffered. Inner city scenes were portrayed by some of the social realist painters discussed later in this chapter.

The art of the 1930s illustrated a new wave of thought and, to a certain degree, discontent. The painting of the traditional Australian landscape and of European-influenced, post-impressionist painting meant little to a group of Melbourne painters who felt that art affected society and that art could even change the world. The social realists were concerned in particular with the effects on Australians of World War II, the Spanish Civil War and the Depression.

Painting, the Contemporary Art Society and the Australian Academy of Art

By the middle of the 1930s the reaction to the modernists had become hostile. The public was not interested in buying this style of art and the Director of the National Gallery of Victoria, J. S. MacDonald, disliked Modernism so vehemently that he did not want any modern art in 'his' gallery.

Many art students returned from overseas with new ideas and were keen to share their knowledge. These artists included Grace Crowley, Rah Fizelle, Eric Wilson and William Dobell. They returned with such new abstract painting styles as Cubism and Constructivism. While the group of modernists were thinking about ways to promote their cause, another group of people were arranging to establish an Australian equivalent of the British Royal Academy.

In 1937, an Academy of Art was set up in Canberra by the then Attorney-General and later Prime Minister, Robert Menzies. Its aim was to provide a forum for Australian art, and foster art appreciation and art education. Other groups of painters, however, felt that an academy would serve only to strengthen the powers of the conservatives and eventually stifle contemporary art and expression. They felt something had to be done to oppose the Academy.

In July of 1938, George Bell made plans to organise strong opposition to Menzies's Academy. He set up a society that would be supportive to modernist sculptors and painters. He also felt that this society should stimulate public interest and awareness of contemporary art. So it was that on 13 July 1938 the Contemporary Art Society was founded, with George Bell as its president and Rupert Bunny as its vice-president. The society's philosophy can be summed up in this paragraph which came from the catalogue for one of its annual exhibitions:

> Art does not stand still. Its movement is always forward, so each new year sees some new step taken. If the Contemporary Art Society is to be deserving of its name and the fundamental objects of its constitution, it, too, must move forward. When you cease to find in the annual exhibition of the society any new thought or feeling or any urge to explore the possibilities of the unknown, then you may be sure that the society no longer carries the banner it was intended to bear.

A similar society was set up in Sydney. Formed in 1937 as the Teachers' College Art Society with members Bernard Smith (the author of *Australian Painting*), James Gleeson and Rah Fizelle, it was later renamed the Sydney Contemporary Art Society.

The Melbourne CAS had its first exhibition in 1939. The artists included representatives from both Melbourne and Sydney. There were works submitted by Noel Counihan, Vic O'Connor, Joy Hester, Albert Tucker, James Gleeson, Russell Drysdale, Sali Herman and others. The CAS proved a valuable forum in which artists could show and sell their work, heighten their awareness and voice their feelings and ideas about modern art and life. The society also proved to be so strong that after only five shows the Australian Academy of Art dissolved.

There were many influences on contemporary artists during the early war years. The strongest came from the return of students who studied overseas, while another was the Herald Exhibition of Modern Art which began in 1939. This show was sponsored by the Melbourne *Herald*. It brought to Australia a wonderful collection of modern European art. The artists represented included such famous names as Gauguin, Matisse, Cézanne, Pissarro, Seurat, van Gogh, Bonnard, Vuillard, Vlaminck, Léger, Ernst, Dali and others. The show proved to be one of the most significant influences on contemporary painting. The most controversial of all the paintings proved to be the work of Dali. The show drew large crowds of up to 40 000 in its opening days and, of all the works exhibited, the Dali painting created the biggest stir. It was reported that the painting would corrupt Melbourne's youth. J. S. MacDonald said: '… the work called "modern" is the product of degenerates and perverts and the public and press have been fed with it.'

Despite the criticism from MacDonald, young painters still persisted with their interest in Modernism.

Another wave of enthusiastic modernists came when a large group returned to Australia in the early 1930s. Armed with 'weapons' to fight conservatism in art, they introduced in diluted doses Cubism, Constructivism and other forms of abstraction. The painters concerned—Rah Fizelle, Paul Haefliger, Eric Wilson, William Dobell and others—all made contributions to local art. Although Surrealism never gained as much support as it did in Europe, it emerged in some of Albert Tucker's work and especially in the painting of James Gleeson.

Gleeson (b. 1915) was most impressed by the unusual nature of the work of the Spanish surrealist, Salvador Dali. He used elements of Dali's work to create paintings dealing with the horror of war, at this time so close. *The Sower*, 1944, was first exhibited at the 1944 CAS exhibition. It is a very violent painting, symbolising the destruction of humanity. Gleeson has shown a figure almost totally torn apart, rising out of a rocky landscape. There is a nude female torso as well as two flesh-eating monsters and two skulls, one of which occupies the eye socket of the figure. The work is very similar to Dali's war paintings, in particular the gruesome *Soft Construction with Broiled Beans; Premonition of Civil War*, 1936. Apart from playing a small role in shaping some of the work of Tucker, Nolan, Boyd and Drysdale, Australian Surrealism died out and did not have an important influence on 1930s painting.

The other major influence upon painters in Australia came with the arrival of two Europeans, Danila Vassilieff and Josl Bergner. Their art was based on European developments and contained the excitement and vigour of contemporary European painting.

'Social Realism' was the term given to the work produced by a group of Melbourne painters working in the early 1940s. It commenced, aptly enough, at the same time as the beginning of World War II. The main artists involved in this early group were Josl Bergner, Noel Counihan and Victor O'Connor. A group of painters who had similar concerns to the social realists developed later. They became known as the 'Angry Penguins' because of their association with a cultural magazine called *Angry Penguins*. These painters were Nolan, Tucker, Perceval and Boyd.

Tired of people being so complacent about developments in world politics, they wanted to shout out and awaken people to what was happening. Painting was their voice. The social realists believed that art should reflect society and expose social injustice. They were political artists, making statements and questioning the values and standards of society.

BELOW:

JAMES GLEESON (b. 1915)
The Sower, 1944
Oil on canvas, 72 x 51 cm
Art Gallery of New South Wales
Purchased 1966

BELOW RIGHT:

DANILA VASSILIEFF
(1897–1958)
Children Playing, Fitzroy
(date unknown)
Oil on canvas, 49.1 x 60.8 cm
Collection: Geelong Art Gallery
Purchased with the assistance
of the Caltex-Victorian
Government Art Fund, 1979

Arguably the first Australian social realist painting to be produced came from the streets of Fitzroy, Melbourne, and was painted by **Danila Vassilieff (1897–1958)**. Born in Russia, he arrived in Darwin in 1923. After a brief stay there, he moved to Sydney and finally to Melbourne in 1937. Almost immediately he started painting the local life, the street scenes and his surrounding environment. His style was unlike anything seen in Australia before. It was free, vibrant and expressionist, with a child-like spontaneity. It was unstylised and uninhibited. Vassilieff often looked to the work of van Gogh, the Russian Chagall, and Vlaminck for inspiration.

The painting *Children Playing, Fitzroy* depicts a street scene of inner suburban Melbourne. While the brushstrokes are lucid, free and expressionist, the paintwork is thin and raw. Although his subject matter is quite detailed and thought-provoking, the painting style is quite the opposite. This new style of painting brought a variety of responses. The overriding one was disbelief that someone could paint such a depressing scene. Depressing scenes were considered unworthy of being painted. Consequently, such work seldom sold and was often criticised. The social realists were among the first artists to show the impoverished life in the inner city and the effects of the Depression years.

Unlike Vassilieff, **Bergner (b. 1920)** was not concerned with local issues. His concerns lay in depicting the gross injustice of the world. He was born in Austria into a Jewish family and, on arrival in Melbourne, settled into its Jewish community. Bergner was a keen admirer of the work of the French social realist Daumier (1808–79) and felt that he could identify with Daumier's social conscience.

Shortly after his arrival in Melbourne, Bergner was employed selling food at the Victoria Market. Here he frequently saw the poor, the drunk and the homeless—people in a similar predicament to himself, scavenging for any food they could find. It was during these years that he painted *The Pumpkin Eaters*, c. 1942. Painted in muddy browns and yellows, it was typical of social realist subject matter. It shows a terribly thin-looking family, including their shoeless young boy, walking beside a cart full of pumpkins which is being hauled by the father. Although not a good piece of drafting, the message of the painting is adequately conveyed: the misery and plight of the impoverished during the Depression.

Bergner's lively personality and character, coupled with his European background, made him popular with local Melbourne artists. He influenced quite a number including Tucker and Perceval, and was friendly with **Noel Counihan (1913–86)**.

Counihan entered art school at the age of sixteen. In fact, he was a storeman during the day and attended lectures at the Gallery School at night. Two years later, after losing his job and going on the dole, he became active in the Communist Party. He then became a freelance artist for many newspapers including the *Sun* and the *Bulletin*. Between 1931 and 1940 he completed six linocuts. Counihan was admitted to hospital with tuberculosis in 1940 and was too ill to work, although he was determined to start painting as soon as he was discharged. Bergner visited him in hospital two or three times during this period.

The memories of the Depression remained clear in Counihan's mind. Many of his paintings from these years were powerful reminders of life in Australia at the time of the Second World War, particularly his painting *At the Start of the March 1932*, 1944, in the Art Gallery of New South Wales. Speaking about this work in later life Counihan said that, while a powerful work, it was one which cast him in a role as a social realist for the rest of his painting life. Counihan felt this title was too limiting and restrictive.

JOSL BERGNER (b.1920)
The Pumpkin Eaters, c. 1942
Oil on composition board,
79 x 96.4 cm

Collection: National Gallery of
Australia, Canberra

Counihan blamed the capitalist system for the Depression, and he aimed to show this in his art. Counihan's later work dealt with a variety of subject matters. His 'good life' series is a metaphor for materialistic society sending young men to the Vietnam War. In 1938 he spent about four months in Broken Hill, mainly drawing unionists and mine workers. Many of these works were later produced as a collection of linocuts, of which *The Miner*, 1947, is one of the strongest in the series.

The horrors of war were also brought to light with the works of **Albert Tucker (b. 1914)** and Sidney Nolan (1917–92). Tucker never attended art school but was self-taught. He and Nolan responded to the influence of war on Australian society. Tucker's antiwar themes were similar to the war paintings of the German expressionists from the North: Otto Dix and George Grosz.

During the war years in Melbourne there was an influx of soldiers, particularly Americans. Khaki uniforms became part of everyday life in wartime Melbourne; soldiers were constantly looking for a 'good time'. This was all part of the 'moral decay' that Tucker believed went hand in hand with war. Tucker explores these issues in his *Images of Modern Evil* series. He explained where his inspiration for this series came from:

> They came out of wartime Melbourne. I remember a newspaper story about girls in a back alley, with some diggers, doing a strip-tease for them—great old fun and games. This was part of the image stock-piled in my mind. Beer and sexual contests along Swanston Street, all along St Kilda Rd from Princess Bridge, down to Luna Park at St Kilda. The GI, the digger, schoolgirl tarts, Victory girls. All these schoolgirls from fourteen to fifteen would rush home after school and put on short skirts made out of flags—red, white and blue—and go out tarting along St Kilda Road with the GIs and of course, diggers—when the diggers could get a look in, because they were all poor men compared with the Americans.[1]

---

[1] Mollison, J. & Bonham, N., *Albert Tucker*, Macmillan with the co-operation of the Australian National Gallery, Melbourne, 1982.

RIGHT:

ALBERT TUCKER (b. 1914)

Victory Girls, 1943
Oil on canvas, 64.6 x 58.7 cm

Collection: National Gallery of
Australia, Canberra

BELOW:

ALBERT TUCKER (b. 1914)

Man's Head, 1946
Oil on cotton gauze on
cardboard, 63.4 x 76.0 cm

Collection: National Gallery of
Australia, Canberra
Gift of the artist 1981

BELOW RIGHT:

SIDNEY NOLAN (1917–92)

Head of a Soldier, 1942
Enamel on cardboard,
775.8 x 63.3 cm

Collection: National Gallery of
Australia, Canberra

The *Victory Girls*, 1943, is an image taken directly from this experience. Despite its horrifying subject matter, the painting is superb in its execution. Large colourful brushstrokes in blue, red and white were slapped on to the canvasboard. The women's faces are dominated by the large, brilliant, orange–red 'V'-shaped mouths filled with teeth. While the women are portrayed as sexual toys, the soldiers' image is not one of Anzac heroes, but one of drunken sleaziness.

The common problem associated with war was the traumatic effect it had on the soldiers' mental and physical health. If they were not suffering from physical injuries, they were suffering from mental illnesses including severe depression and war neurosis. For a short time Tucker was attached to a hospital where he was required to make drawings of soldiers' facial injuries.

The remainder of Tucker's work from these years dealt with the outcasts of society. For example, *Man's Head*, 1946, was inspired by a newspaper photo of a man convicted of kicking a dog to death. Another work was based on a report of a man who had murdered his mother, mutilated her in the lounge room, and then had attempted to cremate her in the lounge-room fire.

Sidney Nolan also depicted the effects of war; however, he later ventured into landscape painting. His painting *Head of a Soldier*, 1942, was actually reproduced on the cover of a book on war psychosis called *Psychiatric Aspects of Modern Warfare*. The work depicts the face of a soldier with large, popping, bloodshot eyes, and twisted, sucked-in cheeks. The soldier's tongue is hanging out of his mouth. Childlike in its simplicity but powerful in its message, the work all too readily conveyed the horror of war.

Nolan moved on from these scenes to rediscover the Australian landscape. Not in the same tradition as the 'gold and blue' school—it was a modern approach.

SIDNEY NOLAN (1917–92)
MacDonnell Ranges, 1949
Oil on ripolin, 91.5 x 122 cm

Collection: Art Gallery of South Australia, Adelaide
Government Grant 1952

He travelled extensively throughout South Australia and the Northern Territory where he painted vast panoramic views of the desert. *MacDonnell Ranges*, 1949, is one of these works. It is an unusual painting in that it has two horizons: the first is of the mountains in the foreground while the other, the true horizon, is evident in the background. The painting has a very broad and distant view that goes on indefinitely, only broken up occasionally by clumps of carefully painted, silver-trunked, gum trees. For the mountains and landscape Nolan relied on natural ochres of reds and browns, while for the sky he used the contrasting traditional Australian blue.

Nolan continued to paint consistently. His works include paintings of Central Australia, Queensland and other Australian landscapes, and series depicting Burke and Wills, and Ned Kelly. After being knighted in 1981, Nolan spent most of his time in England.

The devastating effects of war also confused and angered the young **Arthur Boyd (b. 1920)**. Like Norman Lindsay, Boyd was born into an artistic family, which had a history of involvement in the arts. He did not attend art school but was taught art by his family.

Boyd's work of the 1940s was like Tucker's in that it depicted scenes of horror, degradation and twentieth-century sophistication, and the century's barbarism—the ultimate act being the dropping of the atomic bomb on Hiroshima in 1945. Boyd felt so strongly about this that he painted a holocaust scene of Melbourne in 1945. This made quite a few people think about how close the war was to home. While he was serving at the war, Boyd worked on a series of superbly expressive and powerful drawings. Executed between 1941 and 1943, they were similar to Tucker's *Images of Modern Evil* series and, in particular, *Victory Girls*.

In his earlier years, Boyd was influenced by the painter Pieter Brueghel (c. 1530–69). This Flemish painter portrayed panoramic views and paid particular attention to detail and human activity. Boyd used these features in his *Melbourne Burning*, 1946–47. While many figures in the work are Brueghel-like, most of them are depicted screaming and running from the raging fire. Other figures are shown lying dead among the trees. Even animals are shown fleeing across the river.

The drawing *Prostitute on Soldier's Hat and Soldier with Prostitute*, 1942, truly confronts the viewer. Drawn with a reed pen and ink, it has lines full of expressive spontaneity. Boyd relies upon the trick of making some of his figures disproportionate, a device that children frequently use when they want to stress a point in a drawing. The soldier appears dwarfed, tucked under the arm of the woman.

John Perceval (b. 1923), a good friend of Boyd's, studied and enjoyed the work of both Brueghel and Hieronymus Bosch (c. 1450–1516). Perceval first began to paint after copying the work of van Gogh. He went to art school but disliked the conservative and rigid training.

Perceval's early paintings were mostly of children, painted during the Depression years—disturbing and depressing subjects. In particular *Boy with Cat*, 1943, shows a horrifying scene of a little boy holding a cat. Under normal circumstances such a scene would be expected to be typical of the beautiful paintings of French Impressionism: delightful works of children and leisure were common. This work, however, is quite the opposite. It is vicious. The brushwork is appropriately rough and crude, while the colour range is dull and muddy, consistent with the feeling of Perceval's image. The boy is holding the cat in his hands: the cat's mouth is open and

RIGHT:

ARTHUR BOYD (b. 1920)
Melbourne Burning, 1946–47
Oil and tempera on canvas,
90.2 x 100.5 cm

Collection: The Robert Holmes
à Court Collection

BELOW:

ARTHUR BOYD (b. 1920)
*Prostitute on Soldier's Hat and
Soldier with Prostitute*, 1942
Reed pen and ink,
26.4 x 29.6 cm

National Gallery of Victoria,
Melbourne
Purchased 1966

BELOW RIGHT:

JOHN PERCEVAL (b. 1923)
Boy with Cat, 1943
Oil on composition board,
58.5 x 43.2 cm

Collection: National Gallery of
Australia, Canberra

its claws are attached to the boy's cheeks. Although a terribly violent painting and a disturbing work, this could also be interpreted as black humour.

In his later years, Perceval worked on landscape paintings and, during 1957 and 1958, produced a series of ceramic angels. He travelled to Europe but returned to Australia where he is still painting and exhibiting.

Sculpture

The Depression years weighed heavily upon the sculptors of this period. Many artists suffered from financial difficulties. Even the rich were feeling the pinch. Despite this predicament, artists kept working. In particular, two modernist sculptors, **Lyndon Dadswell (1908–86)** and Clive Stephen (1889–1957), established their identities during these years.

In 1929 Dadswell was a student of sculpture at the East Sydney Technical School where he studied under Rayner Hoff (see Chapter Eight). While working on the Shrine of Remembrance in Melbourne, Paul Montford invited Dadswell to work with him. He was employed to sculpt relief panels depicting the various tasks undertaken by the AIF (Australian Imperial Force) on the Shrine's exterior. It took more than four years. In 1935 Dadswell travelled to England with a scholarship to the Royal Academy, where he studied for two years. He returned to Sydney in 1937 and taught sculpture at the East Sydney Tech.

Dadswell became a significant sculptor and teacher while producing many modern pieces of sculpture, one of these being *Man and Horse,* 1950. The simplified figure reclining on the back of this rather chunky modernist horse is actually a transitional piece of modernist sculpture. As years went by Dadswell's later work became less figurative and more abstract.

Immediately after the war, Melbourne sculptors also became interested in exploring the modern style, and the most significant work came from a doctor and part-time sculptor, **Clive Stephen**. He was interested in all spheres of art but particularly sculpture. At a time when Australian sculptors were breaking new ground, Stephen was looking to the modernist trends in Europe. While serving in the Royal Army Medical Corps in Europe, he had seen modern art exhibitions and had been influenced by them.

On his return to Australia, Stephen practised medicine and in his spare time worked on his sculpture. Stephen's situation was different from most other artists in that he already had an income and therefore was not totally dependent on a patron or a gallery buying his work. Stephen's work was unique: he was the only modern Australian sculptor to be strongly influenced by primitive sculpture and art from Africa and the Pacific Islands.

The original sandstone block that Stephen chose for his piece *Garden Sculpture,* 1950, was selected for its closeness in shape to a planned design. The figure shows a crouching woman, one leg tucked underneath her arm. The beautifully carved forms are rounded and smooth while at the same time eliminating unnecessary detail. The head, with a face not unlike that seen on an African mask, is turned at an angle. The hair has been depicted by the careful carving of thin lines. For the reminder of his life Stephen involved himself in many art groups in which he constantly encouraged discussion of the role and future of modern sculpture.

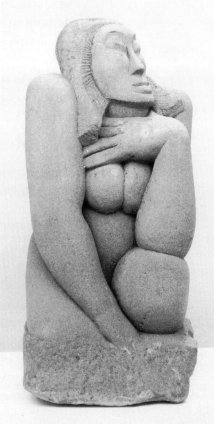

Civil architecture

During the Depression years there was virtually no significant contribution to architecture. The building industry was badly affected by the Depression; architecture has always been a good barometer of a country's economic situation. However, in the early 1930s the economy gradually improved and building recommenced.

The strong horizontal, the conscious elimination of decoration, and the sweeping curved balconies were typical of the 1930s. It was an efficient style but also rather bland and, at times, sterile. At its best, it was suited to and became a popular style for hospitals. Melbourne's Mercy Hospital is a typical example. Designed by the architects Stephenson and Turner, it was the first modern work Stephenson produced after his return from Russia and America. Other hospitals he designed were the Royal Melbourne (1939–43) and the Freemasons' Hospital (1936). The trend swept the country, partly because the style was so well suited to hospitals. The long sun-drenched balconies were therapeutic for convalescing patients. The balconies contrasted aesthetically with the vertical structures housing the administration and lift wells.

This early modern movement became a popular style for blocks of flats, apartments and office buildings. The new techniques and materials made constructing buildings of different shapes and designs easier: the concrete slab, the steel frame and curved glass revolutionised both commercial and domestic architecture. Of the office buildings, Mitchell House (1936) by Norris on the corner of Elizabeth and Lonsdale Streets, Melbourne, is evidence of this new streamlined movement. In Surry Hills, Sydney, the Hastings Deering building is similar. Designed by Samuel Lipson, its bands of windows and concrete make for a rather streamlined, modern, tall 1930s design.

The 1930s also saw the construction of a number of buildings either built in the style of the exotic Art Deco or flaunting its elements. The origins of this flamboyant yet geometrical style lay in the art of Ancient Egypt, the American Indians and the Aztecs. Owing to the overwhelming success of the International style, Deco did not develop into any significant architectural trend. The style became much more popular in other areas of design, such as jewellery, furniture and statuary.

Some Art Deco buildings are:

- City Mutual Life, Sydney, 1936 (Emil Sodersten)
- Alkira House, Melbourne, 1937 (J. Wadrop)
- Sands and McDougall building, Adelaide, 1933 (Claridge, Bruer and Fisher)
- War Memorial, Adelaide, 1930 (W. Bagot)
- Anzac Memorial, Sydney, 1930 (B. Dellit)
- National Film and Sound Archive, Canberra, 1929–31 (W. Hayward Morris and R. Casboulte)

Melbourne's contribution to the building of war memorials came in 1930. Built with unemployed labour from local granite, it commands a broad view of the city. The

STEPHENSON AND TURNER
Freemasons' Hospital, East Melbourne, 1936
Photographer: Jon Rendell

two architects, Philip Hudson and James Wadrop, were inspired by one of the Seven Wonders of the World, the Mausoleum at Halicarnassus.[2] Many of the Shrine's marble elements and decorations were borrowed from fifth century Classical Greece—in particular, the Doric columns and entablature, which are not unlike parts of the Parthenon in Athens. The Shrine stands as a symbol of, and memorial to, the people who served in the Great War, 1914–18. Of the monument it is written:

> They chose to build in the Classic style of Ancient Greece whose monuments surviving the storms of the centuries proclaim the truths by which men live and for which alone they are prepared to die.

Domestic architecture

Domestic architecture became known as the P & O (Peninsular and Oriental Steamship Company) style. The long decks, flat roofs, strong vertical chimneys and porthole windows (all flush to the wall) resembled the functional simplicity of an ocean liner in the P & O fleet.

The architect **Frederick Romberg (b. 1913)** designed one of the first modern blocks of flats, called Newburn. They enjoyed views of Melbourne's Albert Park Lake and were quickly filled with tenants. The interesting feature of the building was that not one flat looked on to another and each had views of the lake.

---

[2] The remnants of the Mausoleum are situated in Bodrum in the Gulf of Kos, south-western Turkey. It was built for King Mausolus, ruler of Caria, 377–53 BC.

HUDSON AND WADROP
The Shrine of Remembrance, Melbourne, 1934
Photographer: Jon Rendell

Romberg's other block of flats, just a little further down the road, is called Stanhill. This building is much higher and uses much more glass. While long verandahs occupy one side of the building, on the other side windows with views of Port Phillip Bay face on to the lake.

The 1930s style in housing manifested itself in a style called Waterfall, so called because of its shape. It became very popular in the years immediately after World War II. With carefully rounded corners, it was a streamlined style in contrast to the weightiness of the Californian bungalow and Spanish mission styles. The Waterfall style lacked decoration and, as a consequence, a certain amount of attraction.

P & O style flats, South Melbourne
Photographer: Jon Rendell

Characteristics of the Waterfall style are:

- horizontal windows with steel casement
- front door with porthole window
- cream-coloured paint or trimmings
- occasionally a combination of brick and stucco bands
- tiled roof
- often 'waterfall' curtains (Austrian blinds)

FREDERICK ROMBERG
(b. 1913)

Stanhill Apartments, Queens Road, South Melbourne

Photographer: Jon Rendell

Waterfall style house,
Thornbury, Victoria

Note characteristic 'waterfall'
curtains, an original feature of
this style

Photographer: Jon Rendell

ACTIVITIES

1. Compare and contrast the work of the Spanish painter Dali with that of Gleeson.

2. Look at the differences between art from this period and that of a century earlier. Discuss, with references to the work of at least three artists.

3. Look at the work of the German Expressionists. Can you draw any similarities with that of Australian artists?

4. Using news items or political pictures from a newspaper or magazine, make a drawing or painting. Try to make the work a 'political' statement.

5. Find out more information about the Angry Penguins.

6. Using the guide in Appendix One, analyse Boyd's painting *Melbourne Burning* (page 130).

7. As a class, discuss one of these topics:

    (a) Are depressing scenes such as those painted by the German Expressionists and the Australian social realist painters suitable subject matter?

    (b) Do you believe, as J. S. MacDonald said, that 'art can corrupt the young'?

8. Using simplified shapes and forms similar to the work of Dadswell, carve a figure sculpture.

9. Compare and contrast the sculpture of Dadswell with work from fifty years earlier.

10. Research the work of the American architect Frank Lloyd Wright. How does it compare with the work produced in the 1930s and 1940s?

	AUSTRALIAN EVENTS	GENERAL EVENTS	ARTISTIC EVENTS	
1950	**1951** ANZUS treaty is signed. **1952** Uranium is discovered in the Northern Territory. **1954** Uranium is discovered at Mary Kathleen, Queensland. The Petrov affair, with accusations of communist espionage in Canberra, occurs.	**1952** Radio-carbon technique is used to date archaeological finds. **1953** Colour telecasts begin in the United States. Edmund Hilary conquers Mt Everest.	**1951** Dali: *Crucifixion*. **1952** Matisse: *Seated Blue Nude III*. **1953** Pollock: *Blue Poles*.	**Australian artists** Sali Herman Russell Drysdale William Dobell Grace Crowley Rah Fizelle Ralph Balson Mark Haefliger Eric Wilson Godfrey Miller Frank Hinder Ian Fairweather Leonard French Roger Kemp Robert Dickerson Charles Blackman John Brack Joy Hester Clifton Pugh Danila Vassilieff Margel Hinder
1955	**1956** Olympic Games are held in Melbourne. The first Australian abstract expressionist exhibition is held. Television is introduced into Australia. **1957** The Danish architect Joern Utzon wins the Sydney Opera House Design Competition. **1958** The first Australian nuclear reactor is built at Lucas Heights, Sydney.	**1955** Polio vaccination is first used. **1956** Trans-Atlantic telephone links are established. **1957** The USSR launches *Sputnik*, the first satellite. **1959** A Russian satellite photographs the moon.	**1955** Johns starts his *Flag* series. Rauschenberg: *Bed*. **1956** Hamilton: *Just what is it today that makes today's homes so appealing?* **1958** Van der Rohe: *Seagram Building*. **1959** Rauschenberg: *Monogram*.	
1960		**1960** Egypt begins building the Aswan High Dam on the River Nile.	**1960** Johns: *Flashlight* (S).	
	1964 Lake Burley Griffin is completed.			
1965	**1967** Aborigines become accepted as Australian citizens by being included in the Census.			**Architects and architecture** Harry Seidler Roy Grounds Prefabricated housing The 'Austerity' House International Style Academy of Science building Myer Music Bowl Queensland and Northern Australian domestic architecture
1970				

CHAPTER TEN

Figurative versus Abstract 1951–60s

Social and political background

In the summer of 1956 Melbourne played host to the sixteenth Olympic Games, opened by the Duke of Edinburgh. It was the first time the Games had been held outside America or Europe and it created much excitement and energy. The flaming Olympic torch was flown from Olympia in Greece, and then carried on foot all the way from Cairns to Melbourne. Melbourne's streets were lined with tens of thousands of cheering Australians as Ron Clarke ran with the torch into the Olympic stadium. Australia won thirteen gold medals at these Games, most of them for swimming. Two Australian winners were Dawn Fraser and Betty Cuthbert.

With a big push from television came the biggest influence to hit the teenage Australian—rock'n'roll. American artists such as Bill Haley and the Comets, Little Richard and Elvis Presley, showing as much excitement as the teenagers who watched them, burst on to our screens. Shows such as 'Bandstand' and, later, 'Six O'Clock Rock' echoed the American rock shows. Eventually Australia had its own rock'n'roll star in Johnny O'Keefe.

The rock'n'roll dance became popular with the young as did the desire to be seen looking suitably 'cool'. While the boys slicked back their hair with Californian Poppy or Brylcream, the girls preferred to have theirs pulled back into a ponytail. The clothing worn by the 1950s young was just as provocative as the clothes worn today. The boys pulled on blue jeans and brightly coloured shirts, and fluorescent socks and blue suede or black pointed shoes. The girls frequently wore jeans, jumpers and shirts;

however, the wide, knee-length dress was 'big' on dance nights. It was all an attempt to emulate their American idols whom they heard on the radio or watched on television. The 1950s was a time of renewed prosperity and also a period of materialism and mechanisation.

Since the war, Australia has gone through many changes—political, economic and social. Of the social changes that have taken place, one of the most significant has been the mass immigration of Europeans between 1947 and 1960. This influx of new Australians changed the face of the nation. As the country became culturally richer, cities took on a cosmopolitan feel. The increased population created a consumer demand which increased productivity and brought economic bonuses for the Government.

Foreign investment increased. Mining and chemical production increased, particularly with the discovery of uranium in the early 1950s.

Despite ties with Britain, another big influence on Australians and their way of life during the 1950s was the United States. After their assistance and intervention during the Pacific war, the American influence was still strong. American culture filtered into areas such as cinema, music, books, magazines and food. Australians' dress, attitudes and eating habits started to become Americanised. Mickey Mouse and the peanut butter sandwich were here to stay. This trend became increasingly powerful during the 1960s until there was a conscious move in the 1970s to resist it.

The biggest development in technology that came from America was television. That much talked about 'box' took off in Australia as other electrical appliances did in the 1930s. Families who could afford to purchased a television, and in 1956 watched the telecast of the Olympic Games in Melbourne, along with a few American situation comedies, cartoons and drama.

Painting

Cubism is no different from any other school of painting. The same principles and the same elements are common to all. The fact that for a long time Cubism has not been understood and that even today there are people who cannot see anything in it, means nothing. I do not read English, an English book is a blank book to me. This does not mean that the English language does not exist, and why should I blame anybody else but myself if I cannot understand what I know nothing about.[1]

Sali Herman (1898–1993) arrived in Australia in 1937. Born into a family of eighteen, he had studied in Paris. Once in Sydney Herman set to work painting the local people and their houses. Rendering them carefully and then using a palette knife to apply paint, he sought to produce a vision of Sydney's inner city dwellings. In remembering these works Herman said: 'Houses are part of people, and people part of houses, and when I paint them I look for the character of prettiness or dirty walls.'

His work *The Law Courts*, 1946, is a painting of Greenway's Hyde Park Barracks (see Chapter Three). Scraping away at the surface of the paint on the canvas, Herman also highlighted the texture and quality of Greenway's building. Although Herman did not have a guiding influence on Australian art, his prodigious output earned him a retrospective in 1982.

---

[1] Picasso, 1923

Two prominent Sydney painters of the late 1940s and the 1950s were William Dobell (1899–1970) and **Russell Drysdale (1912–81)**. Until this time Australian landscape painters had mostly concerned themselves with the 'attractive' side—the beautiful wide rivers, the bush, and the blue and gold visions of the Heidelberg tradition. The art of Drysdale changed the way Australians saw their country.

A student at the Bell School of Art, Drysdale worked his way through a variety of styles, all crucial to his development as a serious artist. His paintings from the post-war years depicted the new vision of the Australian outback. *The Rabbiters*, 1947, relies upon a touch of Surrealism to add to its mood. The predominant and dramatic use of black, as seen in the cast shadows and rock formations, all add to this impression. Interestingly enough, Drysdale also painted the rock formations with a certain ambiguity. The strong, vertical rock formation on the right of the painting is reminiscent of the lower leg bone of a cow. Similarly, the uprooted tree looks very much like skeletal remains. There is a feeling of uneasiness amid eeriness as the two rabbiters are dwarfed by the large lifeless formations. Overall, it is a forbidding and overwhelming landscape.

From the same year came the painting *Sofala*, which in 1947 won Drysdale the Wynne Prize.[2] Painted in warm ochres of reds and browns, it depicts the rundown and deserted gold town in New South Wales. The buildings stand as monuments to the once busy and frantic life of Australia's many gold towns, now deserted.

Drysdale was also a brilliant draftsman and continually made drawings, often in pen and ink. In his later work he explored the world of the Aborigines and people in the outback. Drysdale believed that the Aborigine held a certain mystique for him. He said they had a 'peculiar dignity and grace'.

Another significant Sydney painter, though not of landscape, was **William Dobell**. A portrait painter, he won three Archibald prizes.[3] After initially training in

BELOW:

SALI HERMAN (1898–1993)
The Law Courts, 1946
Oil on canvas, 61 x 81.5 cm
National Gallery of Victoria, Melbourne
Felton Bequest 1946

BELOW RIGHT:

RUSSELL DRYSDALE (1912–81)
Sofala, 1947
Oil on canvas on hardboard, 71.7 x 93.1 cm
Art Gallery of New South Wales
Purchased 1952

[2] In the terms of the bequest of Richard Wynne who died in 1895, the Art Gallery of New South Wales runs an annual competition for landscape painting or figure sculpture. The prize is $10 000.

[3] In the terms of the bequest of J. F. Archibald, who died in 1919, the Art Gallery of New South Wales runs an annual competition for portraiture, preferably of some person known for services to Art, Science, Entertainment, etc. The prize is judged by the Gallery's Trustees and is worth $20 000.

RUSSELL DRYSDALE
(1912–81)
The Rabbiters, 1947
Oil on canvas, 76.2 x 101.6 cm
National Gallery of Victoria,
Melbourne
Purchased 1947

Sydney and winning a travelling scholarship, he went to London in 1929 where he continued his studies until he returned to Australia in 1938.

Dobell produced many naturalistic portraits throughout the late 1930s and 1940s, one of them being the superb study *Boy at the Basin*, 1932. Dobell's portrait painting hit the headlines in 1943 when a work he exhibited in the Archibald prize of that year won first place. The painting, a portrait of his friend Joshua Smith, created a huge controversy when a couple of other entrants in the show claimed that the painting was not a portrait but rather a caricature, in which case the prize should be set aside. The argument finally reached the Supreme Court, where after much cross-examining and deliberation, Dobell won.[4] Bernard Smith says this about the victory:

> Consequently, the judgment was rightly heralded as a significant victory for the modern movement in Australia, regardless of whether Dobell was a classic, academic or modern painter. As a result, expressionist painting acquired some status at law and the angry voices of the old prophets for whom portraiture would always mean tonal matching in the manner of Velázquez and Raeburn, Hall and Meldrum, were heard less in the land.[5]

Indeed the modern movements in Australia were well on the way towards creating their own prophets and their own establishment.

The case was a major victory for Dobell and his supporters but, despite the outcome, it upset Dobell terribly. His nerves suffered and for a while he was unable to paint. However, he returned to work with a painting of a Sydney restaurateur, *Chez Walter*, 1945. Rococo in its charm and style, the warm red painting portrays Walter

---

[4] An account of the trial can be found in Gleeson, J., *William Dobell: A Biographical and Critical Study*, Angus & Robertson, Sydney, 1981.

[5] Smith, B., *Australian Painting, 1788–1970*, Second Edition, Oxford University Press, Melbourne, 1979, p. 271.

WILLIAM DOBELL
(1899–1970)

Chez Walter, 1945
Oil on composition board
44.5 x 54.8 cm

Collection: National
Gallery of Australia,
Canberra

sitting on a chair, larger than life, and, to the right of him, a large crayfish standing on its tail. Walter's face is full of life and personality and it is this quality that makes Dobell such a fine portraitist.

Although some of the first Australian abstracts painted were by de Maistre and Wakelin in 1919, there were other attempts to get the movement off the ground. The first serious attempts came in the 1930s, with artists Grace Crowley and Rah Fizelle (known to his friends as 'Fizz'—and to others as 'Rough-as-'ell'). Crowley and Fizelle set up an art school in Sydney, primarily to introduce and teach the concepts of Cubism and Constructivism. Forums were frequently held at the school where groups met regularly to discuss the nature of these new styles. While Crowley's early work was basically figurative (see Chapter Eight), her later work tended towards geometric abstraction. Fizelle showed his uncertainty with this style by staying with a kind of academic, subtle form of abstraction.

The other abstract artists who took their lead from cubist experiments were **Eric Wilson (1911–46)** and **Paul Haefliger (1914–82)**. Haefliger's *Abstract with Violin*, 1938, takes its style from the cubist painters—in particular, Juan Gris and Picasso.

Wilson returned from Europe at the outbreak of World War II and set to work painting, drawing and spreading the new word. Of abstract art he said:

No longer a window through which one views a charming piece of nature, but [it] is itself the object. This is the final reality [the artist] is alone concerned with, not at all an illusion of nature's appearances.

With this in mind, Wilson turned his attention to making renditions of stoves and kitchens of which the synthetic cubist work *The Kitchen Stove*, 1943, is a superb example.

Although there was constant prodding by the abstract artists, the late 1930s and 1940s were largely eclipsed by Social Realism. However, in the 1950s there was a rebirth of a serious interest in abstraction by a group of painters. They were Ralph Balson (1890–1964), Godfrey Miller (1893–1964), Frank Hinder (1906–92) and Ian Fairweather (1891–1974).

Their motivation and inspiration came partly from their knowledge of European trends, and partly from the touring French painting exhibition which arrived in Sydney in 1953. This show proved to be quite a catalyst for the young painters, just as the *Herald* exhibition had been to Melbourne artists a decade and a half earlier. The French show displayed the works of Vlaminck, Chagall, Matisse, Derain, Braque, Ernst and more.

Ralph Balson's earlier contact with Crowley and Fizelle inspired him to produce a few figure paintings of a highly abstracted and geometric nature. In the late 1950s he exhibited work that looked like pointillist experiments. One of these was *Non-Objective Abstract*, 1958, which presents dancing daubs of pigment, almost like a close-up of a Seurat or a Signac. The daubs look cramped as each colour struggles for dominance while at the same time wanting to remain within the confines of the canvas. By creating a cluster of smaller, thinner brushstrokes, Balson produces an illusion of depth. At first glance one could be forgiven for thinking the painting to be an aerial view of a crowd, but on closer inspection it can be seen as a selection of different coloured brush marks, daubs and spots.

Godfrey Miller's work shows similar intentions, of laying down various shapes and colours. His work *Nude and the Moon*, 1954–58, shows an abstracted reclining

PAUL HAEFLIGER (1914–82)
Abstract with Violin, 1938
Oil on canvas, 51.5 x 61.8 cm
Collection: National Gallery of Australia, Canberra

RALPH BALSON (1890–1964)
Non-Objective Abstract, 1958
Oil on hardboard,
137.2 x 162.4 om

National Gallery of Victoria,
Melbourne
Purchased 1968

female figure in a landscape. It is a tight and controlled landscape, with an overall linear structure of diagonals, verticals and horizontals which frequently overlap, creating a myriad of diamond, mosaic patterns. Over these lines Miller has placed alternating and tonally different layers of paint. Visually this technique is highly exciting as the variation in tone gives the work a shimmering quality.

Abstract but totally different from Miller's work is the work of **Frank Hinder**. Hinder socialised with the Crowley–Fizelle group and became an important figure in the early Abstract movement. He was interested in mathematical problems, geometry, the structural effect of colour and the dynamic illusion of movement.

Like the Italian futurists, Hinder was interested in the qualities of machinery, mechanisation of the twentieth century, motion and, to take one of the futurists' words, 'dynamism'. The painting *Subway Escalator*, 1953, is a superb study of figures in motion. The multicoloured work is a rhythm of buzzing, fragmented figures all making their way up the escalator. The diagonal push upward of blues, violets and greens is surrounded by the strong vertical and diagonal yellows and oranges of the modern mechanical stairway. The figures move across, up, and out of the subway, up to the light in the street. This work is one of only a few Australian futurist paintings ever produced.

Another eccentric and unusual artist is **Ian Fairweather**. A keen and consistent traveller, he believed travel held the key to freedom. He had a varied career from working on farms in Canada to working in China, Bali and Sri Lanka, constantly on

ABOVE:

ERIC WILSON (1911–46)
The Kitchen Stove, 1943
Oil, paper, sand on canvas
(collage), 96.8 x 53.3 cm

Collection: Queensland Art
Gallery
Gift of the Godfrey Rivers Trust
1948

ABOVE RIGHT:

FRANK HINDER (b. 1906)
Subway Escalator, 1953
Tempera and oil on canvas,
92.8 x 72.5 cm

Collection: Art Gallery of South
Australia, Adelaide
Elder Bequest Fund 1972

RIGHT:

GODFREY MILLER (1893–1964)
Nude and the Moon, 1954–58
Oil on canvas, 61.6 x 104.2 cm

Art Gallery of New South Wales
Gift of the Art Gallery Society
of New South Wales, 1959

the move until he finally settled on an island off the Queensland coast just north of Brisbane.

One of his great stories is of the journey he made out of Darwin by sea at the age of sixty. Yearning for a lush tropical climate, Fairweather built himself a raft made of aeroplane-wing tanks and planks. Armed with fresh water, some cans of beef, a compass and a few other items, he set off across the sea for Bali. Sixteen days later, owing to tropical gales, heat and strong sea currents, he was blown ashore on Indonesian Timor. The Indonesian Government was quick to act and, after detaining him for a couple of months as a spy, shipped him to Singapore. He later ended up in England, where he was forced to dig trenches in order to raise money for the plane fare home.

IAN FAIRWEATHER
(1891–1974)

Roi Soleil, 1956–57
Gouache on paperboard,
99 x 72.5 cm

Art Gallery of New South Wales
Purchased 1957

Fairweather's paintings are wild and exciting, with lush paintwork and calligraphic linework. The work *Roi Soleil*, 1956–57, is a response to the Asian culture which he so much admired. Representing an Asian sun god, *Roi Soleil* is depicted in large gestural sweeps of the brush in white and brown. With touches of red throughout the work, it is beautifully rhythmical and relaxing.

Broadly speaking, Melbourne in the 1950s was more conservative artistically than Sydney. Although Melbourne artists were more concerned with figurative painting, there were a handful of non-figurative painters at work, two of whom were Roger Kemp (1908–87) and **Leonard French (b. 1928)**.

French is well known for his work in designing the stained-glass ceiling in the Great Hall at the National Gallery of Victoria. Originally a signwriter, he went abroad to study art and different cultures. French became interested in the use of literary sources as inspiration for his paintings; he also frequently used religious stories as the basis for his work. French paints using abstracted symbols arranged in aesthetic harmony.

Death and Transfiguration, 1961, is one of these religious works. Heavily built up with layers of glazes, the painting almost takes on a ceramic, glazed effect. This painting is divided in two: in the lower half fish are shown in what appear to be coffins, while above, glittering in gold leaf, is the resurrected martyr transfigured into

ABOVE:

LEONARD FRENCH (b. 1928)
Death and Transfiguration, 1961
Enamel on canvas on hardboard, 122.6 x 137.9 cm
Art Gallery of New South Wales
Sir Charles Lloyd Jones
Bequest Fund 1962

ABOVE RIGHT:

ROBERT DICKERSON (b. 1924)
The Tired Man, c. 1956
Synthetic enamel on hardboard, 137.1 x 152.7 cm
National Art Gallery of Victoria, Melbourne
Purchased 1957

a fish and raised in the sky. Consistent with French's preliminary work, the painting is very carefully planned and carried out. French actually builds the painting. As well as using glazes, he often builds up his surfaces with layers of hessian, producing a surface similar to a relief. In recent years, French has been working on large abstract murals, one of which can be seen in the Commonwealth Bank tower in Elizabeth Street, Melbourne.

Roger Kemp's paintings in the 1950s were highly original and as Kemp himself said, 'not easily understood'. His paintings are concerned with the relationship of humans with the cosmic order. In Kemp's later work of the 1960s and 1970s, he explored the symbols of the cross, the square and circle. The painting, *The Cross*, c. 1967, is an example of this theme. Kemp painted in almost total isolation, exploring this abstract world.

Among the figurative Sydney painters of this time, other than Dobell and a handful of others, was **Bob Dickerson (b. 1924)**. Despite the 1950s trend of abstraction, Dickerson remained interested in figurative painting. He joined the RAAF and, while stationed in Indonesia, took up painting. On his return to Australia he had many occupations, including boxing, which he gave up for health reasons. At the encouragement of a signwriter friend, Dickerson started to paint.

His work displays the loneliness and isolation of the modern individual, whose inability to communicate is evident even when Dickerson places two figures together on the same canvas: there is no eye contact, no acknowledgment of each other. *The Tired Man*, c. 1956, a simple composition, depicts such a theme. The man is presented in a chunky and cubic form and is weighted heavily to the seat. He appears totally exhausted—legs limp, and one arm hanging down. His other arm clutches the bench in a last effort to support himself. The red bench juts into the canvas where it helps to show the vastness of the uninhabited landscape behind him. While the paint surface

ROGER KEMP (1908–87)
The Cross, c. 1967
Synthetic polymer paint on
composition board,
183 x 137.5 cm

Monash University Collection,
Melbourne
University funds 1968

is smooth and carefully modulated, there is no feeling of passion or excitement in the paintwork.

While Dickerson's *The Tired Man* rests on his seat, **John Brack's (b. 1920)** robot-like commuters are making their way up Collins Street, Melbourne. Called *Collins Street, 5 o'clock,* 1955, it deals with the themes of urban living and monotony. Brack's figures go to work, do their job and return to the suburbs, and then are destined to repeat the process again and again. The almost monochromatic colour and the tight, ordered, fine line work was a trait of Brack's work throughout the 1950s and 1960s. His reputation was firmly established when the National Gallery of Victoria purchased this painting in the late 1950s. Brack has also produced many paintings in which he explores the figure. His portrait commissions have been frequent.

The work and world of **Charles Blackman (b. 1928)** is full of colour, imagination and fun. During the 1950s he produced an *Alice in Wonderland* series, in which the famous children's story comes alive. *Dreaming in the Street,* 1960, is quite different from this *Wonderland* series. A group of figures, hidden behind shadows, appears withdrawn and in a dream state, almost hallucinatory. The dark shapes that appear to be shadows are, in fact, further figures. Although the shapes are figurative, an element of the abstract is evident. This painting was one of several which won Blackman a travelling scholarship.

The emotions that run through the faces of **Joy Hester'**s drawings also draw upon the imagination. Born in 1920, Hester produced images of pain, passion and emotion. She was part of a group which included Tucker (whom she married in 1941), Perceval,

JOHN BRACK (b. 1920)
Collins Street, 5 o'clock, 1955
Oil on canvas
114.6 x 162.9 cm

National Gallery of Victoria,
Melbourne
Purchased 1956

Boyd and Nolan. She exhibited with the Contemporary Art Society until her death from Hodgkin's disease in 1960.

The disease which she fought for thirteen years would no doubt have influenced the images she made. Hester was also influenced by the work of the Norwegian painter, Munch, with whom she shared a vision. Hester rarely used colour and felt that the strongest medium to complement her images was black ink. Like Munch, Hester achieved an emotional impact by distorting the face, eliminating the nose, distorting the eyes or placing them on wheels outside the face and by giving the face an expression of despair. It has only been since the mid-1970s that her work has been rediscovered and fully appreciated.

Working on a totally different theme from Hester and the others is **Clifton Pugh (1924–90)**, the painter of nature and portraits. Possibly better known for his portraits of famous people, such as entertainer Barry Humphries and former Prime Minister Gough Whitlam (which won him the Archibald Prize in 1972), his early work explored the theme of native animals and their survival and environment. Pugh lived in the bush on the outskirts of Melbourne, in a wattle and daub house that he designed and built.

In Pugh's paintings of nature, he exposes the law of the bush—both its beauty and its charm. He shows the bush as a battlefield where only the fittest survive. Strength, speed, aggression and agility are the animal traits he attempts to put down on canvas. His colours are all natural ochres, while his designs and compositions are always well planned and executed. Pugh also has an ability to give his works strong and exciting rhythm. *The Eagle and the Baobab Trees*, 1957, is a painting that shows the harshness of the Australian landscape. The jagged shapes of the eagle's wings are echoed in the shapes on the ground. A touch of evil seems present in the bush and this is symbolised by the look in the bird's eye while it searches for its prey.

As a portrait painter, Pugh's work *Hon. E. G. Whitlam*, 1972, displays his ability to capture the personality of his sitter particularly well. Of Whitlam, Pugh said: 'Mr Whitlam's personality is very elusive. Each time I tried [to paint him] it was different.'

There was growing uncertainty in the late 1950s about the spread of abstract art. These feelings motivated a number of artists to form a group to counter abstract art and promote figurative work. Formed in 1959, the Antipodean Group included Brack, Blackman, Arthur and David Boyd, Perceval, Pugh, Dickerson and the writer Bernard Smith. The group was firmly against the promotion of abstract art as its members believed abstracts could only damage Australian art. They published a manifesto and in it stressed the importance of looking to Australia for their ideas rather than going 'international'.

RIGHT:

CHARLES BLACKMAN
(b. 1928)

Dreaming in the Street, 1960
Oil on composition board,
122.2 x 183.2 cm

National Gallery of Victoria,
Melbourne
Purchased 1960

BELOW:

JOY HESTER (1920–60)

Woman in Fur Coat, 1950
Chinese ink and brush on
cartridge paper, 37 x 26 cm

Collection: Georges Mora

BELOW RIGHT:

CLIFTON PUGH (1924–90)

*The Eagle and the Baobab
Trees*, 1957
Oil on hardboard, 66 x 88.9 cm

Art Gallery of New South Wales
Purchased 1957

CLIFTON PUGH (1924–90)
Hon. E. G. Whitlam, 1972
Oil on composition board,
130 x 410 cm

Reproduced by courtesy of
Historic Memorials Committee,
Parliament House, Canberra

The manifesto created a lot of fuss and critical response from abstract painters and critics alike. By far the most open-minded comment on this whole issue of figurative versus non-figurative art came from the Sydney painter Lloyd Rees, who said:

> It is obvious that the work of only a few abstract painters will survive, but that is true of any art movement. I can see a great deal in abstract painting, even if I don't accept the abstractionists' presumption that they are working in the only acceptable modern idiom. I am convinced that there will always be room for the representational painter.[6]

Other painters working throughout this period included Jon Molvig (1923–70), Donald Friend (1915–89), John Passmore (b. 1904) and the religious artist Justin O'Brien (b. 1917).

Sculpture

Until the 1950s, sculpture was only just holding its own. Apart from artists such as Stephen and Dadswell who constantly pushed sculpture, it was never as popular as painting. A painter who also turned his talent towards carving was **Danila Vassilieff**.

Vassilieff, earlier known for his social realist paintings, began to explore the three-dimensional in art. He involved himself with Clive Stephen, from whom he received a lot of assistance and guidance, particularly with carving. Once he had collected his ideas he travelled to the local Lilydale quarry, well known for its superb pieces of limestone, where he chose suitable pieces.

For the most part, Vassilieff's sculptures were figurative, and their size and shape were dictated by the colour, texture and shape of the stone. He roughed out the areas he needed to work on and then carved away, firstly by hand then by a machine which

---

[6] Catalano, G., *The Years of Hope: Australian Art and Criticism, 1959–1968*, Oxford University Press, Melbourne, 1981.

made the laborious task quicker and more accurate. On completion, his sculpture was highly polished. This tended to highlight the beautiful colours and veins in the rock.

In the work *Stenka Razin*, 1953, Vassilieff was concerned with producing a harmony between the positive areas (the mass) and the negative areas (the void). The repetition of the forms, the angles of the arm, and the overall shape are all largely dictated by the stone itself and are carefully planned to produce a powerful work. Stenka Razin was a Russian folk hero, similar to Australia's Ned Kelly. In his sculpture, Vassilieff attempts to show Razin's character by using jagged shapes: the powerful arm thrown up into the air, the winking eye and the gash in the other arm.

The sculpture that Vassilieff produced during these years was ignored, except by a patron of the arts, John Reed. Vassilieff's sculpture, like his painting, has been revived in the past decade and now is being appreciated for its originality and vision.

Sydney was home for another modernist sculptor, **Margel Hinder (b. 1906)**. Hinder's style had not been seen before in Australia. Her contemporaries claimed she was far ahead of her time in her investigation of the qualities of enclosed space, line and shape, and it was these issues that saw the development of *Revolving Construction*, 1957. Like her husband Frank's attempts at painting, Margel too wanted to capture the dynamism of movement. The sculpture incorporates a similar element and shows the viewer a multitude of linear shapes and patterns.

For other, similar work to this, Margel Hinder was awarded the Contemporary Art Society of Australia (NSW) prize. A review at the time read:

> Margel Hinder's superb *Construction 1956*, would dominate most exhibitions. Within the net of a revolving silver sphere, she has imprisoned a subtle starlike shape—a thing of air and movement, of implied planes and contrasting tensions. It is a wholly satisfying work of art, compounded in equal parts of geometry and poetry.[7]

The sculpture of Hinder was highly regarded and she enjoyed an extremely well-respected reputation throughout her career.

[7] Scarlett, K., *Australian Sculptors*, Nelson, Melbourne, 1980, p. 253.

BELOW:

DANILA VASSILIEFF
(1897–1958)
Stenka Razin, 1953
Lilydale limestone,
51 x 40 x 13.5 cm
Collection: National Gallery of
Australia, Canberra

BELOW RIGHT:

MARGEL HINDER (b. 1906)
Revolving Construction, 1957
Wire and plastic,
35.5 x 56 x 49.5 cm
Art Gallery of New South Wales
Purchased 1959

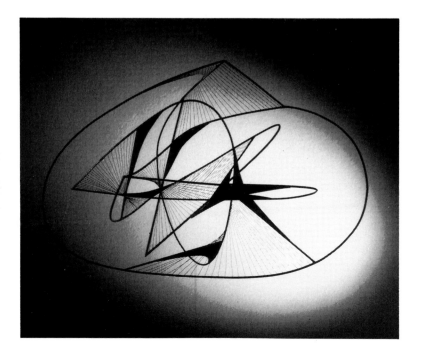

Civil architecture

As mentioned in Chapter Nine, new technology and techniques of prefabrication, and building with steel, concrete and glass were in vogue. Modelling their work on the skyscrapers of modern America, after 1955 architects designed large 'curtain wall' office buildings.

Curtain walling was so named because it had a curtain of glass, held in by metal frames that were all prefabricated. The skeletal structure of the building was hidden behind the glass walls. Simply rectangular, these big boxes were built in most Australian capital cities. In Melbourne an example is ICI House, while Sydney, Adelaide and Perth had MLC buildings, all designed by Bates, Smart and McCutcheon.

The aesthetic quality and appeal of these buildings were negligible. Their appeal lay entirely in their simplified box shape with their grid patterns of glass wall. Unfortunately, little attention was paid to the local environment or climate, both important considerations in architecture. If the air-conditioning failed these buildings turned into hot houses. Technically they were also problematic in that, owing to expansion under hot conditions, the tinted windows frequently cracked and were even known to pop out of their frames and crash to the footpath below. Until this problem was dealt with, walking under these buildings was a challenge to any daring pedestrian. Later designs were modified and skyscrapers of the 1960s and 1970s became more conscious of aesthetics and the environment.

By exploiting the new techniques and materials, **Sir Roy Grounds (1905–81)** designed the country's first domed building. Built for the Australian Academy of Science in Canberra, it was designed to a circular formula. The concrete dome was

BELOW:

BATES, SMART AND McCUTCHEON
ICI House, Melbourne, 1960
Photographer: Jon Rendell

BELOW RIGHT:

ROY GROUNDS (1905–81)
Academy of Science, Canberra, 1959
Photographer: Brownyn McCoy

later capped in sheets of copper which blend well into the surrounding landscape of Canberra. At the base of the dome Grounds designed a moat that separates the building from its environment (similar to his later design for the Victorian Arts Centre in Melbourne). The building sits in a semicircular piece of land that was incorporated into Griffin's early designs of Canberra.

There were also other modern but innovative designs built in Melbourne during the late 1950s, including the Olympic Swimming Pool, 1956 (now the Entertainment Centre), and the Myer Music Bowl, 1959. The Bowl was designed by Yuncken, Freeman Bros, Griffiths and Simpson. At first glance the Bowl looks like a huge metal tent. Capped by a shell of aluminium, it is supported by two huge steel poles at the entrance and many steel ropes which secure the roof to the ground. The acoustics are excellent and it appears to grow out of the ground—an aesthetically superb design.

YUNCKEN FREEMAN BROS, GRIFFITHS AND SIMPSON
Myer Music Bowl, Melbourne,
1959

Photographer: Jon Rendell

Domestic architecture

The war effort had consumed all the good-quality materials and housing became critically short. In addition, the population had greatly increased, and there was a shortage of craftspeople. For the Commonwealth Government this was a problem. To compensate, the Government ordered the manufacture of prefabricated housing. Houses could be quickly established on any block of land in any suburb. Made from steel frames, fibro sheeting and a little wood, these houses could be put together by virtually anyone. This saw the development of the 'do your own' house.

Alongside the 'prefab' home came a more solid and permanent home. Modest in appearance and minimal in decoration, it was aptly called the Austerity design. When compared with Californian bungalow and Spanish mission styles the Austerity design was exactly that. It was mundane and plain, yet it was in great demand. Australian cities grew rapidly during this period; the suburban sprawl—symbolised by the Hills Hoist, the motor mower and brick veneer—had begun.

Characteristics of the Austerity style are:

- plain window frames, in standard wood or metal
- small cantilevered verandahs
- plain, often unattractive, burnt-red bricks
- cement tiles
- glazed tiles on porch floors
- square chimney
- lack of decoration

For the people who wanted and could afford something different, architect-designed homes of the 1950s were modern and international in style. The contemporary American style of domestic architecture was an influence here. At another level, this import injected life into contemporary forms of architecture. The architects of the late 1940s and 1950s believed that their structures could change the world and make it a much better and more comfortable place in which to live. Their aim was to make the houses more in tune with the nuclear age. Open living, sunlight and views of the environment were all characteristics of the new style.

The new American style was introduced to Australia by the Viennese-born **Harry Seidler (b. 1923)**. An immigrant like Burley Griffin, Seidler contributed to the changes in local architecture. Seidler's style—basically rectangular, like a chocolate box with a flat roof and large walls of glass—was revolutionary.

Seidler arrived in Australia in 1948 after studying under German architect Walter Gropius (1883–1969) at Harvard University, USA. One of the first houses he designed was for his parents at Turramurra, a suburb of Sydney. Completed in 1950, its blatant modernity created quite a reaction. It was built on a slight incline out of local sandstone, and was supported by steel poles. The other forms of support were the sandstone walls which acted as a carport and entrance area. The windows did not face the sun but opened on to the superb native bushland. The mullions and transoms formed a Mondrian-like design. Basically, the accent of the house was on open plan and open living.

Within a few years of its completion, Seidler's design became the inspiration for numerous other architect-designed homes; however, there were both good and bad imitations. After this time, Seidler went from strength to strength, improving his reputation to such an extent that he is now one of Australia's best known architects. This house, as well as later ones, was criticised for being both too modern and totally inappropriate for the Australian climate.

While Seidler was busy designing more houses in Sydney, Roy Grounds was doing the same in Melbourne. Grounds had a taste for the geometric and, although better known for his design of the Arts Centre complex, he was actually a leader in Melbourne domestic architecture. He went into partnership with two other architects, Frederick Romberg and Robin Boyd, and together they were among the most powerful and influential architects of the post-war period.

Grounds's aversion to the rectangle culminated in a series of designs based on the triangle, circle and even the square, pierced by a void in the centre. (The Victorian Arts Centre incorporates this last plan.) He was very innovative architect who had a particular skill for producing exceptionally tasteful and simple houses.

The Henty House at Olivers Hill, Frankston, embodies all of Grounds's innovation. A circular plan designed around a central staircase, it was built out of timber and stands elevated upon steel poles. With its wooden facade and circular shape it fits comfortably into the surrounding natural bushland.

The architects of the new styles throughout the 1950s sought to create new environments for a new era and, above all, hoped to improve the quality of life for modern Australians. Apart from the enthusiasm and controversy, the new houses created much food for thought.

ROY GROUNDS (1905–81)
Henty House, Frankston, Victoria
Photographer: Jon Rendell

Queensland and northern Australia

Australia is a country with diverse climatic conditions—mild to cool in the far south, hot and tropical in the north. Architectural styles are also diverse. Houses in Tasmania have vastly different requirements from those in Cairns or Darwin.

Most houses that were built in Queensland before 1930 were designed in a vernacular style. Generally, they were made of timber and elevated on high stumps with wide verandahs.

As timber was freely available in the Queensland forests, it became the most desirable material for building. The other favourable feature of timber was that, unlike stone and brick, it did not retain the day's heat. Aesthetically timber fitted in better with the environment as it tended to blend into the landscape and natural surroundings.

It is important to realise that not all Queensland houses are on stumps. Like all other places there are regional differences. Houses in southern Queensland, and in particular Brisbane, display a variety of styles. However, in the far north, the prevailing style tends to be the house raised on 2-metre stumps. This concept of design originated in South-East Asia where the tropical climate is similar.

Queensland style house, New Farm, Brisbane
Photographer: Donald Williams

There are many reasons for placing the houses on stumps. These range from considerations such as tropical rain and floods to the problems of keeping out snakes, toads and, in some places, crocodiles. There are also other benefits from this design, including better air circulation under the house, which makes the house cooler in the hotter months. The space can also be used as a laundry, carport or play area.

These often 'romantic' weatherboard houses tend to be simple in construction and decoration. Surrounded by tall, wavy, coconut palms, frangipanis and vividly coloured hibiscus, these homes bring a touch of the exotic to Australia. Often the verandah is embellished with lattice, louvred shutters, iron work and decorative glass-panelled windows. The tin roof is also a decorative feature and when slightly pitched projects on to the verandah, improving the look of the house. The verandahs are well suited to Australia's climate. Their design originated in India, and they are most popular in Australian architecture. In Queensland houses they are frequently used as sleeping quarters where the cooling night breezes drift through the opened louvred windows.

Houses designed in these regions today still rely on traditional means of construction and planning. However, particularly in Darwin and far north Queensland, architects are more aware of designing houses that will withstand the cyclones and heavy rains that often plague these areas. Darwin was destroyed by Cyclone Tracy in 1974, and today architects are going to great lengths to ensure that houses are cyclone-proof while at the same time aesthetically pleasing. The use of solar panels on roofs has also become popular.

ACTIVITIES

1. Compare the styles and aims of Drysdale with any other landscape painter of earlier years. Refer to particular works of art.

2. Discuss the three types of Cubism with reference to particular artists and their works.

3. After carefully looking at some cubist portraits, make a cubist drawing of someone in the classroom.

4. Can you draw any similarities between the work of the Italian futurist artist Balla and of the Australian Hinder? Explain.

5. Choose any Australian portrait and answer the following questions.
   (a) What is the artist, title and year?
   (b) Is it an abstract or purely naturalistic portrait?
   (c) What does it show about the person's personality and character?
   (d) Is it decorative ? What are the predominant colours?
   (e) How is the style or technique typical of the period in which it was painted?

6. Research the Antipodean Manifesto. Why do you think abstraction could have endangered Australian art?

7. Find out all you can about the international style of architecture outside Australia.

8. Make a drawing of your house showing the facade and plan. Explain its plan, function, aesthetic appeal and style.

9. What is the Archibald Prize?

10. What was the Dobell controversy?

11. Research some old newspapers and find out what other controversies have affected the Archibald Prize.

	AUSTRALIAN EVENTS	GENERAL EVENTS	ARTISTIC EVENTS	
1960		**1961** The Berlin Wall is built.	**1960** Caro: *Midday* (S). Klein: *Anthropometrics of the Blue Period, Paris* (Performance).	**Australian artists** Fred Williams John Olsen Janet Dawson
	1962 Iron ore deposits are discovered in the Pilbara region, Western Australia.	**1962** The United States establishes a military presence in Vietnam.	**1963** Riley: *Fall*.	James Doolin Dale Hickey Alun Leach Jones
		1963 President Kennedy is assassinated.	**1964** Smith: *Cubi 19* (S).	Peter Booth Robert Jacks Martin Sharp William Delafield Cook Ivan Durrant
1965	**1965** Australian troops are sent to Vietnam. Roma Mitchell is the first woman appointed to the judicial Bench (Supreme Court of SA).	**1965** Australia is a top exporter of iron ore. **1966** The Russian spaceship *Luna 9* lands on the moon. The temple of Abu Simbel, Egypt, is moved to save it from destruction as the Aswan High Dam is built.	**1965** Beuys: *How to Explain Pictures to a Dead Hare* (Performance) **1967** Warhol: *Marilyn Monroe* series. Estes: *Foodshop*.	Jeffrey Smart Brett Whiteley Lloyd Rees Jenny Watson Davida Allen Elizabeth Gower Lesley Dumbrell
	1967 Prime Minister Harold Holt disappears while swimming at Portsea, Victoria. **1969** The American artist, Christo, wraps up part of the coastline of Little Bay, Sydney.	**1969** An American astronaut, Neil Armstrong, is the first man to walk on the moon.	**1968** Stella: *Sinjerli Variation*. **1969** Close: *Portrait of Bob Craig-Martin: 4 Identical Boxes with Lids Reversed* (S).	Clement Meadmore Robert Klippel Inge King Michael Young Clifford Last Lenton Parr
1970	**1970** The Henderson inquiry into poverty is held. **1971** Gough Whitlam becomes Prime Minister. The Labor Government abolishes conscription.		**1970** Bacon: *Triptych*. Oppenheim: *Parallel Stress* (Performance).	Ron Robertson-Swann Clive Murray-White David Wilson Bert Flugelman George Baldessin Rosalie Gascoigne
	1972 The first Sunbury Pop Festival is held near Melbourne. **1974** ABC television launches 'Countdown'. Cyclone Tracy hits Darwin.	**1972** The United States returns Okinawa to Japan. The Watergate scandal forces President Nixon to resign as President of the United States.	**1973** Estes: *Alitalia*. **1974** Nitsch: *48th Action* (Performance presented at Munich). Judd: *Untitled* (S).	John Davis Kevin Mortensen Stelarc Ken Unsworth Mandy Martin Susan Norrie
1975	**1975** Colour television arrives in Australia. The first ethnic radio station is launched by ABC radio in Sydney. The Whitlam Government is dismissed. Malcolm Fraser becomes Prime Minister.	**1975** The Vietnam War ends. **1976** Jimmy Carter becomes President of the United States. The USSR lands a spacecraft on Mars.		David Larwill Colin Lanceley Mike Brown Ross Crothall Norma Redpath Tom Bass
	1978 A New Parliament House is planned for Canberra. The Northern Territory becomes self-governing.	**1978** Pope Paul dies. A new Pope is elected and dies after thirty-fours days in office.	**1979** Chicago: *The Dinner Party* (S).	
1980	**1980** The first woman commercial airline pilot, Debbie Wardley, flies for Ansett Airlines.	**1980** The Olympic Games are held in Moscow. The US calls for a boycott.	**1980** Hockney: *Harlequin*. **1982** Hockney starts producing his polaroid photo-collages.	**Architecture** Sydney Opera House National Gallery of Australia High Court, Canberra
	1983 Malcolm Fraser requests a double dissolution of Parliament and calls an election. The Labor Party sweeps to victory with Robert Hawke as Prime Minister. **1984** The controls of Uluru (Ayers Rock) is given to the Aborigines.	**1983** Australia wins the America's Cup with *Australia II*.		Victorian Arts Centre Australia Square Tower BHP House 'Nuts and Berries' school Ministry of Housing projects Contemporary houses Parliament House, Canberra
1985	**1986** Picasso's painting *Weeping Woman* is stolen from the National Gallery of Victoria by a group calling itself the Australian Cultural Terrorists. The painting is later returned undamaged.	**1986** The world's worst nuclear power station accident occurs at Chernobyl, Ukraine. The US space shuttle *Challenger* blows up in mid-air, killing seven astronauts.		
	1987 The stockmarket crashes. **1988** Australia's Bicentennial Year, celebrating 200 years of European settlement.	**1987** American pop artist Andy Warhol dies. **1989** Salvador Dali dies.		
1990				

CHAPTER ELEVEN

Contemporary Art 1960s–80s

Social and political background

The 1960s and 1970s brought about great change in the way people lived their daily lives. More Australians became conscious of their role in society and also much more politically aware. They questioned both decisions of the Government and standards of the day. The Vietnam War and the Women's Liberation Movement were two of the most significant challenges of this period.

When Prime Minister Menzies committed Australian troops to fight in the Vietnam War in 1965, he bitterly divided the country. The 1960s youth acknowledged the horrors of war to which their forefathers had been subjected: the majority of them were hesitant to follow in their footsteps. Consequently, mass demonstrations were held in most Australian capital cities to protest the involvement of Australia and the United States in Vietnam and to promote the issue of peace. Conscientious objectors were sentenced to gaol, until conscription was finally abolished in 1972 by the Australian Labor Party, led by Gough Whitlam.

Teenagers, too, experienced changes in attitudes and it could be argued that the Vietnam War was partly responsible for doing this. For some, long hair, faded blue jeans and marijuana became the order of the 1960s. Many young Australians were being subjected to American culture, particularly through television and the multimillion-dollar cinema industry, which was extremely popular during these years. Sixties music is remembered for such people as Joan Baez and Bob Dylan who sang about the Bomb and the continuing search for peace, and the Beatles. It was also the era of the 'pop' concert, when Melbourne played host to the Sunbury Pop Festival, an Australian version of the American Woodstock.

Melbourne was taken by storm when The Beatles arrived in 1964. Thousands of hysterical teenagers screamed and cheered while hoping to catch a glimpse of their favourite Beatle.

The increased flood of immigration in the 1930s, 1940s and, later, in the 1960s led to Australia's becoming a particularly multicultural society. The 1960s and 1970s saw our cities become much more cosmopolitan, especially in the areas of food, fashion and culture. Radio and television stations began to produce multicultural and bilingual programs, while government agencies and departments introduced interpreters as a much needed public service. Originally migrants were subjected to considerable antagonism, as xenophobic Australians found it difficult to understand their different ways. Later, however, as overseas travel came within reach of more people, Australians began travelling to Europe. It was here that they became much more aware of other cultures and lifestyles. Schools, too, became aware of their responsibilities in this area and were quick to establish multicultural programs and bilingual education.

Partly led by Germaine Greer, the Women's Liberation Movement fought for such rights as equal pay and opportunity through the elimination of sexist and conservative attitudes. The group became increasingly powerful in the 1970s and working women became accepted into previously male-dominated areas, such as the law, industry and the media.

While some Australian families in the 1970s tended to be more affluent and materially better off, other families found their experience to be the reverse. In 1970, Professor R. F. Henderson made a study into poverty in Australia. The findings led to an inquiry being set up by the McMahon Government in 1972. Headed by Henderson, the *Commission of Inquiry into Poverty* expanded with the Whitlam Government in 1973. Henderson's poverty line is still used today to measure poverty in Australia.

This was also the period when, in order to make ends meet, more women entered the workforce, creating the two-income family.

Other issues that concerned Australians of the 1970s included conservation, the mining of uranium, unemployment, increased sexual liberation and political consciousness. In 1975 Australians became more politically aware when the Whitlam Government was dismissed by the Governor-General Sir John Kerr, who installed Malcolm Fraser as replacement Prime Minister. Many Australians took to the streets to voice their disgust and outrage, seeing these events as a threat to their democratic rights. In the election which followed, however, the Liberal – National Party coalition won with an overwhelming majority.

Painting

The 1960s was a period when international art trends became prominent while the older and more established painters such as Fred Williams, Lloyd Rees and John Olsen truly established their careers. Just as Drysdale had a vision of the Australian landscape, so did **Fred Williams (1927–82)**. His reputation was slow to develop but his work today is admired and his status in Australian painting is of the calibre of Streeton. He was an innovator. Williams has also been described as the best landscape painter of the 1960s and 1970s.

The young Williams was encouraged to paint by his family doctor, Clive Stephen (see Chapter Nine), who was impressed with his talent. Williams studied at the Gallery School, then travelled to Europe. After a few years away he returned to paint a new and imaginatively distinctive view of the Australian landscape. He painted landscapes around Melbourne: the You Yangs, Sherbrooke Forest and Upwey. Williams was also a highly respected printmaker and produced more than 8000 etchings of subjects ranging from English landscapes through to Australian subjects.

On his return to Australia in 1964 he produced a series of landscapes of Upwey. Characterised by their ochre ground, high horizon line and luscious swirls of curved daubs of paint, they became the new vision of the landscape. *Upwey Landscape*, 1965, is from this series. The reading of the work is a little ambiguous in that there is a bird's eye view and a ground level view where you can see the silhouetted trees against the sky. The bush and scrub are depicted by the use of the gestural arcs of black, grey and white which swirl into the ground colour. The tree trunks, both standing and fallen, break up the surface as they are plotted throughout the canvas in white and black strokes. In order to achieve a sense of distance and perspective, Williams has clustered together groups of trees in the background, while in the foreground he has placed them in wide open spaces. At first glance the landscape looks as if it has been ravaged by bushfire and is now starting to rejuvenate. Williams's approach to painting has changed the way people look at the landscape; when flying over the country it is difficult not to see a 'Williams' image.

A Sydney painter who interpreted the landscape in his own manner was **John Olsen (b. 1928)**. His landscapes are very linear in style. In fact, Olsen's lines could almost be roadways on a map. They curl and move throughout the painting in a kind of linear expression. In *Journey into the You Beaut Country, No. 2*, 1961, Olsen explores the land from many different perspectives, from afar and from an ant's view; the land is a hive of activity buzzing with daubs of colour and a mapwork of lines. His colours too are all reminiscent of the ochres of the land.

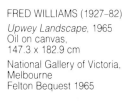

FRED WILLIAMS (1927–82)
Upwey Landscape, 1965
Oil on canvas,
147.3 x 182.9 cm

National Gallery of Victoria,
Melbourne
Felton Bequest 1965

The 1960s and 1970s witnessed a mixed bag of styles, mostly international in origin. These styles were Colour Painting, Op Art, Pop Art, Minimalism, Conceptualism and Photo-Realism; it was the time for any kind of 'ism'.

Janet Dawson (b. 1935) had been painting and travelling in Europe between 1957 and 1961, and it was here that she saw an exhibition of contemporary American painting. This show had a big impact on the direction of her work and, like Norah Simpson half a century earlier, Dawson introduced the new American style of Colour Painting into Australia. The new style's aim was to exploit colour for its own sake so that painting itself became the significant factor, not the meaning of the work. Armed with the new acrylic paint, masking tape, broad brushes and, occasionally, air guns, the young artists produced paintings that were in total contrast to the abstract expressionism of the previous decades.

The Field exhibition opened in Melbourne in 1968. It coincided with the opening of the new premises of Melbourne's Victorian Arts Centre in St Kilda Road. This show exhibited paintings and sculpture in the new style. The paintings were basically 'hard edge' and geometric. Some were simply flat shapes of colour. Sculpture, too, was similarly simplified.

The 'hard edge' works tended to show flat areas of unmodulated colour dominated by straight lines and curves. Often, too, the traditional rectangular canvas gave way to odd-shaped ones of the type made popular by the works of the American Frank Stella. One of the first artists to do this in Australia was Janet Dawson.

Artists who were working in this 'hard edge' manner were James Doolin (b. 1932) with his *Artificial Landscape 67-5*, 1967, and Dale Hickey (b. 1937) with *Untitled*, 1967.

The next stage was Op Art in the style of the English painter Bridget Riley. Mainly concerned with the retinal effects on the eye, these optically active paintings did not appear to be so widespread. The shaped canvas, too, was used; Stanislas Ostoja-Kotkowski (b. 1922) produced works in this style.

The third style of colour painting was a little less concerned with lines, geometry and order. In fact it made a concerted attempt to avoid such things. Often colours were applied to unprimed canvas. This created a staining effect similar to the effects

RIGHT:

JAMES DOOLIN (b. 1932)
Artificial Landscape, 67/5,
1967
Acrylic on canvas,
130 x 101.5 cm
National Gallery of Victoria,
Melbourne
Purchased 1969

FAR RIGHT:

DALE HICKEY (b. 1937)
Untitled, 1967
Liquitex on cottonduck,
173 x 173 cm
National Gallery of Victoria,
Melbourne
Felton Bequest 1968

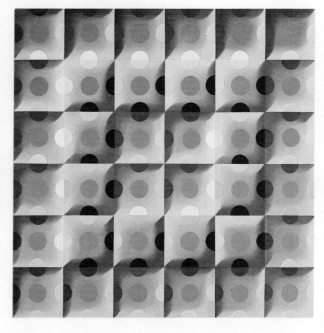

JOHN OLSEN (b. 1928)
Journey into the You Beaut Country, No. 2, 1961
Oil on composition board, 185.8 x 124.2 cm

Collection: Queensland Art Gallery
Purchased 1961

often achieved by Americans Mark Rothko and Helen Frankenthaler. Particular attention was paid to the surface of the painting. Most of the painters who exhibited in The Field exhibition in the late 1960s worked through this style to later develop their own personal language and direction. These artists included David Aspden (b. 1935), Robert Jacks (b. 1943), Alun Leach Jones (b. 1937), Dick Watkins (b. 1937), Sydney Ball (b. 1933) and Peter Booth (b. 1940).

As an outcome of the simplified subject matter seen in the colour field paintings, a new movement called Minimalism was born. It was concerned with reducing the huge canvases to areas of pure colour and surface texture. It also questioned the need for meaning in art, as the minimalists believed their work to be meaningful in itself. This movement, too, was in total contrast to the previous figurative expressionist styles. Sydney Ball's *Canto of XXIV* and Alun Leach Jones's *Noumenon XXXII Red Square* are indicative of works produced during these years.

Traditionally a lot of people are angered by this type of art because they feel they are being cheated. They feel offended that an all-black painting or a block of steel for sculpture could parade as an artistic form, and take its place in a gallery. Cries of 'my little sister could do better than that' or 'to think people paid money for that' seem to be the usual reaction. Possibly, in looking carefully at this movement, its reasons for

SYDNEY BALL (b. 1933)
Canto of XXIV, 1966
Synthetic polymer paint on
canvas, 175.5 x 175.5 cm

Collection: Art Gallery of South
Australia, Adelaide Arndale
Development Pty Ltd Trust
Account 1968

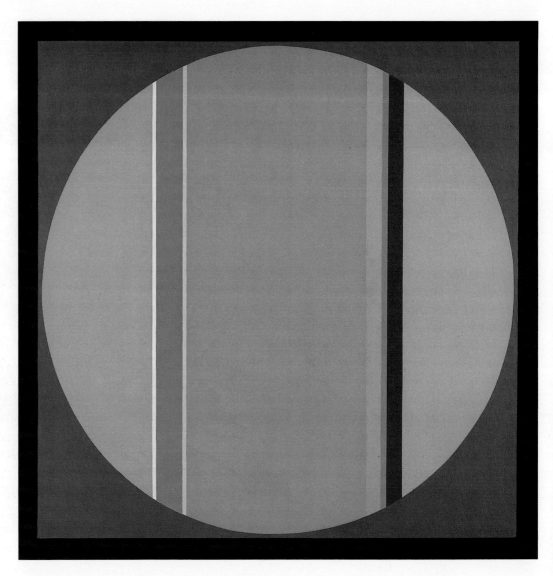

coming into existence, and the environment in which it evolved, can lead to a better understanding of it. Artists who produced minimalist paintings included Robert Hunter (b. 1947), Robert Jacks and Peter Booth.

Although the English–American movement of Pop Art never really established itself in Australia, it did influence a handful of painters at different stages in their development. One artist in particular who used some of the Pop Art imagery and philosophy was **Martin Sharp (b. 1942).**

Sharp has held a wide variety of jobs, including cartoonist, cartoon animator and publisher. He is also an avid collector of kitsch and memorabilia. Sharp has had an obsession with van Gogh since his high school days in Sydney and this is evident in his art. His work is both witty and exceptionally humorous. About his work as a Pop artist, Sharp says,

> … that he feels a certain responsibility to 'look after' certain images which he revitalises and reinterprets then returns to contemporary culture. This is most obvious in his van Gogh paintings.[1]

---

[1] *The Seventies: Australian Paintings and Tapestries,* Catalogue from the Collection of the National Australia Bank, National Bank of Australasia, Melbourne, 1982, p. 95.

Fancy Our Meeting, 1970, combines the American Disney cartoon character Mickey Mouse with the image of van Gogh from his painting *Artist on the Road to Tarascon*. In this work Mickey is shown greeting van Gogh. It is a most unlikely combination. In another work, Sharp combines images from both Australian and European art to make the collage *Billy Boy Visits Saint Remy*, 1970. Dobell's Billy Boy is shown standing in van Gogh's landscape of Saint Remy. The image of Dobell's tattooed boy contrasted with the expressionist painting *A Starry Night* seems incongruous yet highly amusing. In some ways Sharp is also commenting on the preciousness of art.

A far-reaching and influential movement of this period was Photo-Realism, also called New Realism, Hyper-Realism or Super-Realism. Whatever its title, it developed in America and basically aimed at a return to realism in art. Artists working in this manner frequently used photographs as their source material. Photographs were used in two ways: first as a reference, that is, as a way of obtaining specific information about the subject, for example, the way drops of water form on a sink; in the other instance the photo was used as the work, that is, painters wanted to produce an image of a painted photograph that would include such things as distortion of the objects in the background, reflection and focus. Often, too, in order to achieve a texture similar to a photo, some of these painters discarded their hand brushes for the air brush.

Two painters who used the photograph as their tool and strove to produce a 'painted' photograph were **William Delafield Cook (b. 1936)** and Ivan Durrant (b. 1947). In Delafield Cook's *A Haystack*, 1982, what appears at first glance to be a large photograph of a haystack is in fact a carefully rendered painting of thousands of pieces of hay, each one meticulously painted, no doubt with a very fine brush. Such banal objects as haystacks were typical subject matter for the new realist artists. Delafield Cook spent time in London where he was influenced by David Hockney who was, at one time, involved in the English Pop Art movement and often used banal subject matter such as park benches, chairs, haystacks and gardens.

Ivan Durrant burst on to the art scene in a most controversial way in 1975 when he dumped the carcass of a slaughtered cow in the forecourt of the Victorian Arts Centre. Durrant was making a statement on hypocrisy: he claimed that although people readily eat meat they don't like to think about animals being slaughtered to

BELOW:

ALUN LEACH JONES (b. 1937)
Noumenon XXXII Red Square, 1969
Synthetic polymer paint on canvas, 168.5 x 168.5 cm
Collection: National Gallery of Australia, Canberra

BELOW RIGHT:

MARTIN SHARP (b. 1942)
Fancy Our Meeting, 1970
Enamel, metalinc, wax on perspex, 195 x 133 cm
Reproduced by courtesy of the artist and Roslyn Oxley 9 Gallery

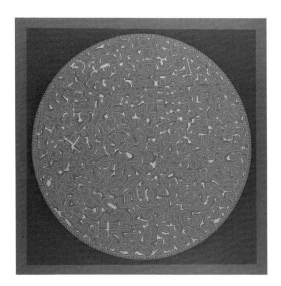

WILLIAM DELAFIELD COOK
(b. 1936)

A Haystack, 1982
Acrylic on canvas,
183 x 305 cm

Collection: Queensland Art
Gallery
Purchased 1982

provide it. Likewise people wear fur coats but are horrified by the clubbing of baby seals. He says:

> Art to me, is the invention of visual material that previously didn't exist in the context I put it. My reasons for making art are aligned with those of a philosopher. He may put facts or words down that help us to see what he wishes us to see more clearly.[2]

Durrant's work *Three Jockeys*, 1975, is a highly photographic work in that he has blurred the background just as in the use of depth of field on the camera. The image, too is framed in a photographic way.

Although **Jeffrey Smart (b. 1921)** is a realist painter, he does not use the camera in the same way that the previous two painters do. He uses photographs only for references in learning something about his subject. In fact, his sources are sketches and drawings taken from life. He does not want to 'paint' a photograph. On this topic Smart says:

> I am sure Da Vinci, Piero della Francesca, etc., would have used photographs if they had been available then. But to copy from a photo, the artist has to know what he is seeing. The camera does not know, it only sees. And the only way anyone can 'know' what they see is by long training and discipline ...[3]

Smart's images are richly coloured and meticulously painted; he has a discerning eye for detail. A resident in Italy since 1963, many of his images come from his immediate environment—in particular *Control Tower*, 1969, which is taken from Rome's international airport, Leonard da Vinci. Ironically, the tower is a symbol of modernity in a country known for its antiquity, and the concern for geometry, careful rendering and painting are all evident. The shadows, the variety of reds and greys all unify the work. The concern for meticulous detail is seen in his painting of the curved brickwork and the people on the observation deck.

[2] *Survey 8* Catalogue, National Gallery of Victoria, May–June 1979.

[3] *Aspects of New Realism: 1981 Travelling Art Exhibition* Catalogue, National Gallery of Victoria, Melbourne, 1981.

IVAN DURRANT (b. 1947)
Three Jockeys, 1975
Synthetic polymer paint on
composition board,
86.5 x 109.5 cm
City of Caulfield Art Collection
Purchased 1976

Footbridge from a decade later is concerned with showing the loneliness and isolation of modern living. A figure stands on the top of a footbridge contemplating … what? The cold, lifeless quality of industrialisation is presented. The painting is highly geometric, hard edge and repetitious in its structure. It even takes on a surreal quality.

Other painters to work in this new realist phase were Jenny Watson (b. 1951), Geoff LaGerche (b. 1940), Marcus Beilby (b. 1951), Robert Boynes (b. 1942), Dale Hickey and Ken Wadrop (b. 1952).

In the 1960s **Colin Lanceley (b. 1938)** produced art with two friends Ross Crothall (b. 1934) and Michael Brown (b. 1938) by exhibiting things found on the local garbage tip. They assembled pieces of rubbish and produced non-traditional works of art that for their time were extremely rebellious. Called the Annandale Realists (the name coming from the suburb in which they lived), the group exhibited only twice, once in Melbourne and once in Sydney. The reviews were damning, with remarks like this from the *Bulletin* (February 1962):

> At best the show might pass as an offensive, good-natured cavort in the scrap heap, were it not that sometimes the stench of the heap wafts through.

Lanceley left Australia in 1964 on a Helena Rubenstein Travelling Scholarship and travelled extensively before settling in London. He returned to Sydney in 1981. His current works are still collage-type assemblages with brightly coloured areas of lush brushwork. He often attaches to his works objects such as pipes, cogs, wooden wheels, shells and other things, which he often paints. His assemblages from the 1980s largely draw their inspiration from the landscape, beaches and gardens. *Songs of a Summer Night, (Lynne's Garden)*, 1985, is one of these vibrant works.

Having delved briefly into Pop Art in some of his paintings, **Brett Whiteley (1939–92)** has become one of Australia's most commercially successful artists. In the 1960s he travelled to Europe where he settled for a time in London and it was here that he first received recognition—for the *Christie* series. Whiteley became obsessed about this 1950s murderer who enticed women into his home then, after gassing and raping them, he stashed their dead bodies under the floor and between his walls. These events caught Whiteley's imagination and after a great deal of investigation and study, he created some superb semi-abstract paintings, the finest being *Christie and Hectorina McLennan*, 1964.

Whiteley was very successful in 1977 when he won three of Sydney's art prizes: the Archibald, the Wynne and the Sulman.[4] *Self Portrait in the Studio*, 1976, won him the Archibald prize. It is a large oil painting showing Whiteley reflected in a hand-held oval mirror. He is in the process of drawing himself, and positioned throughout the room are a variety of objects: Asian wall-hangings, pieces of sculpture. The window opens out on to a beautiful view of Sydney Harbour. Whiteley's colour and line work in this painting are superb and sensitive, and the work also lets us see into his private world.

For decades the panoramas of Sydney Harbour have held the interest of painters from Martens and Lycett through to Streeton, Roberts and the grand master of

---

[4] Sulman prize: the gift of Sir John Sulman, Trustee of the Art Gallery of New South Wales. It is awarded to the best genre or subject painting done by an artist in Australia during the five years preceding the closing date for entries. The value of the prize is $5000.

JEFFREY SMART (b. 1921)
Footbridge, 1975
Acrylic on canvas,
74.2 x 89 cm

From the National Australia
Bank Collection of Australian
Art of the Seventies

landscape, **Lloyd Rees (1895–1988)**. Although his artistic career spanned seventy years, it is Rees's paintings of Sydney Harbour in the 1970s that we are concerned with. His career started in the early 1920s when he produced superb pen-and-ink drawings of houses and landscapes. In the 1940s he painted large panoramas with a freer, more expressionistic approach; in the 1970s and 1980s his work exploded into a richly painted mass of colour and impressionist brushstrokes, though still maintaining a sensitive vision of atmosphere and mood. *Three Boats—Lane Cove River*, 1978, comes from this period when he produced paintings that are contemporary in both their subject matter and approach to painting.

The Women's Movement also proved to be a powerful force in the 1970s. Although the Movement had pioneered Modernism, women's painting kept a low profile until the 1970s.

Through the Women's Movement, women artists were concerned with identifying and developing a particular imagery that was peculiar to both their sexuality and existence. Women who received critical attention during these years were **Jenny Watson (b. 1951)**, Davida Allen (b. 1951), Elizabeth Gower (b. 1952) and Lesley Dumbrell (b. 1941).

Watson studied at the Gallery School and later trained as an art teacher. During the 1970s her work concentrated on four different themes: portraits in coloured pencil which were produced in the new realist style; interiors; works taken from newspapers and hand bills; and paintings of houses.

The *House* paintings, from 1975 onward, show houses where she lived throughout her childhood and later years. The works initially have the appearance of a real estate

BRETT WHITELEY (1939–92)

*Christie and Hectorina
McLennan*, 1964
Oil, charcoal, collage on
canvas, recessed collage,
162.9 x 214 cm

Collection: National Gallery of
Australia, Canberra

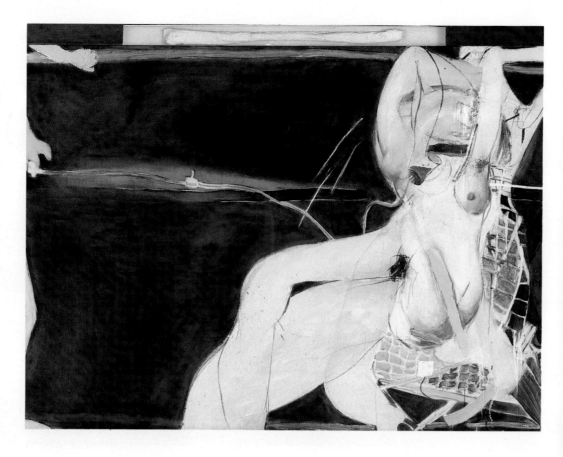

BRETT WHITELEY (1939–92)

Self Portrait in the Studio, 1976
Oil, collage, hair on canvas,
200.5 x 259 cm

Art Gallery of New South Wales
Purchased 1977

LLOYD REES (1895–1988)
Three Boats—Lane Cove River, 1978
Oil on canvas, 124 x 112 cm

Art Gallery of New South Wales
Purchased under the terms of
the Florence Turner Blake
Bequest 1979

agent's advertisements. Despite this, Watson manages to create interest in the banality of such suburban images. The works are painted over a grid on which thick, heavily textured paint has been applied. Often, too, the address is written into the paint's surface in a cream lettering.

The Brisbane artist **Davida Allen** is concerned with her personal experiences and the things that go on around her, such as the death of her father and pregnancy. Her paintings are like a visual diary of her feelings and emotions. Her approach is intuitive and highly expressive, a particular trend re-examined in the 1980s by other painters. Allen's painting is strong in colour, with vigorous brushwork under which lies an intense nervous energy.

In 1983 Allen was invited to show her work in Paris and it was here, while separated from her young children, that she painted *Paris Painting*, 1983.

The images Allen paints are often represented in a childlike manner: free, expressive and spontaneous. In this style, Allen's work is like a return to the Expressionism of Tucker, Perceval and Boyd in the 1940s. Other artists who work in a similarly expressionist style are Jan Nelson, Jan Murray and Peter Booth.

Elizabeth Gower produces collages, or 'paper quilts' as they have often been described. Gower places transparent, opaque and coloured shapes of paper, some covered in resin and wax, over each other to produce highly colourful and exciting assemblages. Initially her work used a rectangular format but later she produced odd asymmetrical shapes of work that are simply attached to the wall. Recurring shapes and symbols that crop up in these collages are the 'X', the 'V' and 'I'. One of her most original and beautiful pieces is *Nylon Tubes within Folded Newsprint*, 1977. It originated

JENNY WATSON (b. 1951)
House: Fifth Address, 2c High Street, Windsor, 1977
Oil on canvas,
177.6 x 213.8 cm

Collection: National Gallery of Australia, Canberra
Gift of the Phillip Morris Arts Grant 1982

from a drawing of tubular steel chairs which, after being abstracted, produced a zigzag pattern. The repetition of the zigzag also relates to the movement made by the hand when rapidly drawing. Applied to this work were layers of coloured resins, washes of colour and pieces of nylon and newsprint.

Originally influenced by the work of British Op artist Bridget Riley, **Lesley Dumbrell**'s reputation took off in the late 1970s. She worked through the Colour Field and Op Art stages introduced in the 1960s, and the concern of these movements with colour and shape have no doubt helped consolidate Dumbrell's present style of painting. On fields of coloured ground, Dumbrell applies vividly coloured lines, some jagged, some 'V'-shaped, diagonals and verticals. Depending on the colours she uses sometimes these lines appear to jump out, move back and skip around the surface of the painting, occasionally seeming reluctant to remain within the confines of the frame. Of her work from the early 1980s, *Untitled*, 1982, is a superb example of her watercolour paintings. In these works, contrasting colours in the form of elongated, jagged fans are the popular motif. The transparency of the watercolour and the contrasting colours all combine to produce a beautiful and sensitive surface.

Other painters from this period include Dale Hickey (b. 1937), Imants Tillers (b. 1950), Richard Dunn (b. 1944), Paul Partos (b. 1943), Suzanne Archer (b. 1945), Fred Cress (b. 1938), Jan Senbergs (b. 1939) and Jeff Makin (b. 1943).

In the late 1980s both Susan Norrie (see Chapter Thirteen) and **Mandy Martin (b. 1952)** have won awards and received commissions to make them very important figures in Australian art. Martin's work developed out of political images concerning the oppression of women into studies of urban and industrial life. Her early 1980s

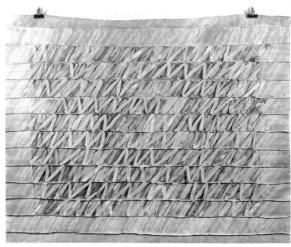

studies of galvanised iron warehouses, and facades of houses with their grid-patterned, mesh-screened windows, were the abstract elements Martin depicted in her painting and drawing. These works tended to verge on the abstract. Martin's later works explored the dark and mysterious industrial landscapes characterised by overbearing factories with saw-tooth rooflines, powerhouses of energy and pollution. All her landscapes are devoid of human beings.

The 1980s also saw a large number of younger artists exhibiting in a non-traditional gallery environment. Working from a place they called ROAR studios, the group worked as an artistic community, often holding weekend auctions of goods with which to pay the rent on their studio space. One of these artists was **David Larwill (b. 1958)**. Larwill and the others in the group drew upon their local environment, personal emotions and experiences to create their art. Their style was largely characterised by semiabstract linear and painterly brushstrokes, often painted over flat areas of colour; it soon became the trademark of the ROAR group. Larwill was also invited by the Ministry of the Arts and the Melbourne Tramways Board to participate in the Transporting Art project and paint a tram. Many other artists have also been involved in this project, including Clifton Pugh, John Nixon, Mirka Mora, Kim Donaldson and cartoonist Michael Leunig.

DAVID LARWILL (b. 1958)
Tram 722
Sponsored by Associated
Communication Enterprises

Photographer: Michael McLeod

LESLEY DUMBRELL (b. 1941)
Untitled, 1982
Watercolour, 57 x 76.5 cm
Possession of the Artist

MANDY MARTIN (b. 1952)
Chasm 2, 1984
Oil on canvas, 232 x 224 cm
Collection: Private

Sculpture

Internationalism spread its tentacles not only over painting and architecture but also over sculpture. The influence from America became particularly popular with the work of **Clement Meadmore (b. 1929)** and **Robert Klippel (b. 1920)**. In the early 1960s, the two Australian sculptors tired of the lack of stimulation in Australia and went abroad, primarily with the intention of broadening their artistic horizons. Both artists went to New York, which had taken over from Paris as the art capital of the world. Klippel went in 1957 to both study and work. On his return in 1963, he started exploring the possibilities of using metal and odd pieces of junk, cast-offs from our consumer society, to make sculptures. His piece, *Junk Sculpture*, 1963, is an assemblage made from cogs, welded devices, parts of machines, splayed out typewriter keys, wheels and other smaller pieces of machinery. The only colour on the sculpture is that which has come about through oxidisation and welding. The piece looks like some kind of strange metal totem pole.

In 1963 Klippel returned from New York and another sculptor, Clement Meadmore, arrived there. Like Klippel, Meadmore studied at East Sydney Technical College under Dadswell and after finding the local art and, in particular, sculpture scene totally boring decided to explore new horizons. On his arrival in New York he studied under Barnett Newman but says that, although Newman's work influenced him, he made a conscious effort not to emulate his style. After living in New York for a while Meadmore's work became much larger. It is also interesting to note that after working in America, the centre of the modern art world, his work sold much more frequently and his status improved. Meadmore still lives in New York.

Awakening, 1969, sits comfortably in the square between two buildings owned by AMP in Melbourne. It twists, stretches and contains a lot of restrained energy, giving the impression of a tense rubber band that is about to break. As the name suggests, this great steel creature has woken up and is about to stretch and expand to its fullest capacity. The work is interesting in that, although steel is not a flexible material, Meadmore tries to achieve an effect to the contrary. Furthermore, rather than paint the sculpture, Meadmore prefers to let the elements colour the work, so a rust colour gives the sculpture a certain warmth. In looking at his means of construction it is interesting to note that he always makes a maquette of the work, which is then made into the finished larger piece by a trained group of professional fabricators. This practice is not uncommon for sculptors, particularly those working in steel of such size. The Melbourne sculptor **Inge King (b. 1918)** also uses this method for constructing her large works.

INGE KING (b. 1918)
Forward Surge, 1973
Steel, 516 x 1514 x 1368 cm
Victorian Arts, Centre
(forecourt), Melbourne

Photographer: Jon Rendell

Forward Surge, 1973, designed for the plaza at the Arts Centre, Melbourne, at first gives an appearance of huge rolling waves. Painted in black, it sits majestically in the grass area of the plaza. Originally designed in maquette form in 1973, it was decided by the William Angliss Fund that this work should be commissioned for the Arts Centre. Of the work art critic Patrick McCaughey said in the *Age* (4 April 1973):

> Along with her rhythmic sense goes a strong predilection for natural balance in the work. Even when her cut blades of steel hover above the ground, the sense of their attachment to the ground, their respect for gravity, is strong.

As we have seen with the work of these sculptors, steel has become popular for creating exceptionally large pieces of sculpture. Until the introduction of abstract forms, sculptors had little use for this industrial quality metal; however, in the work of these artists steel is used for its intrinsic qualities as well as for its symbolic expression of the modern age.

The Field exhibition also included some minimalist pieces of sculpture. These works were formal, and highly finished, and most of the sculptors to work in this style later went on to develop highly personalised styles of their own. **Michael Young (b. 1945)** produced highly polished geometric works in stainless steel which in appearance and simplicity of form are like three-dimensional geometric paintings. Other sculptors working in this style are Noel Dunn (b. 1933), Nigel Lendon (b. 1944) and Wendy Paramor (b. 1938).

In complete contrast to the work of these minimalists is the work of **Clifford Last (b. 1918)**. He carves and shapes wood with a subtractive approach while others, particularly Klippel, add pieces of material to make their work. Last's work is concerned with organic forms and in particular with 'growth'. His forms are usually carved in wood and convey the moods of peacefulness, tranquillity and warmth. They too are always highly polished so that the grain, texture and colours in the wood become important features of his work.

CLIFFORD LAST (b. 1918)
Lucis, 1965–66
Jarrah, height 148.9 cm
National Gallery of Victoria, Melbourne
Purchased 1966

Other sculptors to work in this organic style were **Tom Bass (b. 1916)**, **Stephen Walker (b. 1927)** and **Norma Redpath (b. 1928)**. All three sculptors worked predominantly in metal and their major contribution to Australian sculpture lay in the form of public commissions. Bass has done many abstract relief pieces for facades, foyers and courtyards of buildings in cities throughout Australia (see Appendix Three). Walker has produced many pieces of sculpture for the City of Hobart while one of Redpath's major pieces is the *Treasury Fountain*, 1965–69. Made from bronze, the piece sits in a pool in front of the Treasury, Canberra.

The 1970s saw great changes in both the methods and expression of sculpture. In particular, steel construction became a big feature. In terms of expression and conceptual art it broke down the traditional way in which people regard sculpture.

Another sculptor who had a love of steel was **Lenton Parr (b. 1924)**. He was one of the first Australian sculptors to work in welded steel and, apart from his initial organically derived forms, his work is highly abstracted. The piece at the Chadstone shopping centre in Melbourne is based on Australian flora; in fact it looks like some weird, futuristic plant, both in its shape and texture. In total contrast to this work of the 1960s comes *Astra*, 1970. This large, upstanding piece was designed for its location at the Astrojet Centre at Melbourne's Tullamarine Airport. Constructed from thin planks of steel, its strong vertical forms coupled with the curved rubbery shapes could reflect the expression of this new form of art as well as the scientific and aeronautical advances of the 1970s. Parr is particularly well qualified to work with steel as he once worked for a period of time building locomotives.

The influence of the British sculptor Anthony Caro (b. 1924) on Australian sculpture was felt when **Ron Robertson-Swann (b. 1941)** fell under his spell. For a while Robertson-Swann was much influenced by this sculptor as were others such as Clive Murray-White (b. 1946) and David Wilson (b. 1947). By not dwelling too long on Caro's style, all of these artists moved on to pursue their own personal styles and language.

On his return to Australia, Robertson-Swann exhibited his work in his new style; he received a lot of criticism for deriving his style so obviously from Caro's work.

In 1980 Robertson-Swann made headlines with a sculpture he constructed as a commission for Melbourne's newly completed city square—a large yellow steel work called *The Vault*. The controversy started when it was suggested that the sculpture should be moved. Robertson-Swann was originally asked to design a sculpture specially for that square and after months of work the sculpture was finally put together and constructed on the site. The events that followed were to cause quite a

BELOW:

LENTON PARR (b. 1924)
Astra, 1970
Welded steel painted black,
1006 x 762 x 335 cm
Astrojet Centre, Melbourne
Tullamarine Airport
Photographer: Jon Rendell

BELOW RIGHT:

RON ROBERTSON-SWANN
(b. 1941)
The Vault, 1980
Steel painted yellow
Photographer: Jon Rendell

fuss with Melbourne's City Council, its art establishment and, most of all, the sculptor. One of the former Lord Mayors, Cr Don Osborne, called for its removal on the grounds that it did not look good on that site and that it became a 'hang-out' for so-called 'undesirables'. Finally, after much debate, protest and demonstration the Council decided by vote that the work dubbed the 'Yellow Peril' would have to be moved. At enormous expense and in the early hours of one morning, *The Vault* was pulled apart. The huge slabs of steel were placed on to a convoy of semitrailers and moved to their present site in Batman Park beside the Yarra River.

Clive Murray-White and David Wilson are sculptors who make their work from constructing and welding together standard prefabricated steel sections to create different tensions, shapes and spaces.

It was the rule rather than the exception that steel, when used in these abstract sculptures, was left to discolour through rusting. Most sculptors preferred to leave steel in its prefabricated state, rarely painting it. Stainless steel was used in the sculpture of **Bert Flugelman (b. 1923)** and George Baldessin (1939–78).

Born in Vienna, Flugelman came to Australia and studied in Sydney before settling in Adelaide. In the 1970s Flugelman preferred to use stainless steel: he liked its highly reflective character and used it to make *Pyramid Tower*, 1978. This was a gift from the Sir William Dobell Foundation to the people of Sydney for Martin Place. The *Tower* is a series of pyramids which stretch 19.5 metres in height; the flat top seems to echo the surrounding buildings. Flugelman has done other similar work which can be seen outside Adelaide's Festival Theatre, the Art Gallery of South Australia and the Adelaide Mall.

DAVID WILSON (b. 1947)
Shelter V, 1976
Welded steel,
310 x 320 x 305 cm

Collection: National Gallery of Australia, Canberra

Photographer: Lister G. Clark

CLIVE MURRAY-WHITE
(b. 1946)

Holocaust, 1974
Steel

Photographer: Suzanne Davies

George Baldessin produced a large volume of work during the fourteen years of his art career. Mainly a printmaker who chose to etch, he also produced sculpture in resin, steel and aluminium. Baldessin realised that aluminium, unlike bronze, was cheap to use; it was light, shiny and, owing to its low melting temperature, easy to cast. The sculpture *Performer and Bouquet*, 1969, depicts the figure of a woman dressed in a theatrically striped outfit, the head exploding into a mass of flowers, or a bouquet as the name suggests.

Other sculptors to work in metal during these years were Geoff Bartlett (b. 1952), Jock Clutterbuck (b. 1945) and Tony Coeling (b. 1942).

RIGHT:

BERT FLUGELMAN (b. 1923)
Pyramid Tower, 1978
Stainless steel, height 19.5 m

Photographer: Jon Rendell

FAR RIGHT:

GEORGE BALDESSIN
(1939–78)

Performer and Bouquet, 1969
Aluminium, 170 cm

Art Gallery of South Australia
A. R. Ragless Bequest Fund
1970

The return to the elements of nature are concerns of the sculptors **Rosalie Gascoigne (b. 1917)** and John Davis (b. 1936). Gascoigne is an obsessive collector of natural and synthetic objects such as feathers, shells, old planks of weathered wood and scraps of tin. She then reassembles them into different forms to produce sculptures of varying sizes. Of this practice she says:

> Most of the things I use have been exposed to the weather and, in this sense, mine is an art of the outdoors. I like to use very ordinary material making do with whatever comes to hand within about a 30 mile [48 kilometre] radius of Canberra. I collect anything I like the look of ...[5]

Tiepolo Parrots, 1976, is constructed from discarded pieces of wood combined with images of the 'Arnotts' parrot. The 1930s logo is not only representative of the biscuit company and of the domestic environment but also is a symbol of the Australian bush. Gascoigne's work can also be appreciated for its textures and shapes. They are like three-dimensional visual diaries.

John Davis initially worked in stainless steel like Flugelman; however, in the 1970s he became interested in the landscape and the movement Art Povera. Like Gascoigne and Klippel his art is one of assemblage. He too collects objects from the land. With twigs, leaves, rocks and branches he constructs little environments and towers. This type of sculpture is in total contrast to the high art and carefully constructed works of the other sculptors. Davis's work is made from easily obtainable objects. In this sense his work is a kind of Australian Art Povera.

BELOW:

ROSALIE GASCOIGNE
(b. 1917)
Tiepolo Parrots, 1976
Wood, cardboard, coloured
inks, metal;
61.2 x 56.4 x 23 cm
Collection: National Gallery of
Australia, Canberra

BELOW RIGHT:

JOHN DAVIS (b. 1936)
Cape Schanck, 1978–89
Twigs, string, paper, stone,
canvas, feathers, wood, bones;
316 x 742 cm (floor area)
National Gallery of Victoria,
Melbourne
Purchased 1980

[5] *Survey 2* Catalogue, National Gallery of Victoria, April–June 1978.

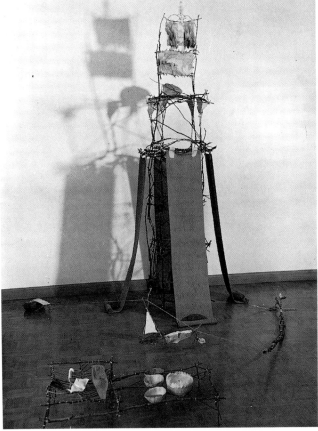

Of the work *Cape Schanck*, 1978–89, Davis says that it is no comment on the area itself and that the rocks placed with the work were actually picked up from Cape Schanck. A review of his work noted his primitive approach to sculpture as well as his affinity with the bush:

> One of a new breed of neo-romantic, ecology-conscious artists, Davis obviously finds fulfilment in emulating the ritualised, communal, art-in-life activities of tribal, primitive societies.[6]

The form of art in which the human body is used in contrast to wood, metal or ceramic is called Performance. This style is a combination of theatre, dance and ritual and it became popular in the late 1970s. **Kevin Mortensen (b. 1939)** performed at many locations, including the Mildura sculpture shows and many galleries.

One of his better documented pieces is the *Seagull Salesman and His Visitors*, 1971. Mortensen, the salesman, set himself up in a gallery. Naked from the waist up, he wore a hand-made seagull mask. Mortensen sat in his chair surrounded by sand, two burnt poles, cast seagulls in cages and two papier mâché figures (the visitors). He sat there motionless and silent except for an occasional seagull-like rapid head movement. In this performance Mortensen was concerned partly with humans' affinity with animals, their interaction and their communication.

KEVIN MORTENSEN (b. 1939)
Seagull Salesman and His Visitors, 1971
Live performer with mask, papier mâché figures, posts of polyurethane and fur, seagulls of painted plaster, and sand on floor

Pinacotheca Gallery, Melbourne

Other forms of performance tended to be more concerned with demonstrations of pain and endurance. Certainly this was true of the work of **Stelarc (b. 1946)** and Ken Unsworth (b. 1931). Stelarc's performance event was certainly about pain and

[6] Borlase, N., 'Two aspects of nature', *Sydney Morning Herald*, 23 July 1977.

endurance. It was performed in Japan only because Australian authorities were fearful for his safety. Stelarc hung suspended from a board with fifteen large fish hooks driven through his body from his lower legs to his elbows. The suspension lasted for fifteen minutes. He later stated that it was psychological rather than a physical experience. He says:

> Then on this idea of suspension … In the past I've been suspended from a balloon with all my body sounds amplified. I've been suspended from harnesses, I've been suspended from upside-down, sideways, upright. So this idea of a gravitationless state has always been an interesting one. But I've found it unsatisfactory that I've always had to use so many props to support the body and so that the idea gradually grew of how you get the body supported in space by its own material.[7]

Ken Unsworth too uses his body in suspension. At a performance presented at the Australian Institute of Contemporary Art in 1975 he suspended himself between two beams of wood which were pressed against his neck. He was situated at the apex of the triangle; this places tremendous stresses upon the body. This performance emphasised the vulnerability of the human body. Other performance artists are Robert Parr (b. 1923), Peter Cripps (b. 1948), Lyndal Jones (b. 1949), John Lethbridge (b. 1948) and Bonita Ely (b. 1946).

STELARC (b. 1946)
Sitting/Swaying
Event for Rock Suspension
Tamura Gallery, Tokyo,
11 May 1980

Photographer: Kenji Nozawa

Civil architecture

> … the architect knows that architecture can be generated only by aspirations for a better world built from life experiences; a hopeful aspect of man's endeavours, not the mirror of his confusion.[8]

With Australia's increasing cultural consciousness and the desire to be seen as part of the world's concert circuits, a competition was launched in 1955 for a design

[7] *Survey 15* Catalogue, National Gallery of Victoria, April–June 1978.
[8] Romaldo Giurgola quoted in Walter, B., 'The Sydney Opera House. A Second Celebration', *Belle*, September 1983.

for a Sydney opera house. Finally in 1957 the winning design and commission was awarded to a Danish architect, **Joern Utzon (b. 1918).**

The radical but inventive design staggered people. It was considered to be a structural and engineering nightmare—a huge plate of granite or rock on which sat a number of ceramic-tiled sails, echoing the huge sails of yachts on the harbour, the structure itself looked like a big yacht sailing into Circular Quay. For part of his design, Utzon referred to the terraced constructions of the Mayan and Aztec temples which he saw when he travelled to Mexico in 1949. He particularly liked the powerful effect achieved by placing a structure on top of a succession of steps. Utzon had faith in his design and said of it:

> If you think of a Gothic Church, you are closer to what I have been aiming at. Looking at a Gothic Church you never get tired, you will never be finished with it—when you pass around it or see it against the sky. It is as if something new goes on all the time and is so important—this interplay is so important that together with the sun, the light and the clouds, it makes a living thing.[9]

JOERN UTZON (b. 1918)
Sydney Opera House, 1956–73
Photographer: Jon Rendell

Construction of the Sydney Opera House 1956–73

Conception

30 November 1954: Premier of New South Wales Mr Cahill announced plans to advise the Government on the building of an opera house.

13 September 1955: Cahill announced a worldwide competition to design an opera house. It was to be designed at the site of the old tram depot at Bennelong Point near the Harbour Bridge, Circular Quay, incorporating one large hall and one smaller hall containing the following:

1. Large hall with capacity for:
   - symphony orchestra
   - large-scale opera
   - ballet performance
   - mass meetings

---

[9] Op. cit.

2. Small hall with capacity for:

- drama theatre
- small-scale opera
- chamber music
- lectures

Winning design 1957

The winning design was from a Danish architect, Joern Utzon. It was announced on 29 January 1957 that the Opera House would be constructed at a cost of $7 million in three stages:

1. foundation and base

2. roof and shell

3. furnishings, fitting and equipment

May 1958: Sinking of test bores to check for stability in the sea bottom undertaken.

2 March 1959: Earth moving and demolition of the old Bennelong Point tram depot carried out. Stage I foundations started:

The base or podium was constructed from pink-grey granite slabs, quarried locally in the Blue Mountains. This podium rests on a bed of sandstone in which are set 550 concrete piers, each 3 feet [1 metre] in diameter.

20 October 1959: Premier Cahill died while in Parliament. Premier Heffron carried on. There was a public outcry at the rising costs of building the Opera House.

March 1963: Stage II commenced:

From the podium rises a row of halls, theatres and foyers covered with dome-like shells or sails.

- This proved to be technically difficult in terms of working out stress points and weight distribution; therefore, the highest degree of accuracy was required.
- It took more than 2000 computer hours and 35 000 worker hours to perfect the roof system.
- Each shell was made up of supporting ribbed vaults with rows of precast ribs, used to reinforce and act as a skeleton for the trays of ceramic tiles.
- One million Swedish ceramic tiles in the form of trays, designed to reflect the sea and sun, were applied to the shells. Of the 4200 trays, the heaviest weighed 4 tons [3.6 tonnes].
- The huge tinted windows, imported from France, supported by millions of shaped steel pins, were attached to bronze bars.
- This stage alone took three years. It was finally completed in January, 1967.

May 1965: A Liberal Government took over and there was increasing pressure on Utzon for another cost estimate and date of completion. The Opera House Lottery was introduced in order to raise revenue.

February 1966: Utzon stated that the new cost was $50 million but gave no exact date of completion. Utzon tendered his resignation, which was accepted. Demonstrations against Government and political harassment occurred.

April 1966: A new team of architects was appointed and many changes were made, particularly to accommodate more people in the theatres.

March 1967: Stage III begun:

- The interior of the Opera House included furnishings and artworks designed by prominent Australian artists. The stage curtains in the concert halls were designed by John Coburn, while a long mural situated in the harbour-side foyer area was painted by John Olsen.

- Fourteen years and seven months after construction began, and at a final cost of $106 million, the Opera House was completed. It was a jump of more than $100 million from its original somewhat conservative estimate. All this expense was covered by the Opera House Lottery established a decade earlier.

1968: The new team expenditure budget ($85 million) and the completion date (December 1972) were announced.

20 October 1973: The Opera House was officially opened by the Queen.

Other important buildings

The building of new cultural centres became popular in the late 1970s and early 1980s, especially in Perth, Brisbane and Canberra where new art galleries were built. In Canberra some superb modern buildings such as the High Court, the National Gallery of Australia, Canberra, and the new Parliament House have also been constructed.

Linked by a walkway to the High Court of Australia, the National Gallery of Australia, Canberra, was designed by Edwards, Madigan and Torzillo. It is situated on the shores of Lake Burley Griffin. In 1982, fourteen years after its conception, it was opened by the Queen. Basically, the National Gallery is a mass of concrete which has been carefully sandblasted on the facade to create texture and soften the colour. The sculpture-like building creates a mass of interconnected spaces and voids. The building is capped with metal, and is rich in natural light, although careful consideration has been given to the conservation of the artworks, most of which are sensitive to direct light. The tall white building is complemented by its neighbour, the High Court building, 1982, which is more like a square box of glass, thereby creating a sense of weightlessness.

Situated on Capital Hill, Canberra, and designed by Mitchell, Giurgola and Thorpe, New Parliament House stands as the symbol of democratic government in Australia. It took several years to build and comprises enough concrete to build twenty-five Sydney Opera Houses. Sunk into the Hill and overlooking Old Parliament

BELOW:

MITCHELL, GIURGOLA AND THORPE
New Parliament House, Canberra, 1983–88
Photographer: Bronwyn McCoy

BELOW RIGHT:

EDWARDS, MADIGAN AND TORZILLO
High Court Building, Canberra, 1982
Photographer: Jon Rendell

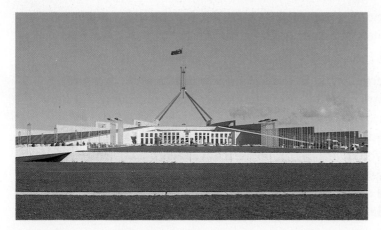

ROY GROUNDS (1905–81)
Victorian Arts Centre,
Melbourne
Photographer: David Parker

House and Lake Burley Griffin, the main building is flanked by two axes: the east–west axis contains the House of Representatives and the Senate, while the north–south axis contains the Great Hall, ministerial offices and function rooms.

The forecourt is dominated by an Aboriginal (Papunya Tula) inspired mosaic design. Inlaid into the ground, it symbolises Australia's first inhabitants and the meeting of the tribes. Beyond the forecourt a massive marble colonnade dominates the entrance. The entire building is capped by a huge flagpole, which stands 81 metres above the roof. Giurgola said:

> It is a national town hall for ceremonies and national occasions. It really should be a people's place. I hope, for example, Parliament hopes to have recitals there on a Sunday.[10]

In total contrast to the dynamic designs of the Canberra buildings is the Victorian Arts Centre complex, designed by **Sir Roy Grounds**. Well known for its controversial spire, the complex is basically a collection of geometric forms and spaces. The art gallery is a rectangle broken up by three square courtyards. In the front of the building are two rectangular moats; the arched entrances are semicircular. The Gallery School is triangular with a pyramid roof, while the theatre is circular. All these features have been previously used in Grounds's other works—the Henty House, Frankston, 1952; the domed Academy of Science, Canberra, 1959; and Grounds's own house in Toorak, Melbourne, 1954.

Prestressed concrete, steel and glass 'curtain wall' skyscrapers began to shoot up in most cities, and companies competed to see who could build the tallest. In 1967 the then tallest building in Australia, Australia Square Tower, was designed by **Harry Seidler**. Built with precast steel, concrete parts and frame, the Tower was faced with

---

[10] Stevens, J., 'The House on the Hill', *Age*, 30 April 1988.

white quartz stone. It set a precedent for significant changes. The fifty-storey tower was the first circular skyscraper constructed in Australia. Its shape responded particularly well to sun and light and, for pedestrians and for other buildings, it increased the space and light.

Although skyscrapers are disliked by many people, Seidler is very happy to design skyscrapers and says of them: 'Skyscrapers can be beautiful, you can make a skyscraper into a work of art, with the same materials.'[11] Australia Square Tower's shape, too, is particularly suited to the open plaza design where people can freely move about, have their lunch, shop and feel part of this construction rather than be repulsed by it.

Tall city towers often reflect the corporate wealth and power of the company. The old BHP Tower in William Street, Melbourne, one of Seidler's favourite Melbourne buildings, is a good example of this. Designed by Barry Patten of Yuncken Freeman, this glass tower reflects the 1970s. The dark glass with its large steel decorative bracing was not like previous steel constructed buildings, in that the steel frame was exposed and used as a form of decoration.

Domestic architecture

While Melbourne's triple-fronted, red brick veneer suburbs were developing, in Sydney in the 1960s a style that was indigenous to Sydney's climate and environment was born. This was called the 'Nuts and Berries' school. Although it did not become as popular as other styles, it did influence to a certain degree the design of Australian homes, particularly in the use of 'natural' materials. The 'Nuts and Berries' designs incorporated such elements as exposed timber beams and bricks, angular sloping roofs, split level interiors, and walls of brick or wood. On the exterior, clinker brick and wood panelling were used while large windows brought into view the natural landscape. It was for this reason that the landscape became of utmost importance when planning these houses. Architects such as Ken Woolley, Philip Cox and Philip Johnson all designed with particular skill and sensitivity in this style to make homes compatible with their natural surroundings, rather than interfere with the landscape as the previous International Style seemed to do.

While the 'Nuts and Berries' architects designed their work for only a small area of Sydney, project housing was introduced and became very popular with many Australians. Groups of architects teamed up with builders to design homes that suited families and the new modern suburbs. The spread of suburbia continued with the construction of freeways.

American-inspired, multilane roads transported thousands of commuters daily. Although they proved time-efficient for people in outer urban areas, for the inner city dwellers they became nightmares of the grandest kind. On entering the inner city areas some freeways became terrible bottlenecks where noise and air pollution became overwhelming concerns for local residents. Despite all this, freeways became the motorist's necessary evil.

[11] Hawley, J., 'Seidler, and what makes Harry wild', *Age*, 23 November 1985.

ABOVE:

KEN WOOLLEY (b. 1933)
*Woolley House, Mosman,
New South Wales*, 1962
Architects: Ancher, Mortlock &
Woolley Pty Ltd

Photographer: David Moore

ABOVE RIGHT:

*Ministry of Housing high rise
flats, South Melbourne*

Photographer: Jon Rendell

At the end of the freeways, however, the newly designed brick veneer homes with their pergolas, swimming pools and carports were sought after. Most of these project houses incorporated some of the features that the 'Nuts and Berries' group had introduced in Sydney.

But there were thousands of families who found it difficult to pay high rents, and food and power bills. State governments, particularly New South Wales and Victoria, introduced their high-rise development plans. In order to construct these buildings and clean up the inner city slums, governments demolished rows and rows of inner city terraces, only to replace them with very unattractive, box-like twenty- and thirty-storey towers. These 'filing cabinets' and 'bee hives', as they became known, filed hundreds of families away from the rest of the community and its facilities. These buildings, as was discovered later, only served to alienate and depress the majority of their inhabitants. Owing to the lack of recreational facilities and the ugly environment, some of the estates became hives of violent activity. The original function of architecture in this instance had failed miserably. These flats were not attractive, nor did they improve the residents' standard of living. In all, these hideous towers ruined the environment and were a public embarrassment for the governments involved. Although they are still in use and maintained, new high-rise projects have been abandoned.

Governments, in consultation with architects, realised that housing conditions had to be improved. It was decided that what most people desired was the 'Australian

Dream' of their own house on a quarter-acre block (0.1012 hectare). With this in mind, architects hired by the Ministry of Housing in Victoria and New South Wales designed some of the most experimental and highly decorative houses, blending them with surrounding homes. This was in contrast to the high rises, which ruined the skyline and streetscapes of inner city suburbs.

Both Norman Day's Candy Houses in Northcote and Peter Crone's modern Victoriana houses in Carlton are respectful of, and architecturally sensitive to, the suburbs in which they are situated.

Day (b. 1947) designed seven houses which were built out of brick, timber and tiles. Each house sat on its own plot of land. Parts of the houses are painted in candy colours of violet, green, pale oranges and creams—colours that are both modern and exciting.

Located in Station Street, Carlton, **Peter Crone's (b. 1952)** houses are even more in tune with their environment, with the exception of the slight modernising of the brickwork, parapet and verandah.

Other Ministry of Housing projects in Melbourne are at Kay Street, Carlton (page 195); Courtney Street, North Melbourne; Port Melbourne and South Melbourne. In Sydney similar projects can be seen in Woolloomooloo and Daceyville.

Apart from the innovative houses for the Ministry, many architects have created exciting and modern houses for the private homeowner. The ongoing search for an Australian style suitable for our modern era and climate became an issue for many architects of this period, including Suzanne Dance, Glenn Murcutt and John Andrews. These architects responded to the landscape and used materials rarely used in domestic building.

BELOW:

NORMAN DAY (b. 1947)
Northcote housing (Candy Houses), Victoria
Photographer: John Gollings

BELOW RIGHT:

PETER CRONE (b. 1952)
Ministry of Housing houses, Carlton, Victoria
Photographer: Jon Rendell

John Andrews (b. 1933) designed Andrews Farmhouse, 1981, at Eugowra, NSW. Here he has employed corrugated iron which had traditionally been used for outhouses, sheds and tanks. With this material, Andrews has cut down the cost as well as made his home particularly individual. The house is energy efficient and practical. The 'energy tower' in the middle of the house contains the header tank, and there is also a place for a solar collector and heater. A sprinkler system has been designed to spray the roof when it gets too hot. The location of the house on the land is well planned, as one side of it is protected from cold winds by a hill planted with trees. In the hot season the prevailing breezes are cooled by the strategically situated dam.

JOHN ANDREWS (b. 1933)
Andrews Farmhouse, Eugowra,
New South Wales, 1981
Courtesy of John Andrews
Photographer: David Moore

The wide verandahs and breezeways are also useful in cooling down the house. Overall the design exploits the traditional plan of the Australian farmhouse but employs new energy-efficient and practical extras.

The use of corrugated iron as a symbol of the rural landscape has become increasingly popular. **Glenn Murcutt**, Suzanne Dance and Peter Crone have all, at one time or another, used it in designing houses. Two of Murcutt's houses which he designed in 1979 actually won the Robin Boyd Award for home architecture. Originally the local council concerned would not approve his plans and wanted him to build in stone and brick, not corrugated iron, but they finally relented. Both these houses sit on land with pre-existing galvanised iron sheds. On Farmhouse A the sides of the house were lined with local timber, while the unusually shaped roof and a couple of sides were made with corrugated iron. On the verandah, the windows were covered with exterior wooden venetian blinds. The inside was lined with pineboard. When designing, Murcutt pays particular attention to winds, sun and views. Both

houses are light and airy but they have an affinity with the designs and mood of earlier rural dwellings. Other innovative architects are Daryl Jackson with his Shoreham Residence in Victoria and Greg Burgess with Hackford House, Traralgon, in Victoria's Gippsland.

GLENN MURCUTT
Mt Irvine House, New South Wales

Photographer: Max Dupain

ACTIVITIES

1. You have had the opportunity to see many different painters interpret the landscape. With all these different approaches in mind, whose work do you prefer? Why?

2. What were the next obvious changes to occur in Australian art during the 1960s and 1970s? Why did they happen? Explain, relating your answer to particular artists and their works.

3. Look at William's *Upwey Landscape* (page 163). What kind of Australian landscape does it remind you of? Why?

4. Research any one of these American painters: Rothko, Stella, Frankenthaler, Warhol or Estes. How does their work relate to the work that was done in Australia during the 1960s and 1970s? Look at colour, size and theme.

5. Research the work and motivation of overseas Performance artists.

6. Why did steel become a popular material to use for sculpture?

7. Having looked at the work of all the architects throughout the past fifty years, design a 'country homestead' for the climate of northern Australia.

8. What features would you include if asked to design an Australian country homestead? Why?

9. Research the controversy surrounding *The Vault*. You will need to look through old newspapers from the period July–November 1980. Look particularly at editorials from the Melbourne *Age* newspaper, 30 July and 4 September. From the information you have uncovered, do you agree with the *Age* editorials? What is your opinion of the entire incident?

	AUSTRALIAN EVENTS	GENERAL EVENTS	ARTISTIC EVENTS	
1989	Newcastle earthquake kills 12 people. Aboriginal Deaths in Custody Report first tabled, in parliament. Australia spends $59 million on AIDS research. Fitzgerald Report on corruption released. Air pilots strike cripples domestic air travel.	Tiananmen Square massacre, Beijing, China. Ivan Lendl wins 'Australian Open' Tennis Championship. President Ceaucescu deposed as leader of Rumania, and is later executed with his wife.	Australian Film Institute awards—Evil Angels wins Best Film of the year. Brian Westwood wins Archibald prize with his portrait of painter/critic Elwyn Lynn. Tandanya, National Aboriginal Cultural Institute, is established in Adelaide.	**Australian artists** Maria Kozic Imants Tillers Tim Johnson Gordon Bennett Ian W. Abdulla Paul Boston Tim Maquire William Robinson Judy Watson Peter Callas Howard Arkley Jon Cattapan Richard Dunn Angela Brennan Rose Nolan Gareth Sansom Peter Booth Hossein Valamanesh Tom Risley Narelle Jubelin Akio Makigawa Bronwyn Oliver Fiona Hall Jennifer Turpin Hilarie Mais
1990	Dr Carmen Lawrence becomes Australia's first woman State Premier in Western Australia. Author, Patrick White dies in Sydney. Paul Keating takes over from Bob Hawke as Prime Minister. Environmentalist and artist Clifton Pugh dies.	Nelson Mandela released from jail in South Africa after 27 years imprisonment. Iraq invades Kuwait with a soldier power of 120 000. Berlin Wall opens after 28 years. East and West Germany join together again. Miniature heart pump used in heart surgery in USA. Tunnel under the English Channel links Britain with France.	Aboriginal artists: Rover Thomas and Trevor Nickolls represent Australia at the 44th Venice Biennale, Italy. New York mural artist Keith Haring dies of AIDS. John Paul Getty Museum in Los Angeles purchases van Gogh's *Irises*, formerly owned by Perth businessman Alan Bond. Christo's *The Umbrellas* installation in USA and Japan. Dame Joan Sutherland gives her last appearance at the Sydney Opera House.	
1991	Australia sends 1631 troops to the Gulf War; there are no Australian casualties.	Mikhail Gorbachev deposed as leader of Russia, new leader is Boris Yeltsin. Mt Pinatubo erupts in the Philippines; more than 280 000 flee their villages. Gulf War erupts when Iraq invades Kuwait. Discovery of new planet outside of our solar system is made by Manchester University, England.	Museum of Contemporary Art opens in Sydney. *Dances with Wolves* wins an Academy Award for Best Film. National Gallery of Australia purchases the surrealist painter René Magritte's *The Lovers*, 1928.	
1992	Australian Airlines amalgamates with Qantas. The Australian film *Strictly Ballroom* starring Paul Mercurio wins worldwide acclaim.	Riots in Los Angeles see the army called out to maintain peace. Bill Clinton wins election from George Bush and becomes new president of USA.	Brett Whiteley dies. Sidney Nolan dies. British painter Francis Bacon dies in Madrid, Spain. Sculptor Ken Unsworth's *Vietnam Memorial* is unveiled in Canberra.	**Architecture** 101 Collins Street, Melbourne. Chifley Tower, Sydney. Adelaide Botanical Gardens Conservatory. Great Southern Stand (Melbourne Cricket Ground) Sydney Football Stadium Box Hill Community Arts Centre St Andrew's Beach House Tent House, Queensland Inner City Townhouses.
1993	Painter Jenny Watson represents Australia at 45th Venice Biennale, Italy. Prime Minister Paul Keating wins election in his own right and returns ALP to power.	Drought and mass starvation continues in Somalia. International Committee selects Sydney to host the Olympic Games in 2000. Earthquake in Los Angeles creates chaos and causes considerable damage to freeway systems and homes.	The cleaning and restoration of Michelangelo's frescoes on the Sistine Chapel ceiling complete. Opinion is divided on whether the works were actually cleaned or ruined. Aratjara—Art of the First Australians (a block buster exhibition of Aboriginal Art) opens in London.	
1994	Population 17.5 million with unemployment running at 9.5 per cent. National Portrait Gallery opens in old Parliament House building, Canberra.	Ex-USA President Richard Nixon of Watergate scandal fame dies in New York. In May, Nelson Mandela (African National Congress) becomes the first black President of South Africa in the first elections to involve black people in 300 years which spells the end to apartheid. Modern technology has finally stopped the falling of the Leaning Tower of Pisa. Tunnel linking Britain and France is opened by the Queen and French President François Mitterrand.	Norwegian artist Edvard Munch's *The Scream* is stolen from the Nationalgalerie in Oslo but returned undamaged months later. Sidney Nolan's *Ned Kelly* works exhibited at New York's Metropolitan Museum of Art. American minimalist sculptor Donald Judd dies.	
1995				

CHAPTER TWELVE

Towards a New Identity 1980s–90s

Social and political background

At last count Australia's population was heading towards 17.5 million. Our multiracial population has added a fertile ingredient to Australia and has influenced the way we live. Influences have been reflected in such things as our food, language, music, film and clothing. This influx has also served to change the way we socialise and has altered the way we view ourselves and our country. American streetwear, the 'grunge' look, 'rap' look with baggy jeans, baseball caps and T-shirts seem to be one of many popular forms of dress codes that has been adopted by many Australian teenagers as they move away from the blue denim jeans of their parents' generation.

The push for increased trade, tourism, education links and communication with Asia has become of prime importance to Australia in the 1990s. In particular, the Japanese tourist dollar has proved to be an important element in developing Australia's relatively young tourist market. Traditionally we have looked to America and Europe, but an increased activity in all these areas, both to and from Asia, has seen Australia becoming more comfortable with its nearest neighbours.

Prime Minister Keating's determination to create a native land title (Mabo) for the indigenous Aboriginal population was another issue that created much controversy from many State governments, mining companies, pastoralists, farmers and even suburban families, many of whom felt that they would lose their backyards! The hysteria eventually settled down and the Bill was finally passed in parliament. Aboriginal art, both urban and traditional, is still receiving increasing success both here and overseas, while environmental concerns such as forest conservation and nuclear power still provoke lively debate.

The early 1990s saw the republican debate raise its head. The call to cut ties with the United Kingdom and make Australia a republic proved to be controversial among all members of the Australian community. The public and private problems experienced by the Queen and her family during this time seemed to only highlight the debate, while for many younger Australians it confirmed the thought that the Royal Family is an outdated and expensive institution irrelevant to current Australian life. A poll conducted in October 1994 discovered that 66 per cent of Australians polled favoured a republic over a monarchy.[1] Suggestions for a new flag were even more emotional and divisive, particularly among many older Australians.

The mystery and horror of AIDS still baffle scientists worldwide as health authorities continue to promote the safe sex message throughout the Western world. This campaign has forced many young people to consider the fatal implications of unprotected sex. On a more positive note groundbreaking advances in genetic investigation could make it possible for doctors to manipulate the building blocks of human life and eradicate fatal hereditary diseases. Homelessness, child poverty and unemployment are issues that still need to be addressed. In 1994 the unemployment level was running at around 954 000, encouraging many students to stay at school and consider tertiary education. The traditional concept and notion of the family is at risk as current statistics claim that one in three marriages ends in divorce. Many families are no longer fitting the traditional mould and we are forced to open our minds to reconsider a new meaning of the word 'family'.

By far one of the most powerful influences on the young—next to the media—was computer technology. Children at primary school level started to master the use of the computer and other pieces of technological hardware, further widening the 'techno' generation gap between them and their parents. The late 1980s and 1990s has seen a great increase in the way we receive information. A communications revolution has developed; the facsimile machine or fax, compact disc players, laser scanning and developments in photographic technology have found many artists expanding their practice to include some of these devices. Many artists explored the mediums of installation and performance; and work with computers and videos has become more accepted and these forms of expression have proved to be both stimulating and provocative.

Painting

Maria Kozic (b. 1957) is a Melbourne artist whose work has developed out of her interest in popular culture, particularly such things as fast food, dolls, toys and characters from television programs. Much of her work raises issues concerning the role of women in society, their relation to men and the way they are portrayed in the media. Kozic uses a range of materials in her work, incorporating film, sculpture, television and painting. Her work from the 1980s was very concerned with issues of sex and violence as seen in her cartoon-style works of people having their heads splattered against walls and other similar such horrific imagery.

A lover of popular culture, especially television and cinema memorabilia, Kozic has a collection of dolls, many of which have been modelled on television and movie

---

[1] Herald Saulwick Poll, *Sydney Morning Herald*, 3 November 1994.

stars. From the series *I, Woman* from 1994 comes Kozic's much larger-than-life portraits of dolls' faces. All have different names but are essentially the same person: they are stereotypes of a certain 'type' of woman, just like Barbie. Kozic draws our attention to their faces: their sparkling eyes, flawless rosy complexions, plucked and pencilled eyebrows and, of course, pink-red glossy lips. Are they toy manufacturers' representations of how we see women? Is it a representation of how they are presented to us on the television, cinema and advertisements? The dolls are wrapped up in a bag of plastic, which reflects across the surface of the doll's face. They are not placed in their gift boxes but are wrapped rather crudely in a cellophane bag—a 'body bag' as Kozic calls it. Painted carefully to hide all the brushmarks in a highly realist manner, they adopt a variety of expressions and emotions, and above all question the way the dolls look and the way in which we look at them.

MARIA KOZIC (b. 1957)
I, Woman (Babet), 1994
Diptych, acrylic on cotton
duck, 198 x 198 cm and
10 x 10 cm
Photograph courtesy of
Anna Schwartz Gallery

Sydney-born artist **Imants Tillers (b. 1950)** is of Latvian descent and much of his work looks at issues of migration, cultural identity and cultural isolation. Originally trained in architecture, Tillers decided to become an artist after working with the international artist Christo, when he was in Australia in 1970 to wrap up Little Bay in Sydney. This experience introduced Tillers to conceptual art, an interest that has remained with him ever since.

In the huge work called *Diaspora*, 1992, Tillers constructs his picture by bringing together 288 individual canvasboards. Tillers has been working in this manner since 1981. The boards are painted independently of each other and then assembled together on a wall. This accounts for the slight changes in colour, linework and texture of the paint from board to board. Each board is numbered and then placed together, like a jigsaw. The reasons for this approach to working are both practical and aesthetic. Tillers said:

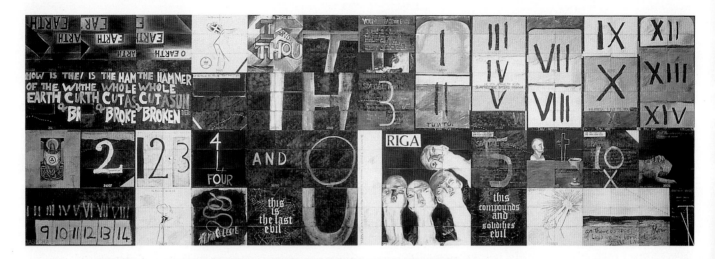

IMANTS TILLERS (b. 1950)
Diaspora, 1992
Synthetic polymer paint,
gouache, oil stick on 288
canvasboard panels
Courtesy of Sherman Galleries
Photographer: Paul Green

I work at a desk, not in a studio. Yet one of the reasons I use this method is to make huge paintings that have a substantial presence. But when I take the picture down from the wall it reverts to a stack of panels. The image disappears …[2]

Tillers 'borrows' images from other artists' works, often referred to as 'appropriation', a common practice during the late 1980s. This is his way of questioning the practice of reproduction of images as seen in art books, postcards and even the electronic media. Consider how a reproduction of an artwork changes our perception of its true scale, colour and texture. In part it is this notion that he is trying to make us aware of. The painting *Diaspora* is about the dispersal of the Latvian people at the end of World War II. Generally speaking it can also relate to the dispersal of different races. Nowhere is this more prominent than in Australia where we have a wide mix of different peoples: Aborigines, Vietnamese, Italian, Chinese, Greek, Middle-Eastern, Anglo-Saxon and the list goes on. The word 'diaspora' actually refers to the dispersion of people belonging to one nation. Tillers makes the point that the word also relates to the physical structure of the picture itself: the breaking up and repositioning of the many boards.

Tillers' parents were part of the dispersal and subsequent migration to Australia. His Latvian background accounts for the subject matter in many of his pictures—this one particularly. Tillers makes reference to Riga, the capital of Latvia, which was the first place in which this picture was exhibited. Much of the text relates to different poems and is painted in a manner borrowed from the New Zealand painter Colin McCahon (1919–87). Words and text form an important element in his art, and he uses words from diverse cultures: Latvian, Maori, Aboriginal Australian and Australian. Numbers written at the bottom of each panel are his numbering system, while the image of the four heads is taken from a painting by the contemporary German painter Georg Baselitz.

The colonisation of Australia by white Europeans has brought about the dispersal of the Aboriginal people and has seen the collapse of much of their rich and complex culture. The artist Tim Johnson and his wife Vivien have been responsible for bringing much of this plight to the attention of the wider population. Since around 1977 **Tim Johnson (b. 1947)** has built up a considerable collection of Aboriginal art—

---

[2] Tillers, Imants, *Origins Originality + Beyond*, The Biennale of Sydney, 1986, p. 270.

in particular the work of the Papunya Tula artists from the Central Australian Desert area of the Northern Territory (Chapter One). Johnson has painted in the same locations as the Aboriginal artists and has even worked with them on a series of paintings. Johnson has been criticised for using the dots and colours of the Aboriginal artists but, as he claims, the dot is not exclusively the domain of the Aboriginal artists:

> Painting in the style that is influenced by Papunya artists has meant developing the dot screen or matrix. It has obvious affiliations in Western culture. For example: halftone screen images, television screens, grain on photographs and films, Pointillism and mosaic. By painting my images primarily in elevation they are different from the schematised maps of sites and the use of an abstract language of symbols and the specific detailing of dreamings that characterise tribal art ...[3]

Johnson has also travelled widely throughout Asia, and has studied Buddhism, which has influenced his outlook on life. In many of his paintings Johnson combines elements of his understanding of Aboriginal painting with images of religious Asian icons and other pictorial inferences to Chinese, Tibetan and Indian art and culture. At first appearance *Amnesty*, 1993, has marked similarities to a piece of highly decorative and patterned Asian fabric. The array of gold dots interspersed with Asian-like figures float in and out of the picture surface, and the gold colour embodies a particular preciousness to the work.

After becoming bored with his job with Telecom Australia, **Gordon Bennett (b. 1955)** enrolled in an art course in Brisbane. His paintings and installations explore his Aboriginal heritage in a European, or as he calls it 'Eurocentric', upbringing. His work is highly political. It is about our colonial history, Aboriginal history from both black and white perspectives, and coming to terms with his own Aboriginality.

[3] Johnson, Tim, *Across Cultures*, University of Melbourne Museum of Art, Melbourne, 1993, p. 10.

TIM JOHNSON (b. 1947)
Amnesty, 1993
Oil on linen, 180 x 240 cm
Collection of the artist
Photograph courtesy of
Tolarno Galleries

Through his paintings, sculptures and installations he aims to redress the disparity of opportunity between the two cultures. Bennett claims that growing up not knowing about his Aboriginality placed him in a unique position. His art is about learnt racist attitudes, the viewing of himself as an outsider, and how Aboriginal culture has been formulated from a European perspective. It is these issues that underpin Bennett's paintings and installations. He said:

> From cocktail parties to backyard barbecues, to workplace parties and coffee breaks, predominantly derogatory opinions about indigenous people are exchanged with unquestioning ease and assurance.[4]

In *Myth of the Western Man*, 1992, Bennett recalls the painting *Blue Poles* by American abstract expressionist painter Jackson Pollock: in developing his drip technique of painting Pollock looked to the traditional sand paintings of the American Indians. The bearded man carrying the pen or pole comes originally from a textbook story about the inexperienced explorers Burke and Wills. The figure holds the pole that was the support to the tent, which was on the brink of being blown away in a desert storm. The symbolism behind the man holding the pole is quite complex. The pole is a reference to *Blue Poles*, and to an old white man holding onto European written history, a form of written propaganda. The blue 'flags' are printed with specific dates in Australia's history including the landing at Sydney Cove, Mabo, the establishment of the Tent City in front of Parliament House in Canberra and the many massacres of Aboriginal people throughout our history.

GORDON BENNETT
*Myth of the Western Man
(White Man's Burden)*, 1992
Acrylic on canvas,
175 x 304 cm
Art Gallery of New South Wales

[4] Bennett, Gordon, in *Strangers in Paradise*, Art Gallery of New South Wales, Sydney, 1993, p. 22.

The paintings of **Ian W. Abdulla (b. 1947)** explore issues similar to those of Gordon Bennett, but they are dealt with in another way. The basic difference is that Abdulla, unlike Bennett, was largely a self-taught artist.

Abdulla was born at Swan Reach on the Murray River in South Australia and belongs to the Njarrindjeri group of people. He spent much of his youth working on farming properties on the Murray, picking grapes and tending to irrigation systems. His interest in art developed around 1988 when he began studying screen printing, and he took up painting the following year.

Abdulla's pictures are recollections of growing up on a 30-kilometre stretch of the Murray between Cobdogla and Katarapko. Written in paint over his pictures, his messages are direct and at times poignant. While his technique is seemingly crude, the works are fresh and lively. Some of the stories are disturbing and tell us about the impact of white man on both the Aboriginal people and the fragile natural environment, particularly around the Murray River waterways.

Living on the fringe of Australian society, Abdulla's past times of hunting, fishing, and exploring along the river beds with his fellow 'Nunga' (Aboriginal) people have supplied him with a rich source of inspiration from which he can draw. The oral history tradition inherent in Aboriginal culture is transferred to a pictorial one, where a descriptive collection of text highlights the radical change in culture and daily life that occurred when the white man arrived.

IAN W. ABDULLA (b. 1947)
Night Fishing on the Murray River, 1994
Acrylic on canvas, 22 x 122 cm

Photograph courtesy of
Paul Greenaway Galleries

As with Tim Johnson, **Paul Boston (b. 1952)** too has strong links with the Buddhist religion, partly due to extensive travelling through parts of Asia. This religious doctrine clearly defines the manner in which Boston operates in the world and governs his beliefs about life, and as a consequence underpins much of his art. His early works were predominantly abstract in style and founded on collections of calligraphic marks, heads, boats and other organic shapes and squiggles, many of which were recognisable as something in particular. His current work has become devoid of any readily identifiable objects and uses repeated forms and curved shapes, all of which are balanced and composed thoughtfully.

The surface quality of Boston's pictures is important. Richly built up with many transparent washes of pigment and glazes, they are then overworked, rubbed back and reglazed. The rich surface quality reflects light and gives the works a further dimension and quality. It plays an equally important role with his restricted choice of colours: olive greens, greys, dark blues, off whites and black. *Painting No. 5*, 1994, is highly ordered and formal: divided in half, curved white lines break the rigidity of the straight lines, and it is about balance, harmony, structure and restraint.

PAUL BOSTON (b. 1952)
Painting No. 5, 1994
Oil on canvas, 137 x 92 cm

Private collection
Photograph courtesy of
Niagara Galleries, Richmond

Abstract art is not about storytelling or depicting realist visions of life; it is about things less tangible, less obvious. The work of Paul Boston is a case in point. His art is not narrative, but one that is abstract, where one is forced to consider less obvious, less tangible issues; things requiring contemplation; and elements such as harmony, balance, colour and tone.

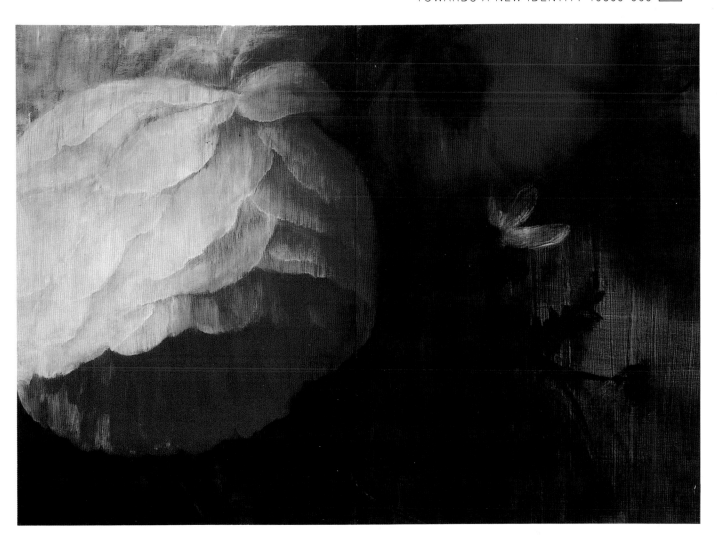

TIM MAGUIRE (b. 1958)
Untitled
Completed November 1992
Oil on sized paper on canvas
diptych, 135 x 181 cm each
Collection of Moët & Chandon

Tim Maguire (b. 1958) first came to the notice of the general public when he won the prestigious Moët & Chandon Art prize in 1993. Maguire was originally a landscape painter, in the spirit of such others as Russell Drysdale, Arthur Boyd and Sidney Nolan. Maguire isolated elements in the landscape, not panoramas or beautiful vistas but particular objects such as corrugated iron water tanks and wooden gates standing isolated in the landscape. These works take on a surreal element and recall some of the early works of Drysdale.

Maguire won his award with the work *Untitled*, 1993. The subject is an enlarged study taken from a detail of a seventeenth-century Dutch painting of flowers. Maguire selected the painting and then chose a specific area of the work to enlarge. This process of selection needs to be carefully considered for its colour, form and texture. Maguire's work is painted on a much grander scale than the original and, like Boston's approach, is then worked over in many glazes and washes of colour in a rather traditional approach.

In the original Dutch context, the flowers and insects would have had particular symbolic meaning, known to many in their time; however, these days most of the traditional stories and symbols are lost. Maguire is not so concerned with these meanings, but seems to focus on the colour, texture and form of the Dutch original. The colours of the flowers are warm and subdued, and come both in and out of our gaze.

One of the most well-known and established Queensland artists is **William Robinson (b. 1936)**, also a painter of nature. Robinson paints the landscape around his home on the Lamington Plateau, 90 kilometres outside Brisbane. This rich and lush environment offers Robinson an abundance of potential subject matter. Trees that wind and twirl around the picture in a rather unconventional way add a sense of the fantastic, and depict the spirit of the life and atmosphere of the rainforest. They are overwhelming panoramas!

Robinson's use of perspective is unusual in that there is often no horizon line. We are given a combined bird's eye and an ant's eye view. Sometimes we peer down onto the landscape from metres above, other times we look up to be confronted by towering trees adorned with vines, other plants, aerial roots, and animal and bird life. Robinson's pictures describe the hive of activity that is found in the forest environment. He often produces works in panels, visually linked by the 'painted' slipstream of a bird or a line of smoke. Robinson's careful delicate brushwork and use of glazes gives his pictures a luminosity and ongoing freshness. His colours are lush, vibrant and evocative and reflect appropriately that particular region of the Australian landscape.

In Robinson's landscapes the human presence is shown as an integral and harmonious element of the landscape, not as destroyer as in many examples of contemporary landscape painting. In many of his pictures Robinson and his wife (Shirley) are shown together wandering through their property or out in the rainforest, not as invaders but as respectful observers. They are painted in a whimsical way, like characters in a fairytale.

WILLIAM ROBINSON (b. 1936)
*Ridge and Gully in Afternoon Light,*1992
Oil on canvas, 137 x 198 cm
Private collection

Photographer: Norman Nicholls

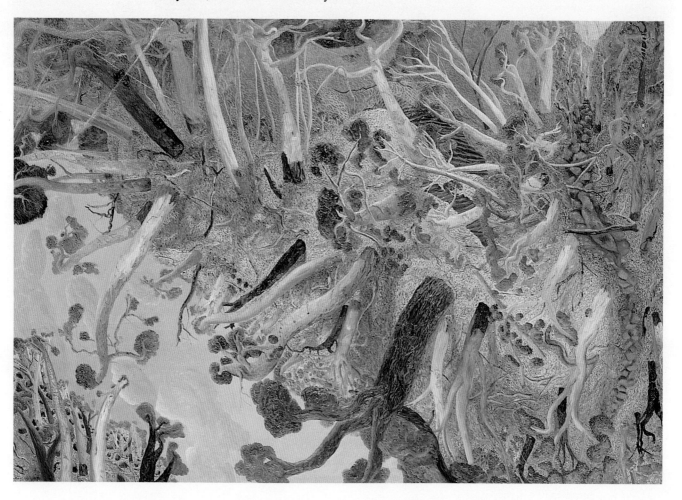

JUDY WATSON (b. 1959)
Exchanges, 1994
Powder pigment and pastel on
canvas, 1880 x 1265 cm

Photograph courtesy of
the artist

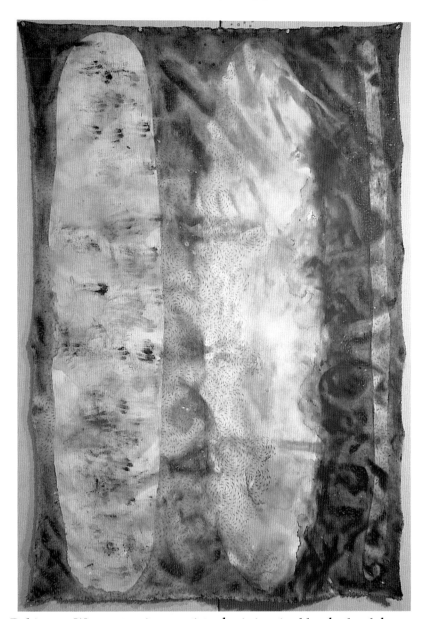

Like Robinson, Watson too is an artist who is inspired by the land; however, her work deals with less tangible and the not so visible elements of her country. The mysterious appearance of **Judy Watson's (b. 1959)** pictures allows them also to fade in and out of our gaze. These large canvas works, which hang unstretched, have associations of pegged-out hides or groundsheets, and relate to the spirit of the desert and its mysterious qualities. Some are autobiographical links with her grandmother's Aboriginal heritage and her grandmother's country in north-west Queensland.

Watson often paints works on the ground, pushing pigments onto the surface of the canvas or suspending them in water with a binder and floating this across the work. In Watson's pictures the land is viewed from above. The red ochres, greys and burnt yellows relate to the soils and the blood staining of the earth as occurred with many of the massacres of Aboriginal people in Australia. The swirling spiral marks refer to change, the obscuring of vision or mirage as frequently experienced in the heat of the desert, the transference of energy. The use of dots and lines placed across the surface of the work suggest tracks, ancestry lines, walkways and long journeys. Like stage lights they also give definition and prominence to what they surround.

Watson also writes superb passages of words, which are often shown together with her paintings. They express Watson's bond to her family and the land on which her ancestors dwell. The following is text from one of her exhibitions:

> The country that I dream about, identify with, is my Grandmother's, mother's country in north-west Queensland Australia.
>
> The ground is a skin stretched over the folds of a living organism breathing.
>
> I can feel the presence of guardians here
> memories from beneath the ground charge up through the soles of my feet
>
> Connecting me with my ancestors, my bloodline.[5]

It is no surprise to find that the technological age is on us—it was inevitable. Computer games, virtual reality, the compact disc player, portable cellular telephones, the satellite, laser, optic fibres (and the list goes on) have entered our lives and will not be going away. This has affected the way we communicate and relate to one another, and in many ways has resulted in a form of a global communications revolution. Many artists have embraced the use of computer technology to enhance the way they work and to enable their messages to be accessed more widely. Artists such as Kim Donaldson, Ellen Jose, Jill Scott and Peter Callas have all used computer technology in their art. Callas is probably the most well known in this field, working in the arts and also in the commercial arena on advertising and marketing projects for different corporations.

Peter Callas (b. 1952) originally graduated from art school in 1980, majoring in fine art and history, and then embarked on a career as a film editor with ABC television. It was here that his interest in the process of film editing and video production developed. Callas has lived for many years in Tokyo, the world capital of such technology. In this environment he has had the opportunity to experiment and work closely with new electronic technology found in much Japanese industry. Callas's technique is an electronic video form of cut and paste. Highly selective in what he chooses, he isolates images on the computer, enhances the colour and then relocates them into a new scene or environment. He is also able to draw onto his graphics pad and then merge these drawings with other images onto the screen.

The use of video as a medium suits Callas: it is immediate and spontaneous, and can give him the effects he wants there on the spot, unlike photography or film which involves sending the film away for processing. The subjects vary: some issues deal with perceived myths in Australian history, such as the romance of the bushman as seen in paintings of Roberts, Streeton and McCubbin (Chapter Five); others are more contemporary in subject and focus on cultural and commercial conflict between different racial groups and how countries construct their own culture with elements taken or borrowed from other cultures.

In the still taken from the series *Neo Geo: An American Purchase*, 1989, Callas juxtaposes cartoon characters from comics and other popular figures, which he places together with a collection of military propaganda slogans and symbols. It relates to American imperialism, global domination and economics. The images flash across the

[5] Text from Judy Watson exhibition at Art Gallery of New South Wales, Sydney, July 1993.

video screens. The colours, sounds and forms are all integrated and remind us of the excitement generated by a pinball game—clearly difficult to show in a static book reproduction.

PETER CALLAS (b. 1952)
Still from *Neo Geo: An American Purchase*, 1989
1 inch colour video, 9:17 mins
Photograph courtesy of the artist

Howard Arkley (b. 1951) is known for his airbrushed paintings of suburbia: the popular triple-brick veneer house, and interior views of lounge rooms and kitchens, complete with patterned wallpaper, lamp, TV and knick-knacks. Arkley has also made furniture and has produced a collection of bizarre portraits of faces that have a tribal African appearance about them. In 1980 his lurid and luminescent colours even found their way onto a Melbourne tram, which sent his art rattling throughout the suburbia he paints.

HOWARD ARKLEY (b. 1951)
Family Home—Suburban Exterior, 1993
Synthetic polymer paint on canvas, 203 x 257 cm
Photograph courtesy of Tolarno Gallery

The suburban culture has long fascinated Arkley as it has many other artists and writers—Let's face it, how many of us have watched an episode of 'Neighbours', or laughed with Dame Edna Everage when she mocks the suburban lifestyle? Suburbia is something we are all familiar with. Most of the population of Australia lives in the suburbs that circle our capital cities like satellites. You and many of your friends probably live in a suburban dwelling, with at least a fence, garden, garage and Hill's hoist in the yard, similar to the one painted in Arkley's picture. Arkley wants to explore the beauty in the suburbs, not the ugliness, and explores it in the way that other artists such as Fred Williams and Russell Drysdale chose the outback landscape or the bush. Arkley has always been interested in the way painters have used the landscape (desert and bush) to describe the Australian experience. Arkley and many others believe the suburban landscape to be more relevant to the bulk of the Australian population.

While Arkley's work might use the same tools and techniques as graffiti artists, he is adamant that his art not be described in this way. The airbrush has been used by Arkley since the early 1970s, and it was not until a few years later that he started to use it as a serious form of artistic expression. He has even worked with other artists to produce paintings. Not surprisingly, Arkley has become exceptionally skilful at using this tool, known traditionally for its commercial use for painting designs on the sides of hotted-up cars.

The urban environment has also been a place that has long held interest for **Jon Cattapan (b. 1956)**. The streets by day and the nocturnal activities of inner city living—car accidents, fights, deaths, conflict on the streets—and personal triumphs and tragedies form the subjects of much of Cattapan's work. A painter and printmaker, Cattapan has travelled widely and has lived in many locations throughout Australia and the world, including St Kilda (Melbourne), Sydney, Canberra and New York. Many of these different experiences have enriched his art.

In the work *Fuse*, 1994, Cattapan continues his interest in exploring the nature of the city, how it is constructed, and how communication channels are established and used in cities throughout the world. Produced from a collection of sources including computer-scanned images, photographs and drawings, they are an amalgam or, as Cattapan himself calls them, a 'generic site'. The computer plays an important role in the development of Cattapan's work:

> A lot of my ideas are now generated on Apple Macintosh computer, scanning in images either of my own making or found images and just simply creating collages on the screen which can be manipulated until they look quite painterly. I'm not so interested in what comes out of the computer, that is the hard copy as an end product, rather I use it as a working drawing, just another tool for my own painting.[6]

Many paintings are also constructed from old photographs, or from dioramas and toys that he sets up into an environment and then paints into a narrative. Drawing also forms an important part of Cattapan's output; while many are produced as preliminary studies for paintings others are seen as finished works of art in themselves. Cattapan is also a wide reader and has been known to refer to novels for ideas, particularly the science fiction writings of John Graham Ballard. Cattapan claims that Ballard's writings inspire in him a particular vision.

---

[6] Kirker, Anne and Cattapan, Jon, in *Eyeline*, Nos 22 and 23, 1993, Queensland Artworkers Alliance, Brisbane, 1993.

JON CATTAPAN (b. 1956)
Fuse, 1994
Oil on linen, 210 x 250 cm
Courtesy of Annandale
Galleries, Sydney

RICHARD DUNN (b. 1944)
Untitled 2 (Grid and a Name)
(#2 of 4), 1989–92
Oil on canvas, 112 x 127.5 cm
Collection of the artist
Photograph courtesy of
the artist

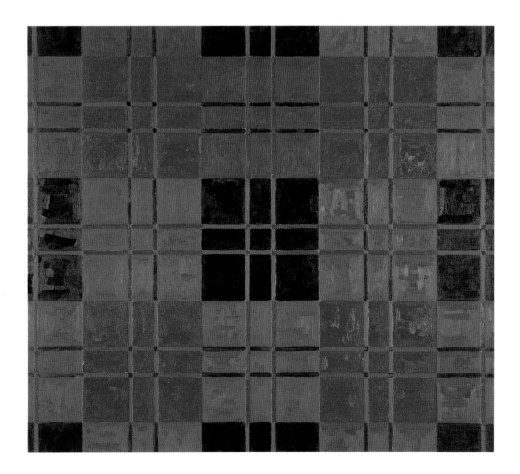

Richard Dunn (b. 1944) is one of a larger group of artists who has been working since the mid-sixties. He has worked and studied in London and New York, and has exhibited widely throughout Australia and parts of Europe. Dunn has moved through many different stages in his career, being affected by many different influences and art 'movements' in one form or another. Dunn is not only a painter—he has worked in a range of media including photography, installation and sculpture. He will often mix many disciplines together, feeling that a range of materials and practices are an appropriate and suitable means of expressing different views and concerns.

Dunn's art is deceptively complex and is largely of a conceptual nature. It is about questioning the role of painting, the psychology concerning the way we observe and see art, and the wider question concerning the nature of art itself. He has a wide interest in a range of other disciplines including film, Greek philosophy, architecture, philosophy and psychology. Through his art his serious interest in these areas can be found.

In *Untitled 2 (Grid and a name) (#2 of 4)*, 1989–92, Dunn's picture resembles a piece of tartan cloth or a kilt but there is more to it than that. It is actually loaded with other layers of meaning, one of which has to do with his Scottish grandparents: MacFarlane, MacGregor, Erskine and Anderson. In this work the oil paint is applied carefully and evenly. On another level, his work seems to recall the formal geometric abstract pictures of European painters Piet Mondrian and Kasimir Malevich and the American abstract painters of the 1950s and 1960s. Dunn's careful rendering and brushwork disguises the qualities of the paint and serves to simulate the texture and weave of the fabric itself.

Of the younger generation of artists, Melbourne-based painter **Angela Brennan (b. 1960)** is primarily an abstract or non-objective artist. She is admired for her position to not move with the 'in crowd' and follow trends in art, but to work through her own personal issues and to think and work for herself. While one should always be careful of placing artists in rigid categories, Brennan can also be described as a figurative artist. In the figurative works her sources are derived from popular culture and include record covers, old and recent photographs, and appropriated images from Western art history. Her colourful large pictures exude a confidence and energy. They are known for their soft, blurred geometric forms, checkerboard patterns, oblongs, squares and circles in pastel and sometimes stronger more intense secondary groups of colours. Brennan's use of paint is careful, and her choice of colour is spontaneous and intuitive. In many pictures she layers the paint onto the surface of the canvas, while in other works she employs a staining technique where the weave of the canvas is still visible and is an important element to the whole painting.

In *Untitled*, 1993, colours and forms weave throughout the canvas and produce a rhythmic and electric atmosphere, almost musical. This picture resembles aerial views of roadways and intersections of right angles, streets and the flashing of vehicles as they intersect and move around each other. In *The Familiar Is Not Necessarily the Known*, 1994 (see Chapter Thirteen), loose and seemingly flexible bands of colour shimmer and vibrate on the surface of the canvas, while thin black lines break up and separate the bands of colour. (See also the interview in Chapter Thirteen.)

Another young Melbourne-based artist who chooses to ignore current trends is **Rose Nolan (b. 1959)**. Her works are made up of painted cardboard assemblages, sometimes flat and sometimes protruding out of the surface, held together by wire and string. For Nolan, it is the forms of the circle and the cross—the overlapping of two rectangular shapes—that seems to dominate her recent art.

ANGELA BRENNAN (b. 1960)
Untitled, 1993
Oil on canvas,
106.5 x 137.5 cm
Collection of the artist
Photograph courtesy of
Niagara Galleries

ROSE NOLAN (b. 1959)
Not Sensitive, With Standards
1993
Mixed media constructions: oil
paint, perspex, cardboard and
tin lid
44.7 x 25.4 x 15.2 cm
Tolarno Galleries

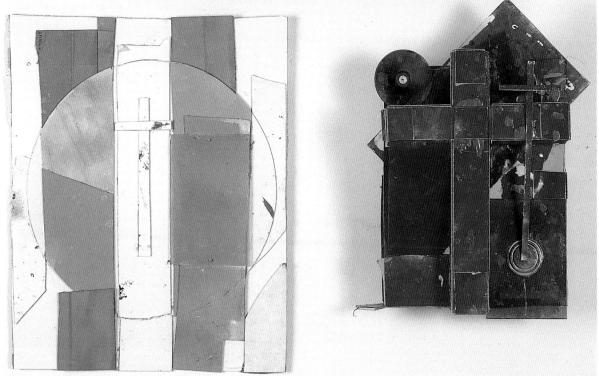

The form of the cross has been explored in the early paintings of Nolan. The cross is one of the oldest symbols. It relates obviously to Christianity but also to the work of the Russian artist Kasimir Malevich and many of the American abstract painters. The cross may also relate to Nolan's childhood, growing up in a strict Catholic environment. It is the meeting of the old with the new. In its use of corrugated cardboard, perspex, tin can lids, string and wood, her art is raw, fresh and earthy. In many ways the materials are secondary to the forms she is creating. The use of restrained colour also recalls the abstract work of the Russian artist Kasimir Malevich. She favours the medium of enamel paint in monochrome colours of blues, greens and reds.

Another significant and well-established artist is **Gareth Sansom (b. 1939)**. Sansom's works differ greatly from the more formal and structured paintings of Dunn. Sansom's pictures are largely autobiographical and tell us episodes and stories about his partners, his travel experiences and his more personal preoccupations such as ageing, sexuality and illness.

The paintings of Sansom are essentially narratives. They can be confronting, provocative and at the same time cheeky. His interest in British Pop art and the work of Picasso and Francis Bacon found him absorbing many different influences and

GARETH SANSOM (b. 1939)

Arthritis, 1993
Mixed media on cotton duck,
213.4 x 152.5 cm

Collection of the artist
Photograph courtesy of
Sherman Galleries

techniques: collage, photo-montage and cartoon-style drawing, and a particular looseness in applying paint. During 1989 Sansom spent some time painting and drawing in India. It was a preliminary visit for his 1991 role as Australia's official artist at the Seventh Triennale in Delhi, India. Many of his experiences on this trip have influenced his subsequent works.

In the pictures from 1993 we see a preoccupation with one's health and states of mind. Like all his works, they are chaotic and frenetic with energy and excitement. Sansom applies his paint generously and his use of colour is bold, expressive and lively. In *Arthritis*, 1993, a spray gun or aerosol can has been employed in selected areas to create another effect, different from what can be achieved through using a brush. The titles of the paintings include such things as *Mortality*, *Retirement*, *Schizophrenia* and *Arthritis*, and relate specifically to his friends and family.

English born, **Peter Booth (b. 1940)** started his career in the 1960s, producing hard-edge abstract pictures (Chapter Eleven). Since then his work has changed dramatically, moving through different phases and constantly challenging both himself and his audiences with the occasional images of the weird and the shocking.

In the work *Winter*, 1993, Booth moves the viewer away from his earlier landscapes that were inhabited by mutants, nuclear explosions, fires and insect people, and barren landscapes suggestive of the collapse of modern civilisation to a more peaceful, new era—a new ice age perhaps, one that is more peaceful, the calm after the storm. Booth started this series in the winter of 1989, at the same time as he had been rereading Shakespeare's *Macbeth*. Maybe Booth's snow-covered forest could be in the vicinity of Dunsinane? Booth shows us a forest denuded of trees; a white carpet of snow is littered with fallen boughs while snowflakes fall and instil in the picture a peacefulness, a sense of solitude and the hibernation of nature. In other works turbulent seas crash onto deserted beaches, and snow storms move across fields knocking down fences and trees in their way. It is the destructive power of

PETER BOOTH (b. 1940)
Winter, 1993
Oil on canvas, 203 x 396 cm
Photograph courtesy of
Deutscher Fine Art

nature—not people. The climate changes affect Booth. It is reflected in his choice of colour and often determines his technique as he explains:

> I like to work in the snow and the rain. I use the rain physically—let it hit the paper and diffuse the ink over waterproof casein paint ... Sometimes the pictures are very still, or they're agitated: it depends on the weather.[7]

Many of the ideas for his pictures come to Booth in the forms of dreams, from episodes in his life, stories and novels. The ideas are then consolidated in the form of rough sketches, drawings and paintings.

Booth's painterly technique maintains its power in these works. Applying oil paint thickly and in a way that makes the paint appear almost edible, Booth is able to build up his paint surface, incredibly richly empowering both the paint and his images accordingly.

Sculpture

Sculpture during the past decade has had a well-awaited boost in popularity and support. An increased interest from the corporate world has seen many companies commission artists to make large sculptures to adorn the foyers and plazas of their buildings, local parklands and gardens. This rather lucrative practice has increased the amount of work for artists as well as enhancing an often harsh and brutal inner city landscape. Multimedia, grunge or junk art, conceptual-based works and installation art became popular in the 1990s. A resurgence of skills-based learning in many art schools has seen the emergence and production of many pieces of sculpture ground in both technique and concept. This was a turn in direction from the mid-1970s and 1980s where the technique suffered at the hands of the idea or concept. Installation-based works became popular forms of expression, particularly when in 1991 it became the theme of the Art Gallery of New South Wales's biennial Perspecta exhibition, the Fifth Sculpture Triennial in Melbourne in 1993, and the Visual arts component of the 1994 Adelaide Festival.

When **Hossein Valamanesh (b. 1949)** migrated to Adelaide from Iran in 1973 he brought with him a rich suitcase of Middle-Eastern culture, which has influenced his painting, drawing, sculpture and installation. Valamanesh prefers to work across all the disciplines. He feels that different messages or intentions require a range of treatments; some drawing, some painting and some installation. As is the case with many immigrants, the sense of dislocation and feelings of isolation are strong; these feelings have been explored in his work. Coming from the Middle East he is familiar with the desert landscape, and since arriving in Australia he has managed to explore some of the desert areas of Australia, visiting many Aboriginal communities as he goes. The desert is reminiscent of his own childhood experiences of living in Iran.

One of Valamanesh's most important pieces of public sculpture is in Adelaide. Valamanesh describes it as his most successful piece to date. The name of the work *Knocking from the Inside*, 1989, is actually a verse taken from a thirteenth century Persian poem of the same name written by Jalâl al-Din Rumi (1207-73). A part of the

---

[7] Zimmer, Jenny, 'Weather helps to paint his pictures', *Sunday Herald*, 15 April, 1990.

poem is inscribed on the polished surface of one of the boulders that makes up the work:

I have lived on the lip of insanity
wanting to know reasons
knocking on a door it opens
I've been knocking from the inside.

Based on the grid shape, the work is an environment that you walk through, with different elements placed at all corners of the space. At one end Valamanesh's silhouette appears to have smashed through a doorway, while opposite his cut-out form, split in two, stands on the top of some steps overlooking the site. He has used this human silhouette form in his painting, drawing and sculpture since 1986. This piece is a highly spiritual work, which creates a story suspended in both the Australian and his native Iranian cultures.

HOSSEIN VALAMANESH
(b. 1949)
Knocking from the Inside
(detail), 1989
Sandstone, bluestone, granite, bricks, ceramic tiles, jarrah

The ASER Collection, Adelaide

Photographer: Donald Williams

Tom Risley (b. 1947), a resident of Herberton (outside Cairns) in far north Queensland, has established a practice of making art from discarded and found objects. Much of his art is made up of objects he has found around his home, including bits of driftwood, painted wood, metal, plastic, fabric and panels from cars. Even the common Australian thong has featured in some early works.

Risley did not undergo any formal training as an artist. He was initially an electrician, which he recalls as being important to the development of his art. His work is not mainstream or consistent with trends in national or international art. In the early 1990s he made a series of chairs from collected pieces of driftwood—silky oak, blackbean, walnut and white beech. These objects question the often fine line that can exist between sculpture and furniture or craft, explored by other artists and crafts practitioners such as Gay Hawkes and designer Marc Newson.

In *Still Life with Vases*, 1991–92, Risley makes a play on the subject matter of the traditional still life painting. This sculpture—or is it a painting?—is constructed from found materials. Their elegant shapes clearly resemble vases and make for a formal and harmonious composition. It is the forms and nature of these shapes that interest Risley.

TOM RISLEY (b. 1947)
Still Life with Vases, 1991–92
Caulking compound and found objects (driftwood and polystyrene fishing float),
388 x 182 x 37 cm

Private collection
Courtesy of Ray Hughes Gallery

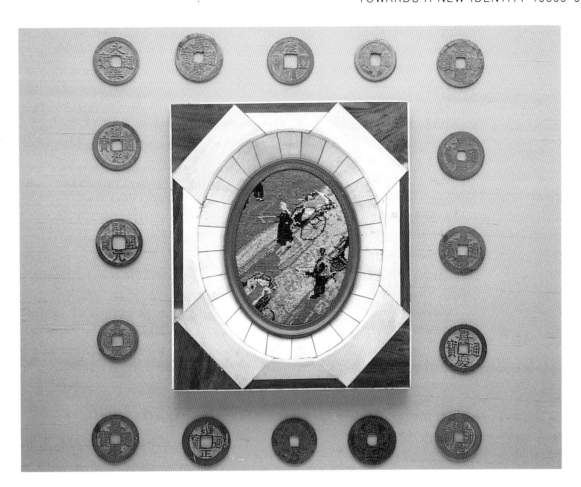

NARELLE JUBELIN (b. 1960)
Legacies of Travel and Trade
(detail), 1990
Renditions of Hedda Morrison
photographs in cotton petit
point; found frames of
ivory, semi-synthetic ivory and
synthetic tortoiseshell and
wood; Chinese bronze 'cash'
coins (museum objects); pair
of Chinese silk petit-point
purses, eyeglass case and fan
case (museum objects);
Chinese ivory cigarette holders
(museum objects); 996 x
590 cm; detail here shows a
rendition of Hedda Morrison's
photograph 'Looking for a
passenger' taken in Peking in
the 1930s, surrounded by
Chinese 'cash' coins

Powerhouse Museum, Sydney

The issue of colonisation evident in the work of Gordon Bennett and Ian W. Abdulla is also one explored in the installation *Legacies of Travel and Trade*, 1990, by Sydney artist **Narelle Jubelin (b. 1960)**. Jubelin works in petit point, a form of intricate needlecraft stitch traditionally carried out by women. She has been using this technique in a range of works since 1984. In this piece Jubelin attempts to redress the imbalance and snobbery that exists between what is viewed as art and craft, and particularly the value given to these examples of craft. These beautiful works are combined with a selection of found objects and items, including icons from other cultures, coins or souvenirs purchased at exotic locations. Many of the other materials Jubelin uses, such as the wooden frames that hold her petit point, are purchased from second-hand shops or collected from discarded rubbish bins and tips.

In the installation *Legacies of Travel and Trade* four petit point works are placed in ivory frames inside an Oriental-style black museum showcase surrounded with coins, ivory, cigarette holders and a selection of embroidered objects. In the detail shown Jubelin draws on a photograph taken by an Australian photographer, Hedda Morrison, who worked in China from 1933 to just after World War II in 1946. It is also significant that Jubelin chooses to use the work of a woman photographer, who in those days before World War II must have been highly individual and brave to have visited such an exotic destination. The image is taken from above and shows women walking with rickshaws along a Peking street. The coins placed around the frames are Chinese and were found on the goldfields in Queensland, but they also relate to the form of the grid as explored in contemporary art. Jubelin also makes the point that they relate to the practice of trade, exchange, history and links between two diverse cultures. They also question how artists and museum collection policies can be selective or biased and can often affect the way we interpret and see history. Consider how few examples there are, in public and private collections, showing the Chinese presence in Australia during the gold rush.

Another significant artist to migrate from his birthplace of Japan to Perth in 1974 was **Akio Makigawa (b. 1948)**. Makigawa's marble sculptures are the complete antipathy of Risley's raw objects. Makigawa's stern and rigid marble forms are highly finished, formal and refined.

Makigawa's interest in coming to Perth was motivated by a desire to study sail making. Once mastering this task he decided to enrol at the Claremont School of Art where he studied painting and later sculpture. His initial exploration into sculpture found him producing installations and later making more permanent objects from metal, wood and fabric—things relating to his study into sails. The mid-1980s found Makigawa turn to working with large pieces of beautifully coloured imported marble from Carrara, Italy.

Makigawa has made many pieces of sculpture for public places, including outside the Hyatt Hotel in North Terrace, Adelaide; Norwich House in St Kilda Road, Melbourne; in front of the Art Gallery of Western Australia; Australian Embassy, Tokyo; foyer of Chifley Square building, Sydney; and various other locations throughout Australia. The large works take Makigawa many months to produce. He

AKIO MAKIGAWA (b. 1948)
Night Sea Crossing, 1992
Chifley Square commission
White Carrara marble,
stainless steel
Main piece: 3.225 x 2 m;
fish 1.5 x 2.6 m;
flower: 1.2 x 3 m

Photograph courtesy of
Sherman Galleries, Sydney
Photographer: Eric Sierens

works tirelessly to carefully finish the surface of the marble, instilling in it a certain preciousness, a seemingly fragile quality prevalent in many elements of Japanese craft. The balance, harmony, serenity and order inherent in Makigawa's work comes through in *Night Sea Crossing*, 1992. The main form is roughly carved and incised, the markings become less frequent and at its top it is highly polished. Interestingly, Makigawa maintains that his early training as a gymnast and knowledge of sailing has helped to shape his development as a sculptor:

> Gymnastics taught me balance, poise, form, harmony, tension and gravity. Sailing taught me force lines, too, because you are defying gravity against nature, the force of the wind, and nature always wins …

> I use symbols that are not East or West but universal—the moon, clouds, flames, buds, pods, shells, spirals, symbols of death, birth, regrowth journeys, shelters.[8]

Bronwyn Oliver (b. 1959) was the first sculptor to win the Moët & Chandon Australian art fellowship (until 1994 it was exclusively a painting prize). Her sculpture made from recycled copper wire, copper and cast metals seems to explore organic shaped forms. Her technique is precise and involves binding, spiralling, stretching, wrapping and embalming. The objects look antique partly because of their foreign forms and because of the aged patina (the oxidisation) they display. Oliver actually mixes up a solution that accelerates the oxidisation process, which gives the works yet another dimension.

Oliver's objects resemble natural objects, nests, shells, cocoons, birth passages and other organic form. Curiously Oliver maintains her work is not based on natural forms:

> I am particularly interested in objects found outside their normal context, for examples objects in museums, debris washed up on the beach, scrap yard junk etc. Objects found out of context pose the questions—Where did they come from? Were they part of something else? What was their role/their former life? What kind of forces have they been subject to since then? These are the kind of questions I hope people might ask of my sculptures.[9]

Many artists are not exclusively painters or photographers or sculptors. Many choose to work across all disciplines, finding that some media suit a theme or subject more appropriately than others. **Fiona Hall (b. 1953)** is a case in point. Hall often merges one discipline with another, as seen where she combines elements of sculpture with photography. Hall is possibly better known as a photographer than a sculptor. Recently she has been making small pictures from aluminium drink cans and sardine cans. The series called *Paradisus Terrestris* was created between 1989 and 1990. The subject is the Garden of Eden and Hall shows us a collection of plants juxtaposed with the human form engaging in acts of sexual passion and exploration. The religious connotation to the Garden is quite prevalent: it was the beautiful landscape, a paradise where man and woman coexisted with plants until temptation reared its head.

In *Grapefruit* (*Citrus paradisi*) Hall produces a botanically correct example of a grapefruit tree. Beneath this, inside the sardine can the key unfolds the form of a

BRONWYN OLIVER (b. 1959)
Eddy, 1994
Copper, 190 x 40 x 40 cm
Collection of Moët & Chandon

[8] Hawley, Janet, 'Shape of the New', in 'Good Weekend', *Age*, Melbourne, 12 June, 1993, p. 22.

[9] The Third Dimension—Sculptures, Assemblages and Installations, Post 1960, The Women's Art Register Inc., Melbourne, 1992, p. 30.

FIONA HALL (b. 1953)
Citrus paradisi
Twenty-three sculptures from the series, aluminium and tin, 24.5 x 11.0 x 1.5 cm each
Collection of the artist

woman's breasts being held as if they were grapefruit, in many ways an appropriate corresponding human form. The intricately modelled hands are holding the breasts as one might hold and sample the fruits in a market or fruit shop. These mundane cans are constructed with delicacy and skill and adopt an almost jewel-like precious quality. Hall has become so proficient at modelling the cans that she has even made a tiara for an artist friend of hers from used aluminium drink cans.

While Bronwyn Oliver makes objects from copper, **Jennifer Turpin (b. 1968)** constructs environments from water and copper piping—she combines the trade of a plumber with the aesthetic sensibilities of an artist. The series of environments are called *Water Works,* 1993. One of nature's elements, water, can be calming and soothing, or violent and destructive. Its corrosive power and force can wipe out towns, while to be deprived of it can be life threatening. Many people think the sound of rushing water has meditative and peaceful qualities; the roar of a waterfall can also be frightening and deafening.

Turpin constructs her installations from copper pipes, which in themselves become sculptural forms. The water is channelled through this elaborate construction. Most of the installations relate to the landscape, whether it be the rainforest or a running creek. They are usually placed inside a gallery, and the lights are turned down and directed onto the dripping water. The combination of light, the sound of the dripping water and the water itself creates a level of humidity, a closeness and intimacy. For many people experiencing the *Water Works* can be peaceful and meditative; for others it may evoke another range of emotions. All the senses are involved—the eyes to catch the light hitting the water, our ears to hear the trickling and echo, and our sense of touch to feel its humidity.

The idea for *Water Works* series derived from a chronic leaking roof Turpin encountered in a house where she was living:

> We had dozens of buckets around the place to catch the drips and it was driving us both crazy.
> It suddenly occurred to us that if we attached cotton to the holes then that would give the water something to drip down, and so we had this spider's web of cotton strings …[10]

---

[10] Baker, Candida, 'Artist hitching water to the cultural stream', *Age*, Melbourne, 24 August 1992.

JENNIFER TURPIN (b. 1968)
Water Works V, 1993
Water, nylon threads, copper pipes and tanks, 6 units, each
4.5 m high x 3 m x 200 mm

Situated in the National Gallery of Victoria, Melbourne
Photograph courtesy of Annandale Galleries and the artist

HILARIE MAIS (b. 1952)
Untitled No. 3, 1993
Oil paint on timber,
60 x 60 x 6 cm

Photograph courtesy of
Sherman Galleries and the
artist, Sydney

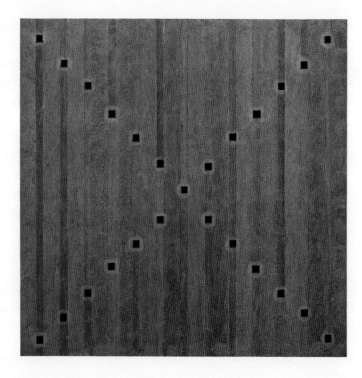

Hilarie Mais (b. 1952) may be known to many for her large, flat, grid-like pieces of sculpture. Placed against walls and sometimes on walls, at first glance these large works run the risk of also being viewed as paintings. These formal flat coloured constructions—in brilliant blue, red, white and grey—are based on the format of the grid that has dominated her work since the early 1980s. The grid design is not new and has reference to classical times and particularly to the disciplines of mathematics, architecture and classical garden design.

In this series of works Mais reduces the scale, and we are confronted with a square made up of an array of joined vertical slats of wood. The surface is punctuated with cut-out squares in the form of a cross. This play of surface tends to produce an illusionistic quality in a seemingly static work. The wood has been delicately coloured, yet maintains its true character and warm nature. (See also the interview in Chapter Thirteen.)

Civil architecture

> We like to think we are dealing with fundamental issues and basic concepts of architecture such as mass, form, space, colour and textures, whilst recognising the social, political and economic values of our times.[11]

Philip Cox—Architect

Currently in Australia there is no predominant architectural style as such. Certainly there is no equivalent of a movement such as the International Style seen during the 1950s and 1960s. Today there are hybrids, eclectic and idiosyncratic styles, most of which derive from both classical and modern designs. One could actually say that the

[11] Australian Architects, Philip Cox, Richardson, Taylor and Partners, Royal Australian Institute of Architects, Canberra, 1988. n.p.

style now is a form of Post-Modernism; however, even this may be too categorical. Post-modernist architecture came into being in the mid-1980s and is partly credited to American architects, such as Robert Venturi and Michael Graves, who looked back to ancient Egypt, classical Greece and renaissance Italy to seek and formulate their ideas and designs. Using a combination of traditional materials and new concepts, these contemporary architects produced some extraordinarily bold buildings, the influence of which has found its way to Australia.

The practice of tearing down old buildings to make way for modern constructions, so common during the past three decades, has appeared to have waned, partly due to ailing economic conditions, environmentally conscious town planning departments and, of course, the rise of diligent heritage consultants. Many architects and corporations have reconsidered their roles in the community and are more sensitive to how their buildings are viewed by the public. The rise of a heritage-conscious public forced many developers and architects to reconsider their former practice of pulling down older, sometimes historically and architecturally significant, buildings. The clever way around this was to produce an amalgam of a pre-existing facade and reconstruct the interior, or incorporate the smaller building as the foreground and back it with a skyscraper. The glass and aluminium curtain wall design was beginning to give way to a stone facade, which produced designs much more sympathetic to the surrounding street level environment. The solving of this problem has seen some imaginative contemporary designs from reworking many old styles and ideas.

Throughout Australian cities there are now many styles being produced by a range of younger architects who find themselves much more inventive in their mode of operating and designing buildings. Computer aided design (CAD) has become one of the more popular ways to design buildings. Today, most architectural firms would use the computer at some stage to assist in the design and construction of their buildings. Many architects are quick to claim that the computer does not replace the architect's vision and sensitivity to our basic human needs. Glen Murcutt (Chapter Eleven) has been critical of the use of computers in architectural practice. He feels that, among other issues, buildings designed by computers have no basis in fundamental design principles and that CAD will serve inevitably to create a sterile city driven not by design but economics. Of course, in terms of economics the computer cannot be challenged. It can draw designs and work out specifications, cutting down the architect's and engineer's time, and therefore costing the client much less.

Like the previous three decades, the skylines of most Australian cities were to be dominated by the ubiquitous cranes, which perched on top of the towering cityscapes like some form of prehistoric bird life. The desire by multinational corporations such as banks, mining companies and insurance firms to flex their corporate muscles through the building of towers has changed considerably. Project buildings designed by groups of architects have become one of the more popular ways to build office towers. Many buildings have lost their corporate identities. Such names as BP House, BHP House, Qantas House and AMP House have given way to more site-specific names such as The Rialto (Melbourne), Melbourne Central, Grosvenor Place (Sydney), Riverside Tower (Brisbane) and QV 1 (Perth).

The building 101 Collins Street is on the site where the Comalco House skyscraper once stood. Denton Corker Marshall designed 101 Collins to be sympathetic to the

DENTON CORKER MARSHALL
101 Collins Street, 1989
Photographer: Jon Rendell

surrounding buildings and environment—predominantly 'Victorian' in style. While the first five storeys reflect the streetscape, the subsequent construction of forty-five storeys is set back and is consistent with the line of the city's other towers. The symmetrical crucifix-like form of the floor plan echoes the exterior of the building as seen in the boxed glass projections, which are placed centrally on all four sides of the building. When floodlit at night the building is not unlike the nocturnal view of New York's Empire State building.

The facade of 101 Collins Street is clad with granite and this makes it the tallest single-tower granite-clad building in Australia. The building is topped with a telecommunications tower, which also shoots out a beam of light into the night sky. The disengaged Doric columns, and the use of black granite on the facade and in the foyer, were designed by prominent American architects Philip Johnson – John Burgee of New York. This is a fine example of Australian post-modern design.

Sport has always featured prominently in Australia's cultural make-up. The 1980s saw the construction of some huge and magnificent sporting facilities throughout Australia, two examples being the Sydney Football Stadium in Moore Park, Sydney, and the Great Southern Stand, which is the southern extension to the Melbourne Cricket Ground. The Great Southern Stand sits with Flemington Race Track and the Tennis Centre (Philip Cox) as an integral part of Melbourne's make-up.

Designed by Tompkins Shaw & Evans / Daryl Jackson Architects, the Great Southern Stand is a shrine to both cricket and football. It dominates the eastern perimeter of Melbourne's city skyline. One of the world's greatest stadiums, it has won an array of architectural awards. Commenced after the 1990 football season, it was completed in eighteen months for the 1992 World Series Cricket match. As well as holding more than 50 000 spectators, it manages to circulate people extremely well. Designed with large corridors, ramp footways and an abundance of exits, it permits speedy arrivals and departures.

The Great Southern Stand is 324 metres in length and seven levels in height. The shape is circular and simple—the design reminiscent of the ancient Greek amphitheatres, the Roman Colosseum and gladiators in battle. Seen from many locations around inner Melbourne, it is essentially a huge concrete drum. The stairs and porthole windows punctuate the sides to break up the rather abrupt exterior surface. The use and colour of the concrete recall Melbourne's use of bluestone as its traditional building material. The steel supports, which hug and hold the roof, give the illusion of lightness to contrast with its weighty base. Inside the stadium, every seat allows for perfect uninterrupted viewing, which was achieved through extensive mathematical equations and many computer hours of information analysis. The architects were concerned that traditionally stadiums have been designed with only the inside view in mind, with the outside being neglected and treated purely as a practical entrance. In this instance, the architects wanted to avoid the sense of coming in from the back.

DARYL JACKSON
The Great Southern Stand, Melbourne Cricket Ground, 1992

Photographer: Jon Rendell

At first glance one may be forgiven for thinking that the Sydney Football Stadium is a roller-coaster ride at a fun park. The stadium's cantilevered roof sweeps up, down and around, and its light airy appearance contrasts markedly with the more static and weighty nature of Melbourne's Great Southern Stand. Holding 40 000 spectators, it was designed by Philip Cox (b. 1939), the architect of Melbourne's Tennis Centre, Yulara Resort at Uluru (Ayers Rock) and Darling Harbour in Sydney to mention a few.

The Sydney Football Stadium is a dynamic building. The design of the steel-frame stadium is generous and shows us its skeleton. Cox calls it the 'bare bones' philosophy of building where the design inspires, delights and informs. Speaking about his work Cox claims:

> They [the buildings] are light, skeletal forms. They have more to do with the Australian windmill or a water tank stand than with 'international high style' imagery. They are buildings which pay homage to the landscape in which they are placed.[12]

The circular form of the stadium surrounds the rectangular football ground required for Rugby. The exciting and fast nature of the game is reflected in the fabric and mood of the stadium. Solid concrete bands contrast with steel masts and cables, which are pulled tight and are almost stressful in mood. The playing field was designed to sit 10 metres below the road level, reducing the required height and cost of the stands.

As a piece of contemporary architecture it is something of a contradiction— Sydney's Chifley Tower looks like something you would have seen built in Manhattan or Chicago in the 1930s, particularly in its use of colour and semicircular form. Designed by Kohn Pedersen Fox / Travis Partners, it was completed early in 1993 and stands as Sydney's second tallest commercial tower. On the edge of the city near Circular Quay, it is an all-steel construction. This is a rarity these days—usually concrete is the most popular material. Each side of the building incorporates a range of different facades. A curved glass wall overlooks the Botanical Gardens, while the

---

[12] Australian Architects, Philip Cox, Richardson, Taylor and Partners, Royal Australian Institute of Architects, Canberra, 1988. n.p.

PHILIP COX
Sydney Football Stadium, 1988
Photographer: Donald Williams

KOHN PEDERSEN
FOX/TRAVIS PARTNERS

Chifley Tower, Sydney,
1992–93

Photographer: Donald Williams

others are faced with stone with varying size windows and look over the harbour. As a way of breaking up the form of the facades, the architects have designed boxes that jut out from the building's surfaces. The tower is topped with what appears to be a three-storey green glass penthouse, but it is actually 'state of the art' microwave communications equipment.

One of the most exciting smaller public buildings to come out of the past decade has been the Tropical Conservatory in Adelaide's Botanical Gardens. An Australian Bicentennial initiative, it won the Sir Zelman Cowen award for (public) architecture.

RAFFEN MARON
ARCHITECTS

Adelaide Botanical Gardens
Tropical Conservatory,
1986–89

Designed by Raffen Maron Architects of Adelaide, it is reminiscent of Joseph Paxton's (1803–65) Crystal Palace exhibition centre in England that was destroyed by fire a century ago. Basically a glass and polished concrete tent or pyramid form and standing approximately ten storeys high, it both preserves and displays the garden's collection of tropical plants and trees.

Domestic architecture

While the suburbs have kept spreading further and further into the country there has simultaneously been a return to the inner cities. Architects and developers worked in tandem to transform old city warehouses and disused corporate buildings into warehouse-studio living spaces and apartments. Particularly around inner Sydney and Melbourne, medium-density housing in the form of the modern townhouse—a rehash of the Victorian terrace—has been developed in locations that were previously factory or light industrial areas. This practice was in part a way of enticing people from the suburbs back into the cities, which after 6 pm had run the risk of becoming wilderness areas.

In many suburban areas local governments have attempted to improve the quality of people's lives by focusing more on the community. Money was injected into local government projects, and architects and designers were employed to produce stimulating and interesting designs for schools, parks, health centres, sporting centres, libraries, arts centres and even public toilets. In outer Melbourne's Box Hill, architects **Greg Burgess & Associates** designed a local community art centre, which now caters to all the local residents and contributes some exciting architecture to an area known historically for its association with the Heidelberg School *plein air* painters a century earlier.

Inner city houses, South Melbourne, 1992–93

Photographer: Donald Williams

GREG BURGESS &
ASSOCIATES

*Box Hill Community Arts
Centre, 1990*

Photographer: Donald Williams

The Box Hill Community Arts Centre is similar in spirit to Burgess' Brambuck
Living Centre in The Grampians in western Victoria. It is a sort of organic, somewhat
whimsical, building designed in consultation with local crafts practitioners and
residents who expressed their individual desires and needs. The building is basically
constructed from a range of materials including bricks, wood, steel and ceramic tiles.
Many of the building's fittings were designed by members of the local community:
Technical and Further Education (TAFE) students, schoolchildren and local artists. The
building is highly expressive and reminiscent of the work of Spanish architect
Antonio Gaudi; however, this work combines elements of Australian corrugated iron
and steel, and is low energy in its design. It stands as an important community
meeting centre and cultural link for all members of Box Hill and its immediate
environs. The building is adorned with Australian native plants and creepers, and
even the steel grates set in the pathways are specifically designed to blend with the
mood and appearance of the building.

The beach has always been a popular holiday location for many families over the
long summer school holidays, and it is an important social meeting place. Melbourne
architect **Nonda Katsalidis** has designed a beach house that clearly breaks away from
the fibro-cement dwelling set among tea-tree tradition, so common in our
architectural history.

The St. Andrews house is highly geometric and is positioned on the landscape like
a shipping container dropped on the wharf. It makes little attempt to blend in an
unobtrusive way but stands defiant as it confronts the elements of nature: the wind,
the sea and the sun. The use of wood and iron are components that are traditionally
associated with boat and ship construction and in this context are appropriate
materials for a beach house. As well as performing an important obvious practical

NONDA KATSALIDIS
Beach House, St Andrews,
1992

Photographer: John Gollings

function, the large windows add a lightness to the structure and help to bring the exterior surrounding landscape into the house. The timber planks were inspired from the colours and textures found on the wharves situated along the Murray River. Iron and steel cap the upper area of the house and glass walls run along the ground storey. The iron has been left to rust, its colour adding a warmth to the building. As can be seen in the photograph, the house is austere in its lack of decoration and detail.

The development of low energy eco-design (ecologically conscious) housing has become increasingly important. Many architects designing houses for clients are emphasising this aspect of design. Also in the northern areas of Australia we can find some of the light and environmentally friendly tent-like constructions of **Gabriel Poole**.

In stark contrast to the weighty construction of the St Andrews Beach House, Poole's houses are the opposite. They are light in construction and are often set up high among hillside bush settings. A form of kit home, its structure is from galvanised tubular steel that is bolted together, appropriate for constructing in rough and hilly terrain. Canopies cover the verandahs and add a lightness and sensitivity to the surrounding environment. There is no desire to disguise or camouflage the dwelling and, as Poole himself claims, the house sits in the bush like a large butterfly or parrot. Known for his ecologically respectful dwellings he feels that his buildings should:

> … give visual pleasure to those who see them and spiritual pleasure to those who dwell in them.[13]

---

[13] Poole, Gabriel, 'Places for Souls to Play', *Artlink*, vol. 11. no. 4, Summer, 1991/92, p. 36.

GABRIEL POOLE
Tent House, 1991
Sunshine Coast, Queensland
Photograph courtesy of
Gabriel Poole

ACTIVITIES

1. Compare the treatment of Aboriginal issues by Judy Watson, Gordon Bennett and Ian Abdulla.

2. What do you think Maria Kozic is saying about the perception of women? How does this compare with Vicki Varvaressos's work of more than a decade earlier? Discuss.

3. Compare William Robinson's treatment of the Australian landscape with that of an artist from the 1940s and one from the 1880s. If possible, compare the following: technique, aims, objectives and appearance.

4. Discuss the effect that computer and other technology has had on the way you and your friends relate to the world.

5. Compare the work of Jenny Watson (Chapter Eleven) with Howard Arkley's picture. Make an artwork of your home.

6. Write a brief essay on the impact that migration has had on Australia's identity. Look specifically at art and culture, discussing specific works of art.

7. Compare the mood and composition of the sculpture made by Akio Makigawa with the painting of Paul Boston.

8. Consider what kind of music you could pair up with Sansom's *Arthritis*. Would it be the same kind of music as you would pair with a work by Richard Dunn or Paul Boston? Explain.

9. Reread the quote made by Philip Cox at the start of the section titled 'Civil architecture'. What does he feel is the role of the contemporary architect? What is your opinion?

10. How do environmental, climatic and geographical conditions influence the styles of Australian architecture?

11. Consider ways you could make your home and life more ecologically sound. Why might these issues be important?

CHAPTER THIRTEEN

Twelve Artists Speak

Introduction

Art in the 1980s and 1990s is incredibly diverse. Artists are responding to their environments and lives in different ways. In this chapter twelve artists have been selected, largely for the different media in which they work, as well as for the different approach they have to their art. These artists clearly demonstrate their dedication to their profession as well as the need to respond to issues that concern them.

The painter Vicki Varvaressos lives and works in Sydney. She studied painting at the National Art School in Sydney and in 1975 held her first solo exhibition. A regular exhibitor of work, her painting is confident, expressionistic and visually exciting. These excerpts from a review in the *Australian*, 29 May 1982, describe her work:

> Varvaressos puts some guts and expressionistic flicks of pink and purple slashes into a group of paintings ...
> ... the canvases are charged with intensity, purpose and energy.

Susan Norrie has been painting for more than a decade and recently came to the attention of the public when she won the Moët et Chandon painting scholarship in 1987. This award comprised a grant and accommodation in France for a year. Norrie exhibits regularly in Australia and overseas.

The sculptors Anthony Pryor and Augustine Dall'Ava shared a studio together in Melbourne, but despite their close working relationship and friendship their art is completely different. At present, Pryor's work is large and dominating, and combines stone, wood and metal. Dall'Ava's sculptures are mainly produced in wood, and of late have been concerned with incorporating natural materials to produce sensitive and highly crafted constructions. His recent sculptures are impeccably finished, balanced and have a magical, mysterious quality to them.

Clive Murray-White has long had a respected reputation in Australia. Primarily an abstract sculptor working in steel, his sculptures often carry humorous messages as discussed in the interview. Clive currently lives and works in Gippsland, Victoria.

For Lyn Moore the experience of carving and working in large chunks of wood is most satisfactory. Using chainsaws, among other tools, Moore produced totem pole-like sculptures. Moore has been exhibiting regularly since 1981 and has work in collections throughout Australia. She lives and works in Canberra.

Architecture of the 1980s is represented by Norman Day and Wood Marsh & Associates Pty Ltd, Melbourne. Day has contributed an article in which he discusses the work of Biltmoderne, Daryl Jackson, and his own building in Melton, Victoria. Day has been a practising architect for more than a decade and in this period has received many awards, including the Robin Boyd Award for his Northcote House (see Chapter Eleven). As well as lecturing in architecture, he has written for the *Australian*, the *Age*, the *Sydney Morning Herald* and ABC television.

Architects Roger Wood and Randal Marsh have formed a company which has designed some exciting and unusual buildings, including Melbourne's Metro Nightclub. They had enough faith in themselves to start their own company rather than work as 'apprentices' under other architects. Wood Marsh & Associates Pty Ltd is a successful and thriving architecture firm located in Melbourne, Victoria.

Sydney sculptor Hilarie Mais is known particularly for her coloured, wooden, flat grid sculptures. These grids, often attached or resting on a wall, have references in classical art, architecture and mathematics but also make us consider the boundaries between sculpture and painting. The realist artist James Gleeson has been painting for more than fifty years and is the only long-standing Australian surrealist painter. His large, meticulous and intriguing paintings are almost 'cinematic' in their fantastic subject matter and are traditional in their execution. Peter Atkins travels extensively and documents each journey by making drawings and paintings. They are reflections of different cultures and personal experiences, and involve a range of media including oil painting, collage and assemblage. Angela Brennan is also known predominantly for her large-scale highly colourful abstract pictures. Her art is spontaneous and lively, and in part explores colour and form.

Vicki Varvaressos (b. 1949)

Painter Studied at National Art School, Sydney.

Q. When did you become interested in becoming a painter?

A. Not sure, When I think back, I realise how lucky I was that I ended up in my profession. One is so young when faced with having to decide what to do—it all seems so nebulous in retrospect.

   I had always enjoyed painting at school but it never occurred to me (and no one ever suggested it) to become a painter. However, in my final year, my art teacher did say something about a fine arts course starting at Sydney University. I was not sure what this was—'just something to do with art'. Fortunately, I did not get in, although didn't think this at the time. So then I did not know what to do. I loved painting but I did not think one could just go and do it—I never knew an artist! Eventually I entered art school.

Q. Who were your favourite artists while at school?

A. I should say first of all that I never saw a work by an Australian artist while at school. Hopefully things have changed!

I remember coming across the Die Brucke and Blue Reiter group and finding them exciting, probably because of their brushwork and colour. I definitely remember not liking people like Mondrian—I just couldn't see why anyone thought he was good. Naturally I was not seeing it in the context of art history—more like a rather boring bathroom floor.

VICKI VARVARESSOS
(b.1949)

Easy-going Hostess 1979
Polymer paint on canvas,
152 x 122 cm

Reproduced by courtesy of the
artist and Watters Gallery

Q. What has your work been concerned with?

A. In my early work I was concerned with media images of women. There are several issues here:

1. In some cases these are what the image makers actually perceive of women.
2. They just reinforce stereotypes and prejudices.
3. Of particular interest to me is how these images and myths affect the female psyche. The bombardment of images playing on fears of inadequacy, stressing youth, beauty, etc., vague references to mystery and allure—always stressing appearance. This is the industry in which one can actually find products on the market like the sort of putty substance that you can rub into your wrinkles and look younger for a few hours! Not to mention more extreme measures like plastic surgery for face lift, bottom lift, etc.

My paintings have always reflected my interests so naturally this is where I get some 'ideas' from. In the early 1970s I was involved in the green ban/resident action movement. There are some early paintings that reflect this. Also I was greatly concerned with the upheavals in 1975, particularly our 'bloodless coup', euphemistically called our 'constitutional crisis'. So political images have also been in my work from time to time.

More recently I have been interested in 'social situations', social behaviour, the nuances which we relate with one another.

Q. What is your work routine? Can you survive from selling your work?

A. I paint daily, on weekdays. I have a policy of not painting on weekends. I think it's important to have time for other things. I think from now on I may be able to survive from my work but the past ten years or so I have needed to teach part-time.

Q. What advice would you give to a student who wanted to become an artist?

A. In the long term, you have to really love it. This may not seem obvious at first. Being an artist is like being a writer—it is an isolated activity! For most students, the first hurdle is when you finish art school and suddenly you are on your own. My advice is not to go into teaching—at least not full-time. It is at this stage that you must continue to paint. Also, do not expect to make money—very few artists ever survive on their work alone! However the rewards are great and it's an interest that can sustain you all your life. I love painting and know that I'm fortunate that I can spend my time doing it.

Q. Where did you get the idea for *Easy-going Hostess*?

A. I found the image of the woman in a magazine. At the time I was concerned with media images of women. Then in another magazine I saw the phrase 'Easy-going Hostess' and I thought 'YUK'—this will go ideally with the image. The title, which I have used in a satirical way, also refers to one of the accepted roles that women are given. Women can spend their lives being hostesses—in subtle ways this is a continuing of the role of seeing that things 'flow smoothly', not just social situations but being the emotional supports of their own families.

Susan Norrie (b. 1953)

Painter   Studied at National Art School, Sydney, and Victorian College of the Arts

Q. What have been the themes and subjects of your paintings?

A. The 'domestic' has always been really important to me in my work, mainly because as a female artist it seemed to be an important zone that I could relate to. By 'domestic' I mean that which is different to the academic painting that lingered on in Australian art history painting until the 1940s. Certain genres were emphasised then as 'correct', subjects such as landscape and historical narrative. I have always found it curious that it was largely women artists who introduced aspects of Modernism to Australia. Artists such as Thea Proctor, Margaret Preston, Grace Cossington Smith in the 1930s, introduced themes to art such as the personal or anecdotal; the still life, the decorative; and there was interest in cross-cultural influences such as Aboriginal art. My earlier 'landscape' works tended to play these two domains off each other as an ironic device—the 'masculinist' landscape against 'domestic' histories.

So in many ways it is the idea of history that is important to me—whether this be personal history, art history or contemporary events. As an Australian artist, however, I am concerned not just with our cultural heritage, but more importantly, with problems of colonialism—continued cultural and economic dependency on Europe and America. You could say that my work is an attempt to define and describe these general problems in a particular, perhaps idiosyncratic, way.

Q. You have travelled, worked and exhibited overseas on a number of occasions. Does this affect your work?

Q. Being out of the country gives one the opportunity to look back at Australia and deal with where one comes from. You sometimes learn more about yourself than the country you are staying in. My work has matured enormously from this process. There is a difference between being a tourist and actually engaging in the contemporary art scene in various countries. These experiences provide you with a breadth of information and ideas.

Q. What about living overseas?

A. Recently I lived and worked in both France and Italy. Being a painter I was able to experience directly the development of painting in the twentieth century, particularly the impact of Orientalism in Europe. It was interesting seeing how the European artists dealt with that type of exotica. I found it most valuable being in Europe which is responsible for a particular painting history, and one that has

SUSAN NORRIE (b. 1953)
Les romans de cape et d'epee
(A swash-buckling romance),
1987
Oil, enamel on canvas,
239 x 189.5 cm

Collection: National Gallery of
Australia, Canberra

been a part of my development, being educated in the Western world. In particular I was interested in the very important art movements at the turn of the century—Cubism, Surrealism, etc. I think the reproduction of my painting, *Les romans de cape et d'epee* illustrates this.

Q. When was your first painting exhibition?

A. My first show was at the Mori Gallery, Sydney, in 1979. I have been painting for thirteen or fourteen years now and it is still difficult exhibiting. In fact I think it becomes harder and more challenging as the expectation becomes more consistently demanding. There are certain responsibilities. One has to create a balance where you have to retain the integrity in your work and also be aware of what is happening in the art scene internationally.

Q. How do you cope with reviews of your work?

A. Of course one worries about critics. It would be dishonest to say that artists don't. I think there is always a trap, that you react against a bad review. But there is a difference though, between reviewers and art writers. I am more interested in people who write about art—what they say is often the result of substantial research and they are not writing or reacting to a deadline.

Q. What is your work routine?

A. I try to work daily. When I work consistently, I work an average of ten hours per day. I might do this for three or four months and be quite isolated and dogmatic about it. At other times I might not work in the studio for about three months. There are times when I research thoroughly new ideas.

Q. Have there been any key influences throughout your early years?

A. Ever since I was very young I have always related to painters. It is a terrible thing to admit I suppose but there have not been too many Australian painters who held my attention for more than a year or so. I'm not in any way declaring war on Australian painting but that's just how it has been with me. The interest, or influences, is often more with the ideas of artists rather than with specific works. I'm interested in artists' ability to make issues, concerns tangible to the viewer.

Anthony Pryor (1951–91)

Sculptor   Studied at Royal Melbourne Institute of Technology, Melbourne

Q. Why did you pursue a career in sculpture?

A. I have always been interested in making things, so after a maths-science course at university and several years of engineering I decided to go back to doing the thing I enjoyed the most—making sculpture.

Changing to an art course involved a lot of catching up, especially in art history as I had no formal art background. I completed the course in three years and decided to go on to post-graduate studies. After graduating I took up part-time lecturing, enabling me to devote most of my time to my own work.

Q. Do you think your background in engineering had any bearing on your sculpture?

ANTHONY PRYOR (1951–91)
Open Stage II, 1984
Steel
Collection: Smorgon Steel,
Melbourne

Photographer: Donald Williams

A. Most of my sculpture is constructed and I think that to a certain degree my engineering background has given me the confidence to explore and combine different materials to suit my work. It also helped me to overcome technical problems encountered during the construction of the works.

Q. You travelled to Japan in 1974 and 1975. How did this affect your sculpture?

A. I was fortunate in that my application for a travel grant to Japan in 1974 was successful. It was my first trip overseas and I hoped to explore what was happening in Japan, in terms of contemporary sculpture, painting and printmaking. I became particularly interested in the traditional methods of construction of early Japanese architecture and torii. I admired the Japanese sensitivity in dealing with materials and their ability to make things special. I returned to Japan a year later with Augustine Dall'Ava and Geoffrey Bartlett to pursue my interests further.

Q. What do you think of the situation with sculpture in Australia?

A. Generally people feel more at ease with a painting that can be conveniently hung on a wall. Sculpture on the other hand directly competes with us for physical space, and people tend not to want things interfering with their space. That is why we find so little sculpture in domestic situations in Australia. As a consequence, there are more professional painters than sculptors.

Q. What advice would you give an aspiring sculptor?

A. I think it is an enormous challenge to create more awareness of sculpture. It can be immensely rewarding to see the completion of a large project or even a small one, and to enjoy the satisfaction of being able to follow your own direction. I suppose it boils down to being stubborn and happy in what you do!

Augustine Dall'Ava (b. 1950)

Sculptor   Studied at Royal Melbourne Institute of Technology, Melbourne

Q. Did you study art while you were at school?

A. Well my secondary education was at a technical school where I did not have much contact with art. After tech. I went to work for a couple of years and soon found I did not like any of the jobs in which I was employed and kept changing them, so I decided to go back to school to do my HSC. I did it at night school and one of the subjects I chose to do was art. I had always made things over the years and I made a lot of sculpture that year and found that I was really enjoying it, so I went on and enrolled in a sculpture course at RMIT. I have not stopped making sculpture since.

Q. In what materials have you worked?

A. It has always been wood. I have always had a link with wood. Some people use steel. I find that, for me, wood is the best medium. I have used other materials but always have gone back to wood. Wood is so versatile I can basically express whatever I want with it.

Q. While at RMIT were there any artists you studied who stood out in your mind?

A. I would probably have to say Miro or even Arp was a big influence, and later Brancusi. But that is putting it very simplistically. There were others but they were the main ones.

Q. Will you discuss your sculpture generally?

A. Well, it's a hard question to answer because you go through different stages. Your life and work are both very much interrelated. The screens are different to what I am doing now. They were contemplative works in search of peace and tranquillity, whereas the sculptures I have been making recently are more to do with humour, sensuality and aggression. The images appear like three-dimensional drawings. *Just a Glance* is more to do with humour and balance. I really enjoyed making that piece. Things always change in your life and it nearly always reflects in the work. Lately I have been painting the works. You can do a lot of things with paint that you cannot do if you leave the material in its natural state, so that has been interesting. It's amazing how it changes and transforms the nature of the material. It can give the work an added dimension.

Q. You teach part-time at RMIT. Do you look forward to the day when you can live solely from your sculpture?

A. Well I would not mind it happening, but I cannot see it happening in Australia just yet. My wife works and if it was not for her, I would not be able to spend as much time here in the studio as I do. She is a big help financially and morally.

It is often the case here that people just don't buy sculpture. Some of the problem has to do with size, but small works are hard to sell too. I think one of the reasons is that sculpture can be made of materials that everyone understands and is surrounded by in daily life and sculptures take up space. However, the attitude is quite different when it comes to paintings. Paintings don't infringe on personal space as sculpture does. I think this is a very important factor as most people live in small houses. There is always wall space but not much space for sculpture among all the household goods. There is still a very traditional view of

AUGUSTINE DALL'AVA
(b. 1950)

Just a Glance, 1984

Polychrome, wood, steel,
copper, rock, linen thread;
206 x 167 x 80 cm

Photographer: The artist

sculpture. For most people, sculpture is made of marble or bronze, giving the sculptures permanence and preciousness. I suppose it basically comes back to attitude. Much of today's sculpture is made from common materials so I can understand people thinking that it's just a pile of junk steel or a bunch of branches stuck together and painted, but it is important to remember that artists reflect the times they live in.

Clive Murray-White (b. 1946)

Sculptor   Studied at Brisbane Central Technical College; Guildford School of Art, UK

C.M.-W.   You know there are all these funny rules that exist in sculpture. The great new tradition in sculpture or in welded sculpture was the introduction of the ready-made part. It's the three-dimensional equivalent of the invention of collage and so you are using real things in just the same way that Picasso originally would have used bits of newspaper and things like that. So that's another element that always intrigues me. I think that sculptors have made great mistakes in the past thinking that things can be abstract: they can't be abstract—you cannot bump into an abstract thing—anything you look at you will try to make something of. And Anthony Caro suffers badly when he says that his sculpture is abstract and 99 per cent of the general public say it looks like an old piece of rusty farm machinery. There is a fact perhaps overlooked by Caro that he is wrong and the public is right. If it can be seen as farm machinery then that's what it is.

So if you can make sculpture and particularly sculpture that looks abstract then you have to be aware of all the readings that someone can make of it. Particularly if you use ready-made bits ... if you use, like I used to use, angle metal and structural beams, they will always remind people of building sites and bridges and all sorts of things like that. So even though there are sorts of abstract qualities I am quite happy for them to be read any way that the public sees fit.

There were all sorts of rules that existed in sculpture ... Calder made mobiles and somehow we were down on mobiles and I had sort of broken that down in my mind. David Smith used stainless steel and it was like you can't use it. It was like 'Oh, no, stainless steel—that's David Smith's; mobiles are Calder's.' Rusty metal seemed to be a little bit more open than that ... it was Caro. Then I started working with stainless steel, the nice things about it is that it doesn't rust. David Smith used to rough the surfaces up with a sander and they were fairly arbitrary. You know, they were. Just to finish off a piece he would get his sander out and whirl it about. It gives this shiny surface and it makes the surface move too. Then I suddenly discovered that because you do have to clean your sculpture up a bit or at least I felt that I had to clean them up a bit, I realised that I could actually start drawing with the grinder and make the surfaces as much a part of the sculpture as the shape. The one with the mower hasn't a highly developed surface on it. It is just sort of polished up, but a couple of the other ones ... this one here, the one you are looking at there, I have actually modelled the surface of the metal so that the people can't even tell if it is round or ... there is a case of straight normal shaping from drawing.

Q.   Tell me about this sculpture, *The Universalist Mobile*.

CLIVE MURRAY-WHITE
(b. 1946)

Foreground: *3rd Universalist
Mobile (Premonitions)*, 1987–88
Stainless steel, steel and
mixed media,
280 x 215 x 119 cm

Possession of the artist

Left background: *Penato 4*,
1988
Stainless steel and steel,
60 x 62 x 269 cm

On loan to Latrobe Regional
Art Centre

Right background: *Penato 3*
Stainless steel,
89 x 36 x 166 cm

Private Collection, Sydney

Photographer: Jon Rendell

A. We are in a room at the moment and right next to us is a sculpture with a lawn
   mower hanging off it, a paddle from a milk churn, a rudder from a boat that looks
   like a chopper, all sort of flying from the ceiling, chains, bits of stainless steel, all
   sorts of things. Each bit of it makes you kind of wonder what their purpose is. In
   fact it looks kind of whacky, I mean a lawn mower hanging on a mobile is bound
   to make a person think of every Australian weekend. It implies a movement, it
   does all sorts of things.

      The mower, apart from the fact that it had been the one that I dragged around
   these several acres, there is a love-hate relationship with this particular mower. It
   had all these functions to do with cutting and transforming people's

environments. Every man has this wild relationship with lawn mowers. It goes perfectly one week and then you can be trying to start it … It takes you half an hour to mow the lawn and three days to fix the darned thing.

Q. Most people who make sculpture now always mention that it's difficult to survive.

A. It's not hard for me to actually survive. I have a full-time teaching job and I enjoy teaching. Painters could quite easily look at the possibility of making a living from their art. Not my kind of sculpture certainly. I would say that people just don't think of putting sculpture around their homes. I don't think that they buy sculpture until they fill up their walls with paintings and have no more room to put the paintings, so they have got to put some sculptures around. I think maybe I should change tack a bit.

I think sculptors have always been very unkind to their audience. Sculptors think that rusty steel is attractive and it is a fine surface, a fine and beautiful thing. The general public sees rust as a sign of decay. It is the last thing we want in our society. You do not want a brand new Volvo with rust coming through at you … Rust was a problem. Paint was even more of a problem because you would have to maintain it. So suddenly someone said "Oh well, rust is not all that different from the patina that goes on bronze.' 'So now we like rust.' And there is historical precedent. People in the country like to put rusty old ploughs outside their houses … people like the aesthetics of old farm machinery. We forget as sculptors that really rust means decay in the public's eye.

Also some things can be too beautiful. If you made a bronze a few years ago, all your friends would say that you were into absolute rank commercialism and you should be despised because only the old artists wanted to make things in bronze. Now we even ask 'Why can't a sculpture be beautiful?'

Lyn Moore (b. 1943)

Sculptor Studied part-time at the Hammersmith School of Art, London, and National Art School, Sydney; and full-time at the Canberra School of Art

Q. How long have you been working as an artist? How do you find it?

A. I finished art school in 1980 and I've been working professionally since 1981. It has sometimes been a very difficult road but highly satisfying because each new work is a new adventure, a kind of enrichment. Often the reward is in the exploration and sometimes the discovery.

Q. Have you always worked in wood? What are the things about wood that you enjoy?

A. My earliest works were from clay, cement fondue and found objects, and at the present time I am working in a new direction altogether. Wood is a marvellous organic material; however, to use a chainsaw continuously is a very exhausting process. Tools for me are only a means to an end. There is no pleasure in the using of the tools but real adventure in what those tools can do.

Q. Where does your work originate?

A. Is it possible to know the origins of one's work? Possibly it comes from life's experiences. I travelled extensively in my late teens and early twenties in Europe, Asia and the Middle East; those experiences had a great impact on my thought processes. In particular I felt quite moved by sculptural objects—sometimes in the natural landscape, other times in ancient sites where only ancient fragments were left standing. In retrospect I think I wanted to make both work with similar feelings. I needed to isolate myself and work through and concentrate on working through many different ideas. Painting and drawing are a part of my daily activities. I work mainly outdoors. The work to date has been very strenuous and needs many hours of physical and mental application. I spend five full days at my workshop and two days, that is including weekends, in paid employment to support myself.

Q. How did you organise your first exhibition? When was it?

A. I worked for three years before I exhibited my work in 1983 at the Arts Council in Canberra. It was arranged through meetings with the Gallery Director and he decided after visiting my workshop that he would show my work. It was the most terrifying experience and still seems that way when showing my work to the public.

Q. Were you pleased with the critics' reviews of your work?

A. I was fortunate enough to have good comments from the critics; however, I have known other artists who have had bad crits and I see this as being a fairly

LYN MOORE (b. 1943)
May, 1987
Ironbark, height to 3 m
Collection: Monash University, Melbourne
Photograph courtesy of Lyn Moore

Photographer: Donald Williams

destructive influence on their development. Artists need to discount good or bad reviews and thereby continue to develop and explore their own ideas without intimidation.

Q. Have there been any international sculptors whose work you like?

A. I have a great love for Picasso's sculpture—such a variety in his work, he was so inventive. Also Brancusi and David Smith for similar reasons. Some of the greatest architecture and sculpture comes from primitive and prehistoric cultures and I have no doubt that this particular area of human endeavour has been a great influence on my work process.

I would also like to say that along with this exhausting work process is a very rewarding family lifestyle. I have been married for twenty years and have two children, one fifteen and the other seventeen.

Norman Day (b. 1947)
Architect   Studied at University of Melbourne

Architecture of the 1980s is disjointed, deconstructed and experimental. No clear expression or unified vision presents itself. Buildings are decorated, superficial and colourful with jagged planning, so they represent a perceived lack of social, political and cultural order.

The simple two-level office building, Biltmoderne, has become a vehicle for Mad Max-type jagged fences, made using standard concrete reinforcing bars and cut-out steel 'spears'. Walls are oddly shaped as if falling over, and oval windows contribute to a general feeling of slipping-away and collapse. Surfaces are decorated with stuck-on concrete medallions. The materials used are standard off-the-shelf rolled steel sheeting, commercial window sections and industrial steelwork.

Modernism was the classical architecture of this century. Modern architects designed for a brave new world—modern glass boxes which blew away visions of dark Victorian interiors and embraced the idea of sun, air and light in buildings, along with open landscapes surrounding high-rise havens.

Post-modern architecture reacted to that rigour (which was a rather hopeful dream) and to other social pressures (like the West losing the Vietnam War) by developing a critical stance to our institutions as represented by their buildings. It placed a check on our recent past and looked carefully at previous pasts.

In the Daryl Jackson House, East Melbourne, the architect has taken clues from the architecture of the neighbourhood and reused them not literally but through a critical sieve, so the elements of Victorian buildings of the area are reassembled in a new way, as one would make a collage or montage of images from the past. Some elements are exaggerated, others are quoted directly from the source. Historicism in post-modern architecture is sometimes developed so we can better appreciate the past. Other times it is used as simply a decorative device of low significance.

The resultant buildings are a hybrid of historical motives with classical structures (used generally only as applied decoration) and one which twists and bends traditional architectural elements in new ways. In suburban Australia, for example, the ordinary houses Robin Boyd criticised some twenty years ago have become the paradigm for a new national architectural expression.

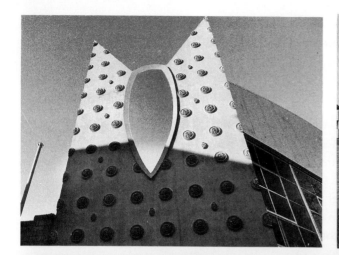

TOP LEFT:

BILTMODERNE
McRae, Way Film Production Studio, South Melbourne
Photographer: Jon Rendell

TOP RIGHT:

NORMAN DAY (b. 1947)
Mowbray College, Melton, Victoria
Photographer: Donald Williams

ABOVE:

DARYL JACKSON
Jackson House, East Melbourne
Photographer: John Gollings

In Mowbray College, Melton, the suburban pattern is deconstructed and reassembled through a critical fresh view of the elements of our common homes. Materials are the same as those abused by Boyd in *The Australian Ugliness* but are locked together as a distinct design, so we can see afresh both the new architecture of the school and the existing architecture of the suburbs.

Our cities are seen as possessing traditional buildings, expressing fine values of urban suitability and continuity between past and present. Architects use the past to inform their new works. There are plenty of Roman colonnades, parapets, entablatures and quoins appearing on new, slick office buildings.

Post-modern architecture could be seen as self-destructive and lacking confidence, which is partly true, but it is so because the artists practising today are questioning basic values underlying their designs, structures, means of building (financial and constructional) and their own role as building designers.

The buildings are a reaction to the inappropriate and unsuccessful utopian vision held by modern architects. They are pushing their ideas by experimenting with new building concepts.

Much of the recent work is an intellectual exercise, relearning old techniques and traditional values and critically reappraising new designs. It is an inevitable artistic exercise to pursue new values and direct attention to fresh approaches, so we may better know ourselves and our society. Post-modern architects are doing just that.

(Norman Day)

Roger Wood

Wood Marsh & Associates Pty Ltd
Architect Studied at Royal Melbourne Institute of Technology, Melbourne

Q. When did you decide you wanted to become an architect?

A. I guess my original desire to become an architect happened relatively late in my secondary school training. I can't say that I had a burning ambition from the age of two to become an architect. It developed out of a pursuit of a combination of things. I was interested in art at school, also theatre and film. As well as all of this I had some interest in mathematics, as connected with structure, and in combination it all seemed to lean towards architecture. I wanted an expressive career and although I didn't see it as a career I saw it as a pursuit that would interest me so I enrolled at RMIT. During the course there I learnt of certain pragmatic and specific things about architecture. The creative side of it was encouraged but basically it is up to the individual to actually choose their direction. I chose a very particular direction which was slightly unorthodox, that was to avoid the long-winded apprenticeship that normally accompanied an architecture course, which is to stay and work in an architect's office. I decided with a couple of friends to form our own practice and express ourselves through our own work, rather than work with another architect, and avoid the associated hierarchy. So in 1983 we formed a company called Biltmoderne and had an exhibition in a furniture gallery in Richmond. At about the same time we received a couple of commissions—Inflation Nightclub, a recording studio in St Kilda and a film production studio in South Melbourne (see page 250). From there we developed into more exhibition work and ongoing architectural commissions. At the end of 1986 Biltmoderne was restructured and I am still working with one of my original partners, Randal Marsh …

Q. How do you see your role as an architect and also the wider role of architecture in the community?

A. I think architects have enormous social responsibility over and above their personal endeavours. It is like the difference between painting and architecture. People have to use buildings. We can look at paintings and find them evocative which is quite a personal thing, but a building affects the whole fabric of our city and within our 'routine' we daily use several buildings, so architecture has a very immediate effect on our society and architects should be held responsible for making that environment worth living in. In an urban sense particularly, I see it as being significant from that point of view. Also it is a corporate art form, whereby large buildings are shaping our cities, manifestations of the greater scheme of things. They have political, commercial and economic connotations and that's no different to Renaissance architecture expressing the commercial and political situation of that time.

Q. How would you describe your work? What style do you call it?

A. Beautiful … We don't actually have a name for it. It has been called Neo-mannerism and all sorts of things. We just see it as probably most aptly called, as it has been, 'New Spirit'. In other words I see it as being inventive and spirited. I don't see it as being Post-modern or Baroque or whatever you might like to call it. That terminology is a job that historians will undertake. In the future they will look back and see how it fits into the scheme of things as they did for instance with expressionist painting. When Rothko started working he didn't say that his painting was 'Expressionism'. That term was invented by historians after Rothko made the work. Likewise with architecture, the title to a particular style is usually given by people who didn't make the work.

Q. What about Melbourne's Metro Nightclub—was it a difficult job?

A. The Metro Nightclub was a project we started designing in February 1987. It was an interesting project because it was basically installing a contemporary interior into an existing old theatre that had gone through numerous uses. The existing building had its own difficulties: being that it was stylistically a theatre, complete with dress circles, a stage and lobby areas; and, secondly, it was a very big space inside. The main auditorium was vast, about 20 metres wide and 20 metres high.

WOOD MARSH &
ASSOCIATES PTY LTD
Metro Nightclub, Melbourne,
1987–88

Photographer: Jon Rendell

Inserted into an existing theatrical cave are steel towers, walkways and mezzanine floors that are boldly supported on cables suspended from trusses and beams. This extends the original dress circles into one, continuous circulation route. Hydraulic, robotic arms move lighting clusters through this space to provide animation. As a contemporary insertion, this new architecture has been shaped to resemble the sensuous curves of the original structure but galvanised so that, by refracting light, the delineation is made clear. The form of this architecture and galvanised finish also work in an unexpected way for an interior by contrasting its industrial appearance against the decorative, theatrical detailing of the old theatre.

We inserted into that interior some contemporary bits of architecture that are almost like small buildings. Galvanised steel towers that are about three storeys high hold draping walkways that connect to different levels in the auditorium. We have built a mezzanine floor, stage and dance floor. It was an effort to celebrate some of the magnitude and festivity that we normally associate with theatrical buildings. They are there to celebrate film or theatre, and nightclubs are perhaps a contemporary extension of that. It's celebrating theatre every night; the audience become the actors, and the stage and set become the architecture.

Hilarie Mais (b. 1962)

Sculptor   Born in Leeds, Yorkshire, England. Arrived in Australia in 1981. Studied at Bradford School of Art, Slade School of Art and also worked in New York on a scholarship.

Q. Was your intention always to become an artist? Was it something that was always with you?

Hilarie Mais in her studio, Sydney, 1994

A. I always seemed to be drawing and painting from my early childhood. I would disappear into a painting and drawing world. I have no other artists in my family, so to be an artist was to enter a very unknown area; yet it seemed rather natural. It was something that just progressed. I attended art school and enrolled in a preliminary arts year where I was lucky enough to be introduced to all forms of art practice, which was where I realised that sculpture, or working with form, was for me. I studied all forms of sculptural media and techniques so as to have a free and wider vocabulary in my later art practice. It again just seemed to be a very natural path for me to take.

Q. Was there any particular painting, building or sculpture that moved you spiritually or emotionally in your early days as a developing artist or student?

A. Yes, I remember as a child discovering art, mainly via books, particularly artists like Matisse, Cézanne, and Picasso. We also visited lots of galleries. I also loved visiting ancient monuments, which are plentiful in England. My very favourite building as a child was York Minster, which is believed to be the largest Gothic structure in northern Europe. I still go back to visit it when I am in England; it is just incredible. As a developing artist I looked at Brancusi and artists from the Constructivist movement, and even Celtic and Romanesque work inspired me.

Q. You use a great deal of wood in your work. What is it about the nature of that material that you find so appealing?

A. I enjoy its versatility. In the recent works you are a lot more aware of the material, so the variety of grain and the random quality of working with or against the structure has been important to me. With the material I choose I like it to have its own personality, and an ability for me to be able to work with it relatively easily. In some of my work all sense of the material is removed—it is just the vehicle, the structure. In works from 1992 to 1993 I introduced other processes like staining or washing the wood to add another dimension, which utilises its natural materiality.

Q. What was it about steel that you enjoyed?

A. I used steel a lot. I like the spontaneity of steel. I like the workshop experience of being in there with it. You can quickly weld something. It has a real flexibility and freedom to it, whereas when you work with wood you have to be a lot more methodical and planned. You can't go hacking and changing your mind too much or you end up destroying the material.

Q. What is your working process?

A. My working process is quite regimented. It is a proper work routine. At a certain point in the morning I expect myself to be in the studio working for the entire day. I think you can't work by waiting for inspiration. You have to be in there working and available so when your ideas are there you can act on them. I usually manage to work five or six days a week.

   When working, one piece often follows another. I don't plan a sequence. One piece often suggests the next—it is like a journey. I often refer to past works in current works so there's a sort of retrieval of previous issues and elements. I also draw continually as I am working, making notations of ideas and the progress of the piece—it is a diary about decisions. It is an important element of my routine.

Q. In the works from 1992 to 1993 (Chapter Twelve) there seems to be a reduction in detail, as well as in size. Are these works more compact?

A. Yes, that's right. It has become more compressed: compression of scale and the compression of density. Those elements are still there but they are becoming almost illusionary. There are some real holes and some painted holes. In these works you are much more aware of the material, yet it also has a strong illusionary element. This element refers to past works—they are like portraits of past works. I've taken the scale down. The intensity is the absence and presence; some voids are real, some are painted.

Q. You have been in Australia since 1981. Did the rather major and disruptive experience of migration affect the way you worked? Did it provide any new influences?

A. Migrating, moving, the sense of being alien, the fresh start, the empty studio is a feeling I really enjoyed. Previously, I migrated from England to America and it was an opportunity to reassess what I had been doing and allowed me the chance to redirect and clarify my work. On a practical level I did change materials when I came here, as I had no access to a metal workshop. I had spent the last years working in steel—it was a major change to start working with wood.

　　As an artist I think you have to make the best of any situation that you are in, so in some ways the move was a compromise at that point; but then for my discipline it was very interesting to move from one material to another. It restructured and reworked what I had once taken for granted with the other materials I had been using.

　　Previously in New York I had been working on my *Weapons* series which were small steel pieces. After arriving in Australia I had a child and this issue of being a woman and what it was to be a woman and to have another life informed and became another issue. Hence, there was another series of work to do with symbols: the femaleness, fertility, sexuality and birthing. This became a major issue, I had never worked with such personal references before. It was a powerful influence.

Q. The grid is a form that has been discussed when people talk about your work. From where does it originate in your work?

A. The grid grew out of the spiral forms (early 1980s). They are both archetypal forms. It is a device used in painting, the structure of perspective. The grid is a modernist, antique and ancient form. It is read in the same way, whether it is ancient or contemporary—it is a pivotal form. I use the grid as a vehicle in which I overlay my own vocabulary; I transform it. The grid works do not describe but evoke. They are in abstract forms, doors, barriers and screens; like most of my Australian work, they are metaphysical. When critics talk about my grids they nearly always relate them only to the movement of minimalism and the modernist grid. They are much more grounded both in historical and personal reference, as well as in their process of making.

Q. Has the urban environment played a role in this interest? For example, many cities are laid out in grid formats—Melbourne for one is based on this form.

A. Yes, it is like New York—no street names, only numbers. It is very methodical. The environment must have informed what my vocabulary was going to be. I grew up in an urban environment, so architecture and structure was my landscape.

James Gleeson (b. 1915)

Painter   Born in Sydney. Studied at East Sydney Technical College, 1934–36. Gleeson is a poet, author, teacher and highly respected Surrealist painter.

Q. What were some of the first influences in your early art education and school life?

A. Well, in Australia in the early 1920s and 1930s access to any first-hand experience of world art was extremely limited—and what was available came second-hand through reproductions in books or prints. However, by the end of the 1930s I had built up a large amount of knowledge of what was happening, or rather what had happened—and as a young artist I found myself being attracted to a wide varying range of 'models'—undoubtedly because I could identify with them. There was Picasso, Blake, Turner, Grunewald, Bosch, Brueghel, El Greco—they all fascinated me. I realise now it was because they were all looking for realities that lay beyond those easily accessible to our limited sensory equipment.

 Of course, then it was the surrealists! By the late 1930s they seemed to be providing pointers for me that would lead me to eventually finding my own direction in art. However even then I couldn't really accept the dogmatic core of Saint André Breton's doctrine—and I eventually came to realise that Surrealism as a twentieth century movement was only one aspect of manifestation of the age-old desire to find realities that exist outside the confines of material realism, and the structures of 'the rational'.

Q. The production of works from the early 1980s are much larger than the earlier works. Is there any specific reason for this dramatic change in scale?

A. Until the 1980s most of my time was taken up by teaching, lecturing, writing, reviewing and travelling. So my earlier paintings—with a few exceptions—tended to be small in scale, as they were really painted in what seemed to be best described as my spare time. It was around 1982 that things began to change. I was able to devote my whole time to painting, so the paintings grew in scale and I was able to concentrate all my attention on them. The larger works take generally between two to three weeks to paint.

Q. How do you go about starting to work on your pictures? Is it a careful evolution?

A. Yes, it is a gradual thing, which evolves through a process of drawing and redrawing and then painting, and at each step there are many changes that tend to occur. First a small rough pencil sketch of something I've sort of perceived in the mind's eye—something that has been sparked by some earlier experience. Then a larger more elaborate drawing usually in charcoal where the forms suggested in the first draft or sketch are given a much more defined role. This is often followed, but not always, by the addition of elements of collage. They can come from any source that I might feel enhances the rhythms or would underscore the emotional impact of the work.

 The final design is squared up and then transferred onto the canvas for the final painting and in this last process many more changes occur, arising out of the necessities of the paint itself. The medium at this stage makes a final input. Technically I draw on all the resources of the oil painting tradition: glazing, scumbling, impasto, drybrush—as many technical tricks as seems necessary to use in trying to achieve the effect I require. In the later paintings I try to cover the whole canvas in a wash of colour, and then work all over it section by section before the final modification of glazing or highlighting with the palette knife.

Portrait of the Artist as an Evolving Landscape evolved from the notion I hold that all things are in a state of transition—an eternal flux in which everything changes. Nothing is permanent. As an individual one changes from moment to moment—from the embryo to the funeral parlour and beyond. The constituents of our present forms are resolved back into the matter of the cosmos—and this deconstructed matter will, in due course, re-form in another guise: air, grass, everything. The landscape element was drawn in charcoal, and a detailed pencil study of the head was cut up and reassembled as a collage within the landscape framework.

JAMES GLEESON (b. 1915)
Portrait of the Artist as an Evolving Landscape
(Self-portrait), 1993
Oil on canvas, 152 x 204 cm
The Agapitos/Wilson Collection, Sydney

Q. Why do you remain a surrealist painter, when Surrealism has never been terribly well received in Australia?

A. Yes, Surrealism attracted some attention among Australian artists at the end of the 1930s and early 1940s, and there were many artists who were touched by it. They were Tucker, Nolan, Boyd and a few others. Most of them either abandoned it after brief experimentations or gave it such an Australian accent as to convert it into a kind of local folklore. I stuck with Surrealism because I was a surrealist. I was born like it and couldn't work in any other way.

Q. How do you feel when you look back over the collection of art you have made?

A. Looking back over fifty years of work, how do I feel? Well, I feel that I'm only just beginning to know about art and what I want to do with it, and I feel that I need another fifty years before I'll be able to do it!

See also Chapter Nine.

Angela Brennan (b. 1960)

Painter   Born in Ballarat. Studied at Royal Melbourne Institute of Technology, Diploma of Painting, 1979–82. Residency in an Australia Council studio in Barcelona, Spain, 1990–91.

Angela Brennan in her studio, Melbourne, 1992

Photograph courtesy of the artist

Q. In an artistic sense who were some of the early influences in your life?

A. Among my earliest recollections of famous images which I saw in art books at home are Cézanne's *Card players*, the Tahitian works of Gauguin, and the pictures by Vermeer and Bronzino. I loved Bronzino's direct portraits on those distilled blue backgrounds and was fascinated by the intricate clothes the sitters wore, to say nothing of their weird facial features. At secondary school I liked Titian, Dali, Magritte, Ingres, El Greco and Chagall, and tried to copy these. I had a teacher who encouraged my interest in art and who introduced me to various techniques and to the history of art.

Q. How did your world change when you entered art school?

A. When I went to study at Royal Melbourne Institute of Technology (RMIT), after completing secondary school, I found that it was quite a shock because during first year the painting exercises were extremely rigid and formal, and we were not allowed to paint what we wanted, as at school. The painting classes focused on exercises such as painting a bunch of onions in only two colours or drawing rotting fish, as well as lots of tonal exercises. The teachers were especially fond of brown paint or variations thereof: burnt sienna, burnt umber, brown ochre and the like. I remember a teacher who used to tell us that using yellow was risky because it put 'a hole' in the picture. I didn't believe this and for a while would go home and paint big, yellow, floaty abstracts.

At RMIT I started to look at American Pop artists. I also liked Italian Renaissance painters such as Piero della Francesca and Uccello. I was especially attracted to the 'design' element of their work, the shallow space and squashed perspective. I liked the way their paintings looked as though they were constructed of cut-out shapes piled on top of one another (Uccello), and the way in which the composition in Piero's paintings fits together: it's calm and well ordered but at the same time dynamic and unnerving. I also liked the work of the Cubist painters, Braque more than Picasso.

Q. What is the role of the artist?

A. What is the artist's role? Artists can provide a whole new way of looking at things. Successful art can help us engage with the world in many different ways, for example politically, emotionally, aesthetically or sensually. In other words we might experience delight, amusement, outrage, horror or pleasure while looking at art and, consequently, can become aware of reactions and feelings which we did not have before. Perhaps such responses may cause us to act differently from how we did previously. It is also challenging to think about why we respond to art in the ways we do.

Q. How do you go about starting a painting?

A. Sometimes I buy prepared canvases; otherwise, I stretch the canvas or linen myself. I prime it with two to three coats of gesso. What I do next depends on how I want the picture to look. For example, I may thinly stain it with a background colour to achieve a washy effect. Usually I paint with oil, occasionally combing this with found objects and/or collage. For the most part I do not rigorously plan my abstract paintings, that is, through preliminary drawings, but rather begin the painting straight off as it were, referring only to the imagination. As far as the portrait figures are concerned, I usually have somebody pose for a few hours in the studio and I finish the painting (most of it at least) in a few hours or a day. However, each painting is different (obviously), so sometimes I will be changing it for a year and sometimes it is finished in about half an hour.

Q. Does your choice of colour reflect your mood, or is it something not so emotional and calculated?

A. The choices of colour are not emotionally based: it is more to do with what the picture requires, yet it is not really a rational decision either. Overall the painting has a 'mood' but colour is not automatically attributable to an emotional state. That is to say, I don't believe that blue or black, for instance, necessarily represents sadness/misery or that pink translates as exuberance. A dark painting can be truly joyous! The colours I choose to use are determined by I'm not sure what (probably the subconscious), anyway the colour dictates itself more than I do. Painting, for me, is not a cognitive process, at least on the face of it, it's not. It is more like the subconscious making the painting, and that is why it is so engaging, indeed at certain times absolutely fulfilling. For me, if making art consisted only of conforming to a formula, you know having an idea and translating it exactly according to plan, then there would be no attraction or seduction taking place and this is important.

Q. What is your response to art critics?

A. Well, some critics get it right and many miss the point, not only with my work but also with other people's work. They can elucidate my intentions as well as point out things in the work which had not occurred to me. But even so, when I read criticism about myself I get embarrassed; even if it is positive, I still get embarrassed! It is something to do with becoming public, revealing oneself. Anyway critics, especially newspaper critics, have a good deal of power and scope to influence; they can influence the public in so far as whether or not it is worthwhile going to see an exhibition; however, I believe that once people get to the exhibition they make up their own minds. Dealers, more than critics, influence a buyer's decision.

When I have an exhibition I'm in the contradictory position of feeling egocentric and exhilarated, but at the same time shy and anxious, concerned with what people think and say: will they be mean or enthusiastic? But in any case I feel that it is essential that I show the work I make (not all of it, of course), although once I had an exhibition in which I covered the gallery from ceiling to floor without leaving an empty space anywhere. Each exhibition calls for its own tempering: some shows will be full of stuff and others quite sparse, but I tend towards crowded shows. It is fantastic if you sell something at the opening. It is always nerve-racking but this feeling abates the day after.

Q. This work is very bold and colourful, isn't it?

A. *The Familiar Is Not Necessarily the Known* is probably about seeing what happens when I repeat the same motif using a given range of colours in an irregular

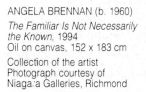

ANGELA BRENNAN (b. 1960)
The Familiar Is Not Necessarily the Known, 1994
Oil on canvas, 152 x 183 cm

Collection of the artist
Photograph courtesy of
Niagara Galleries, Richmond

pattern and varying the size. For this picture I began at one end and worked my way across. The painting dictates itself. It's like following an imaginary rule and then breaking it: yellow, blue, orange, purple, red. Then yellow, blue, orange, green, red. I am interested in the stripe as a motif. It holds a strong position in the history of Modernism—Daniel Buren, Bridget Riley, Morris Louis and Frank Stella, to name a few, have made stripe paintings. It allows for endless permutations and funky combinations and I enjoy playing around with it.

Peter Atkins (b. 1963)

Painter Born in Murrurundi, New South Wales, and currently lives in Sydney. In 1985 won the New South Wales Travelling Scholarship. In 1994 was Australia's representative at VIII—Triennale India, and won one of nine gold awards.

Peter Atkins in his studio, Redfern, Sydney, 1993

Photographer: Richard Ludbrook

Q. What were some of the early influences in your life?

A. I spent much of my early childhood in the country in northern New South Wales and went to high school in Newcastle. I was there for four years and hated it with a passion. It was partly to do with the way I was taught. We were treated as a group, never as individuals; however, my art education, for that era, was actually quite good. I can still remember my art teachers because they really responded to me on a personal level and I responded to them. I went out of my way to listen to them and learn everything I could. I was really eager. At the age of thirteen, I decided to do night classes in art at a tertiary institution in Newcastle.

Q. What made you follow this path at such an early age?

A. Well, I was brought up in a very traditional working-class family where your gender often dictated the kinds of jobs you would do. It was expected I would have a wife and a family, own a house and play that role. But I was exposed to this new thing, this thing called ART. The teachers had opened my eyes to something amazing. They were really good—they gave us lots of books and prints and we were exposed to a whole range of things I had never seen before. I started to cultivate this other idea about being an artist, but it took a long long time to realise that there was another kind of life contrary to what was expected of me at home. To do the night class I had to get permission from the headmaster to say that it would not interfere with my other studies. He wasn't going to let me do it, and I had to really plead with him. Looking back I'm sure that if it had been football or soccer I was wanting to do there would have been no problem, but because it was art there was this big deal. I do think that people should be encouraged to find their way.

Q. Who were some of the artists that impressed you?

A. I can remember looking through books and making my own copies of paintings by Noel Counihan and Stanislaus Rapotec—a fifteen-year-old doing my own version of these great works. Those two artists were probably the most influential. A few years later, when I was eighteen, I actually managed to get a job in a framer's shop and it was through working here that I met lots of artists. They all came in to get their works framed. I was always more interested in talking to them about their artwork than framing their pictures.

I was fascinated by their lifestyle, the practice of doing something they wanted; showing their work and being paid for it—it seemed fabulous! I just found it fascinating and never really thought it was possible for me. I eventually entered art school and my parents freaked right out—they couldn't believe it. I entered art school under the guise of becoming an art teacher, but then transferred to the National Art School in Sydney where I completed my final year. Moving to Sydney gave me the break I needed. I met lots of artists who were working in their studios, big names people I had heard of. They were all practising artists, where the people in Newcastle were primarily teachers. Michael Johnson was really amazing; I found meeting him so influential. I went to his studio. It was fantastic—big art works on the walls and paint everywhere—and he was a really mad sort of character. Seeing his life and his artwork, all those things around him, his book collection, his record collection, the clothes he wore and the way he thought about things—it was great. Artists are always so passionate about things!

Q. How do you feel when you see your work in a gallery?

A. Because my work is so personal, I feel it is beyond criticism. I can't be criticised for doing what I do. It can be challenged for its artistic technique or something, but I just do what I feel. If people don't respond it doesn't worry me. I was once really nervous about all that stuff but I don't care so much anymore. I've gone past that stage. When I saw the work in the Indian Triennale I was mesmerised by it. I had worked on it for such a long time. I could just see my life, where I was at that time. I do get a lot of rewards. I like seeing people respond to it. I suppose I like to be complimented. Everyone does I suspect.

Q. How do the paintings you have selected to be reproduced in this book relate to your three-month residency in India?

A. These works were made while I was in India between October 1993 and February 1994. The hand is the first work in the Indian Journal and is called *Assurance and Protection*. It seemed appropriate to start here because in Indian culture the hand means assurance and protection. It was like a kind of charm for me. It was to be something to ensure I would be able to work well while in India. I was affirming my own self, my own space. It was my own symbol taken from Indian culture to protect myself. I had appropriated it.

The motorbike is from Dalhousi, at the foot of the Himalayas; in fact it is the village next to where the Dalai Lama lives. On the way to this village we passed lots of roadside mechanics, all of which had their own hand-painted pictures of these motor scooters. It was their own advertisement, painted by themselves. They were all so badly painted: the perspective was so wrong, the forms were wrong but it didn't matter, I loved them. I like the honesty involved in that approach to working. I like that kind of sensibility. I couldn't stop looking at these paintings. It was almost like everyone fixes motor scooters—everyone drives them in India. There are thousands of them; they almost take on iconic status. By this stage I was really into Indian Pop culture. Everything is handmade in India, even signs; it is not like here where things are professionally done. Rather than ask one of the mechanics if I could buy his sign and create mass confusion, in the end I just decided to commission a local signwriter to do a picture for me. I specified the view, size and colour. He did it in six hours. I signed it 'Motor Scooter from Dalhousi' and I put his name down.

I consider it to be my work even though Parkash painted it. It is his painting but in the whole group of pictures—the Indian Journal—it was relevant at the

PETER ATKINS (b. 1963)
Assurance and Protection
(Indian Journal)
Delhi. 18 October 1993
(Imprint of right hand)
Mixed media. 30 x 30 cm
Collection of the artist

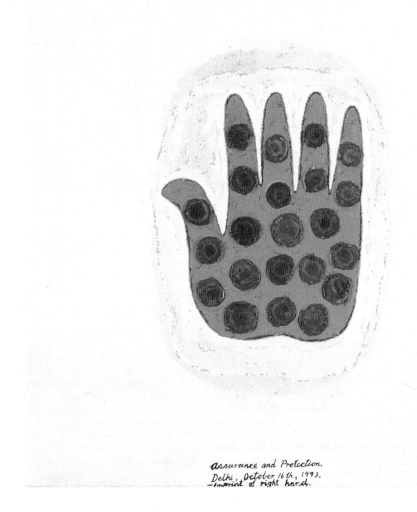

Assurance and Protection.
Delhi, October 16th, 1993.
—Imprint of right hand.

PETER ATKINS (b. 1963)
Motor Scooter. Dalhousi (Indian Journal)
Himachal Pradesh,
5 November 1993
(Scooter painted by Parkash)
30 x 30 cm
Collection of the artist

time. It was something I was thinking about, and it was appropriate that it should be done like this. I often collaborate with other people in my work.

Q. What do you see as the role of the artist?

A. Well, this is a really hotly debated thing isn't it? My ideas about being an artist are very simple and I think it comes from the fact I grew up in a very orthodox environment where basic things were seen as quite important. My work deals with me and how I relate to certain things, like the environment. I have a very personal relationship to the things I make, to the extent where it is difficult for me to sell them. The role of the artist is varied in many ways. The artist is a monitor of society. They exist outside the function of the normal things that happen in society—they can look at things really objectively. They look at things and come to conclusions.

I think a lot of people working in their daily routine become complacent about life. I think they close down lots of their emotions, especially males. It is hard here for men to be emotional; it is not accepted in Western society. I think commercial galleries and public galleries are really important so people can see a whole range of things, see beauty, let off steam. All the arts are there to draw something out of people, and to make them feel something not experienced before.

Looking at Art— a Guide

Use this guide to assist you when writing about art, particularly painting.

Preliminary information

1. Name the artist.
2. Give a brief description of the artist's background.
3. Give the name and date of the work.
4. In which 'artistic period' was the work produced?
5. Is the style similar to other work the artist has done? Explain your answer. (You might have to seek out other examples of the artist's work.)
6. What is going on in the work? Explain what is there.

Intention

7. What do you think was the artist's intention?
8. Do you think it was achieved? Explain.
9. Which word or words best describe the category of the work? For example, historical, social document, religious, abstract, naturalistic.

10. Describe the mood of the work—dramatic, expressive, calm, and so on. Explain.

Design

11. What kind of colour has been used?
12. Has colour been used to add to the 'mood' of the work? Has it been used to influence your emotions? How? Where? Explain.
13. In what way has paint been applied? What is the texture?

Conclusion

14. Quite apart from your personal feelings about the work, do you think it is a 'good' piece of art? Try to relate your answer back to the work of art, and list what you think are its good and bad features.

Suggested Reading

General

Painting

Burke, J., *Australian Women Artists: One Hundred Years, 1840–1940*, Ewing and George Paton Galleries, Melbourne University Union, Melbourne, 1976.

Hughes, R., *The Art of Australia*, Penguin, Melbourne, 1970.

Smith, B. & Smith, T., *Australian Painting, 1788–1970*, Third Edition, Oxford University Press, Melbourne, 1991.

Smith, B., *Place, Taste and Tradition: A Study of Australian Art Since 1788*, Second Edition, Oxford University Press, Melbourne, 1979.

Sculpture

Darby, M., Dover, B. & Zunde, R., *Sculpture*, Curriculum Branch, Education Department, Victoria, 1983.

Scarlett, K., *Australian Sculptors*, Nelson, Melbourne, 1980.

Sturgeon, G., *The Development of Australian Sculpture: 1788–1975*, Thames and Hudson, London, 1978.

Sturgeon, G., *Australian Sculpture Now* Catalogue, National Gallery of Victoria and the Committee of the Second Australian Sculpture Triennial, 1984.

Sturgeon, G., *Contemporary Australian Sculpture*, Craftsman House and Sherman Galleries, Sydney, 1991.

Architecture

Freeland, J. M., *Architecture in Australia*, Pelican Books, Penguin, 1981.

Jahn, G., *Contemporary Australian Architecture*, Craftsman House, Sydney, 1994.

Tanner, H. (ed.), *Architects of Australia*, Macmillan, Melbourne, 1981.

Taylor, J., *Australian Architecture since 1960*, The Law Book Co., Sydney, 1986.

Periodicals

Crawford, A. (ed.), *World Art*.

Lynn, E. (ed.), *Art and Australia*, Fine Arts Press, Sydney.

Timms, P. (ed.), *Art Monthly*.

Chapter One

Amadio, N. & Kimber, R., *Wildbird Dreaming: Aboriginal Art from the Central Deserts of Australia*, Greenhouse Publications, Melbourne, 1988.

Bardon, G., *Papunya Tula. Art of the Western Desert*, McPhee Gribble, Ringwood, 1991.

Berndt, R., Berndt, C. & Stanton, J., *Aboriginal Australian Art: A Visual Perspective*, Methuen Australia, Sydney, 1988.

Carter, J. et al., *Aboriginal Australia*, Australian Gallery Directors Council, Sydney, 1981.

Caruana, W., *Aboriginal Art*, Thames and Hudson, London, 1993.

Crumlin, R. & Knight, A., *Aboriginal Art and Spirituality*, Collins Dove, North Blackburn, 1991.

Ryan, J., *Images of Power—Aboriginal Art of the Kimberley*, National Gallery of Victoria, Melbourne, 1993.

Sutton, P. (ed.), *Dreamings: The Art of Aboriginal Australia*, Viking in association with the Asia Society Galleries, New York, 1988.

Chapter Two

Bonyhady, T., *The Colonial Image*, Craftsman House, Melbourne, 1987.

Gleeson, J., *Colonial Painters 1788–1880*, Lansdowne, Melbourne, 1971.

Smith, B., *Documents on Art and Taste in Australia: The Colonial Period, 1770–1914*, Oxford University Press, Melbourne, 1975.

Chapters Three and Four

Bonyhady, T., *Images in Opposition: Australian Landscape Painting 1801–1890*, Oxford University Press, Melbourne, 1985.

Gleeson, J., *Colonial Painters 1788–1880*, Lansdowne, Melbourne, 1971.

Smith, B., *Documents on Art and Taste in Australia: The Colonial Period, 1770–1914*, Oxford University Press, Melbourne, 1975.

Chapter Five

Bonyhady, T., *Images in Opposition: Australian Landscape Painting 1801–1890*, Oxford University Press, Melbourne, 1985.

Clark, J. & Whitelaw, B., *Golden Summers: Heidelberg and Beyond*, International Cultural Corporation of Australia Limited, 1985.

Gleeson, J., *Impressionist Painters, 1881–1930*, Lansdowne, Melbourne, 1971.

McCulloch, A., *The Golden Age of Australian Painting: Impressionism and the Heidelberg School*, Lansdowne, Melbourne, 1969.

Smith, B., *Documents on Art and Taste in Australia: The Colonial Period, 1770–1914*, Oxford University Press, Melbourne, 1975.

Chapters Six and Seven

Clark, J. & Whitelaw, B., *Golden Summers: Heidelberg and Beyond*, International Cultural Corporation of Australia Limited, 1985.

Eagle, M., *Australian Modern Painting, Between the Wars 1914–1939*, Bay Books, Sydney, 1990.

Gleeson, J., *Impressionist Painters, 1881–1930*, Lansdowne, Melbourne, 1971.

Smith, B., *Documents on Art and Taste in Australia: The Colonial Period, 1770–1914*, Oxford University Press, Melbourne, 1975.

Chapters Eight and Nine

Dixon, C. & Smith, T., *Aspects of Australian Figurative Painting 1942–1962: Dreams, Fears and Desires*, Power Institute of Fine Arts, University of Sydney, Sydney, 1984.

Gleeson, J., *Modern Painters 1931–1970*, Lansdowne, Melbourne, 1971.

Haese, R., *Rebels and Precursors: The Revolutionary Years of Australian Art*, Allen Lane, Ringwood, 1981.

McQueen, H., *Social Sketches of Australia, 1888–1975*, Penguin, Ringwood, 1977.

Merewether, C. (ed.), *Art and Social Commitment: An End to the City of Dreams, 1931–1948*, Art Gallery of New South Wales, Sydney, 1983.

Mollison, J. & Bonham, N., *Albert Tucker*, Macmillan with the co-operation of the Australian National Gallery in Canberra, Melbourne, 1982.

Chapter Ten

Catalano, G., *The Years of Hope: Australian Art and Criticism, 1959–1968*, Oxford University Press, Melbourne, 1981.

Gleeson, J., *Modern Painters 1931–1970*, Lansdowne, Melbourne, 1971.

Chapter Eleven

De Groen, G., *Conversations with Australian Artists*, Quartet Books, South Yarra, 1978.

Lindsay, R., *Vox Pop: Into the Eighties*, National Gallery of Victoria, Melbourne, 1983.

Radford, R., *Recent Australian Painting: A Survey 1970–1983 Art Gallery of South Australia*, Board of the Art Gallery of South Australia, Adelaide, 1983.

Taylor, P. (ed.), *Anything Goes: Art in Australia 1970–1980*, Art & Text, Melbourne, 1984.

Wiliams, D. & Simpson, C., *Art Now: Contemporary Art Post 1970*, McGraw-Hill Book Co., Sydney, 1994.

Discovering Art in the City

These architecture and sculpture maps for Canberra, Melbourne, Adelaide, Perth, Sydney, Brisbane and Hobart have been compiled so that teachers and their students can embark on a walking tour of their city. The maps do not comprise a comprehensive collection of architecture and sculpture, but include a selection of works to which students and the public are guaranteed easy access. Some of the sculptors, architects and architectural styles are discussed in the text.

ACTIVITIES

1. Select part of a building, and then identify and draw *four* of its architectural features. Use line and tone.

2. By making reference to the text or any other reference, identify the styles of any two buildings you have seen.

3. From the buildings you have seen on this walk, which style of architecture do you prefer? Why?

4. Carefully observe the different kinds of decoration on the facades of some buildings. Does the decoration change over the years? How does the decoration reflect the purpose of the building (for example, the Australian Coat of Arms, symbolising the Government of Australia, is placed on the facades of government buildings)?

5. Carefully investigate a traditional bronze statue. See if you can identify the following elements:
   (a) name of the sculptor
   (b) date of the work
   (c) name of the foundry, that is, where the bronze was cast
   (d) the texture of the original modelling, that is, the marks of the artist
   (e) the approximate size in relation to you

6. Research the process involved in making a bronze statue.

7. Compare an old sculpture with a contemporary piece. Then answer the following questions:
   (a) What materials have been used?
   (b) By what means have they been constructed?
   (c) Why were they made? (This may take some extra research.)
   (d) Note the location of the sculptures. Are they situated in prominent positions? If they are, why do you think this is so?

(e) For whom were they made (for example, a corporation, city council or gallery)? (You might need to contact the city council or gallery.)

(f) Are the sculptures consistent with other works from the same period? (You will need to do some research to find other works.)

(g) What classification would you give these sculptures: sculpture as a memorial, sculpture as decoration (that is, as part of the decoration of a building's facade, foyer, plaza, and so on) or sculpture just as a piece of sculpture, for its own sake?

8. There are occasions when sculpture is commissioned to improve the 'look' of an area or environment, or to humanise the city. In your opinion has the sculpture in your area fulfilled this aim? How else would you improve the aesthetics of a city? Do you think these are important considerations for architects, artists and town planners? Explain your answer.

Canberra

Architecture

A *Parliament House*, 1983–88, MITCHELL, GIURGOLA AND THORPE

B *High Court Building*, 1982, EDWARDS, MADIGAN AND TORZILLO

C *Academy of Sciences*, 1959, ROY GROUNDS

D *National Gallery of Australia*, 1982, EDWARDS, MADIGAN AND TORZILLO

E *Old Parliament House*, 1924–27, JOHN MURDOCH

F *Australian War Memorial*, 1941, JOHN CRUST AND EMIL SODERSTEEN

G *National Film and Sound Archive*, 1929–31, WALTER HAYWARD MORRIS AND ROBERT CASBOULTE

Sculpture

1 PETER CORLETT
Simpson and His Donkey—1915, 1988
Bronze

2 ANCHOR MARTLOCK WOOLLEY ARCHITECTS
Australian Hellenic Memorial
Mixed media (including olive trees, cypress and column)

3 KEN UNSWORTH
Vietnam Memorial, 1962–72, 1992
Mixed media installation (water, marble, stainless steel)

4 PETER CORLETT AND ANNE FERGUSON
Return Servicemans League Fountain, 1988
Marble, bronze

5 HENRY MOORE (UK)
Two piece reclining figure, No. 9, 1969
Bronze

6 TOM BASS
Entrance sculpture, National Library of Australia, 1968
Copper

7 LEONARD FRENCH
Stained glass windows in facade of Library, Date unknown

8 GEORGE BALDESSIN
Pear Version No. 2, 1973–76
Painted cast steel

9 LEONARD SHILLMAN
Threshold, 1966
Stone

10 TOM BASS
Ethos, 1961
Copper

11 KERRY SIMPSON, Designer—ACTEA, 1988
Glass bricks, stainless steel, coloured lights

12 ROBERT WOODWARD
Canberra Times Fountain, 1979
Stainless steel

13 JOHN ROBINSON
Eternity, 1980
Bronze

14 MILAN VOJSK
Dreaming, 1974
Bronze

15 EDGAR AUSTRUMS
Chug, 1986
Painted steel

16 BRUCE RADKE
Passacaglia, 1985
Steel

17 PHILIP SPELMAN
Napoleon, 1986
Painted steel

18 LEVA POCIUS
Eagle Queen of Serpents, 1988
Bronze

19 MARY KAYSER
Resting Place of the Dragonfly, 1989
Painted steel

20 BRUCE RADKE
Dance of the Secateurs, 1988
Painted steel

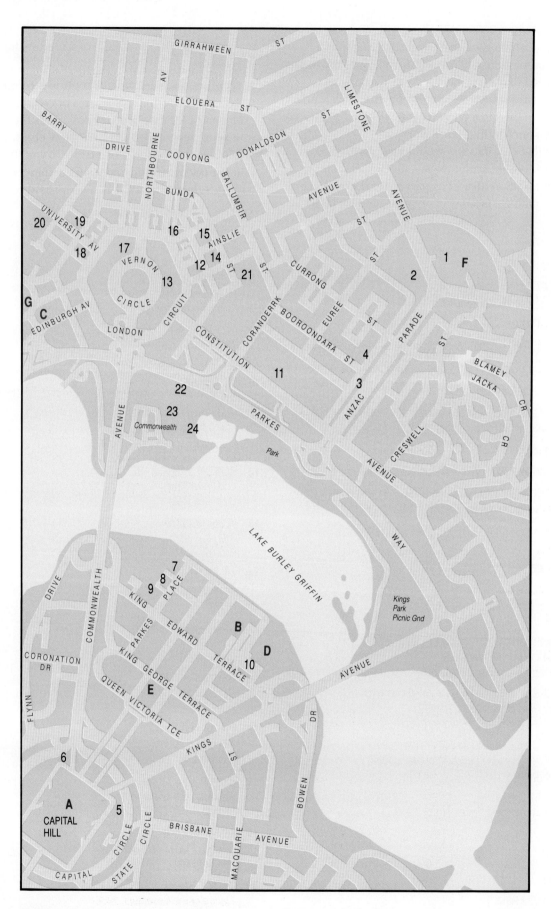

Canberra: *Architecture and sculpture locations*

21 PHILIP SPELMAN
Zngzwang, 1990
Steel

22 BARBARA HEPWORTH (UK)
Two figures, 1968
Bronze, painted areas

23 PETER VANDERMARK AND PAUL LYNZAAT
... Shadow of a Doubt, 1991
Mud brick

24 NORMA REDPATH
Fountain, 1969
Bronze

Melbourne

Architecture

A *Exhibition Building*, 1880, J. REED AND BARNES*

B *ICI House*, 1960, BATES, SMART AND McCUTCHEON*

C *Princess Theatre*, 1886, W. PITT; altered in 1922 by A. WALKLEY

D *Parliament House*, 1856–92, KNIGHT AND KERR*

E *Treasury*, 1857–62, possibly J. CLARK

F *Shell House*, 1988–89, H. SEIDLER*

G *The Forum Theatre*, 1928, J. EBERSON (USA)

H *Gas and Fuel Building*

J *Myer Music Bowl*, 1959, YUNCKEN, FREEMAN BROS, GRIFFITHS AND SIMPSON*

K *Arts Centre Complex*, 1969, SIR ROY GROUNDS*

L *Melbourne Town Hall*, 1867–70, J. REED AND BARNES*

M *Manchester Unity Building*, 1932, M. BARLOW

N *State Library and Museum of Victoria*, 1854–1913, J. REED*

O *Mitchell House*, 1936, H. NORRIS*

P *GPO*, 1959, A. JOHNSON (note the three levels depicting three different orders of columns)

Q *Safe Deposit Building*, 1890, W. PITT

R *ANZ Bank*, 1883, W. WARDELL (note the interior)

S *Alkira House*, 1937, J. WARDROP (superb example of Art Deco)

T *Customs House*, 1858–70, KNIGHT, KEMP AND KERR*

U *The Olderfleet building*, 1889–90, W. PITT

V *The Rialto*, 1890, W.PITT and *The Rialto Tower*, 1987, PERROTT, LYON MATHIESON*

W *Old BHP House*, 1972, B. PATTEN*

X *101 Collins Street*, 1989, DENTON CORKER MARSHALL*

Y *Telecom building*, 1988–93, PERROTT, LYON MATHIESON

Z *300 Latrobe Street*, 1991, NONDA KATSALIDIS

*For further information, see the text.

Sculpture

1 STEPHEN WALKER
Forest Landscape Fountain, 1969
Bronze

2 PAUL MONTFORD
Adam Lindsay Gordon, 1933*
Bronze

3 PAUL MONTFORD
Chief Justice of Victoria, George Higinbotham, 1936
Bronze

4 J. S. MACKENNAL
Figures above entrance to Hotel Windsor, c. 1833–87*
Stone

5 BERTRAM MACKENNAL*
Sir William John Clarke, 1902
Stone

6 WILLIAM BOWLES
Diana and the Hounds, 1939
Bronze

7 CHARLES PERRY (USA)
Untitled, 1988–89
Aluminium (inside the building notice glass ceramic mural of *The Bathers* by Arthur Boyd)

8 MIMMO PALADINO (Italy)
The Paladino Sculpture, 1986
Bronze (commissioned for Hyatt on Collins)

9 CHARLES WEB GILBERT
Matthew Flinders, 1923–25*
Bronze

10 TOM BASS
The Genii, 1973
Bronze

11 JAMES WHITE
Queen Victoria Memorial, 1903
Stone

12 PAUL MONTFORD*
The Water Nymph, 1924
Bronze

13 BARONESS YRSA VON LEISTNER
The Phoenix
Bronze

14 JOHN ROBINSON
The Pathfinder, 1971
Bronze

15 BRUCE ARMSTRONG
Untitled installations (two pieces), 1987
Wood

16 GEOFFREY BARTLETT
The Messenger, 1982
Steel

17 FIONA ORR
Isomorphic Impressions, 1985
Mixed media

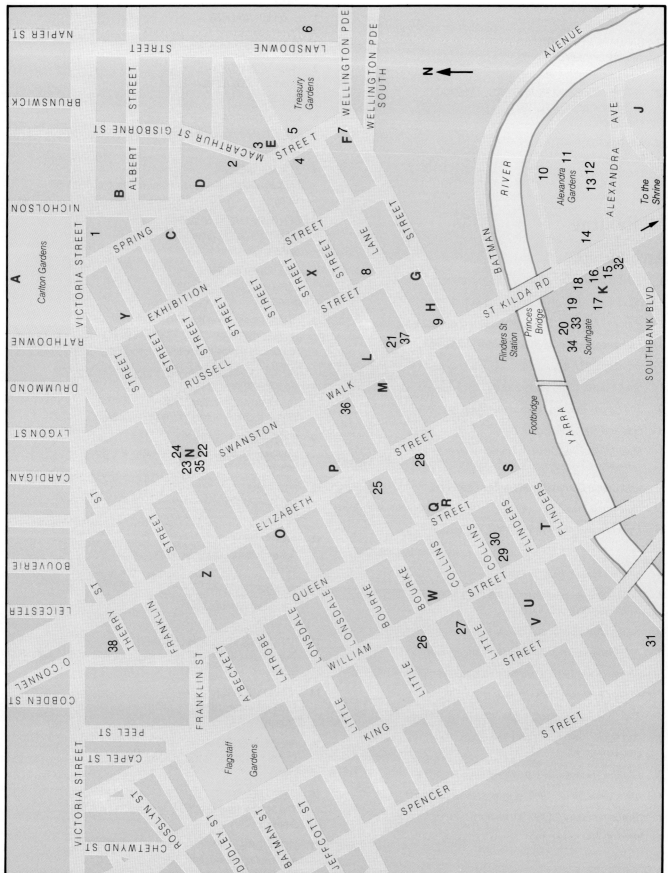

Melbourne: Architecture and sculpture locations

18 WILLEM DE KOONING (USA)
Standing Figure, 1987
Bronze

19 INGE KING
Forward Surge, 1973*
Steel

20 CLEMENT MEADMORE*
Dervish, c. 1982
Corten steel

21 CHARLES SUMMERS
Burke and Wills, 1865*
Bronze

22 EMMANUEL FREMIET (France)
Joan of Arc, acquired in 1907
Bronze (the face of Joan of Arc was modelled on John Peter
Russell's wife Marianne in Paris)

23 G. JAMIESON
Sir Redmond Barry
Bronze

24 J. E. BOEHM
St George and the Dragon, acquired in 1888
Bronze

25 NORMA REDPATH*
Cariatid, 1983
Steel

26 KEN REINHARD
Cubes, 1971
Mixed media (outside Marland House)

27 CLEMENT MEADMORE
Awakening, 1969*
Corten steel

28 TOM BASS
Children's Tree, 1963
Bronze

29 MICHAEL MESZAROS
John Pascoe Fawkner, 1978
Bronze

30 STANLEY HAMMOND
John Batman, 1978
Bronze

31 RON ROBERTSON-SWANN
The Vault, 1980*
Painted steel

32 DEBORAH HALPERN
Angel, 1987–89
Ceramic, steel, concrete

33 TIM JONES
Spirit, 1992
Mild steel, painted steel, copper, architectural paint.

34 DEBORAH HALPERN
Ophelia, 1992
Ceramic, concrete

*For further information, see the text.

35 PETRIS SPONK
Architectural fragment, 1992
Bluestone

36 ALISON WEAVER, PAUL QUINN
*Three Businessmen Who Brought Their Own Lunch: Batman,
Swanston and Hoddle*, 1994
Bronze

37 LORETTA QUINN
Beyond the Ocean of Existence, 1993
Bronze

38 MARK STONER
Passage, 1994
Bluestone

Adelaide

Architecture

A *Parliament House*, 1936–39, WRIGHT AND TAYLER

B *Old Parliament House* (Constitutional Museum), 1855–56,
W. HAYS

C *Adelaide Railway Station*, 1924, GARLICK AND JACKMAN

D *Electra House* (Telecommunications Museum), 1900–01,
J. QUINTON BRUCE

E *GPO*, 1867, WRIGHT AND WOODS

F *Town Hall*, 1863–66, WRIGHT AND WOODS AND D. GARLICK

G *Colonial Mutual Life Building*, 1934–36, HENNESSY AND HENNESSY

H *Edmund Wright House*, 1867–77, WRIGHT AND TAYLER*

J *Sands and McDougall Building*, 1933, CLARIDGE, BRUER AND
FISHER*

K *Adelaide War Memorial*, 1931, WOODS, BAGOT, JORY AND
LAYBOURNE-SMITH, with sculpture by RAYNER HOFF

L *Old MLC Building*, 1955, BATES, SMART AND McCUTCHEON with
CHEESMAN DOLEY, BRABHAM AND NEIGHBOUR*

M *Adelaide High School*, 1940, FITZGERALD AND BROGAN

N *Adelaide Botanical Gardens, Tropical Conservatory*, 1986–89,
RAFFEN MARON ARCHITECTS*

Sculpture

1 MAURICE LAMBERT (son of George Lambert*)
His Majesty King George V, 1938
Bronze

2 OLA COHN
Pioneer Women's Memorial, 1940–41
Sandstone

3 BERT FLUGELMAN*
Continuum, 1973
Stainless steel

4 HENRY MOORE (UK)
Reclining Connected Forms, 1969
Bronze (in front of Napier House, Adelaide University)

5 ALFRED DRURY
Sir Thomas Elder, 1903 (also four relief panels depicting his life)
Bronze

6 F. J. WILLIAMSON
Sir Walter Watson Hughes, 1936
Bronze

7 BERT FLUGELMAN*
Knot, 1975
Stainless steel

8 OWEN BROUGHTON
Steel construction, 1975–76
Steel

9 DONALD JUDD (USA)
Untitled concrete piece, 1974
Concrete (at rear of Art Gallery of South Australia)

10 BERTRAM MACKENNAL*
His Majesty King Edward VII
Bronze (also other figures on this monument)

11 RAYNER HOFF*
Figures on the Art Deco War Memorial, 1930–31
Bronze and marble

12 LYNDON DADSWELL*
Progress, 1959
Welded copper (on facade of David Jones Building)

13 BERT FLUGELMAN*
Spheres, 1977
Stainless steel

14 JOHN DOWIE
The Slide, 1977
Bronze

15 MARGEL HINDER*
Untitled sculpture, 1972
Steel and stainless steel

16 NORMA REDPATH*
Immortal Warrior, 1966
Bronze

17 JOHN DOWIE
Fountain of the Three Rivers, 1968
Cast aluminium
(This depicts the three rivers feeding the water into the fountain:
the Murray depicted by a male Aborigine holding an ibis; the
smaller Onkaparinga River shown by a European woman
holding a heron; and the Torrens by a European woman
holding a black swan.)

18 ADRIAN JONES
Captain James Sturt, 1916
Bronze

19. WILLIAM BIRNIE RHIND
Colonel William Light, 1906
Bronze

20 BERT FLUGELMAN*
Tetrahedra, 1974
Stainless steel (Festival Theatre)

20 PHILLIP KING (UK)
Yellow Between, 1973
Painted iron

20. BARBARA HEPWORTH (UK)
Ultimate Form, 1973
Bronze

20 ROD DUDLEY
Society Ladies, 1973
Wood, fabric, paint and leather

20 OTTO HERBERT HAJEK
Shorthand Adelaide, 1977
Painted sculpture environment

21 OWEN BROUGHTON
Untitled, 1977
Steel

22 ROBERT KLIPPEL*
Bronze sculpture Number 714, 1988
Bronze

23 AKIO MAKIGAWA*
Elements and Being, 1988
Marble

24 MAREA GAZZARD
Mandorla, 1993
Bronze

25 HILARIE MAIS
Wave, 1988
Painted aluminium (blue)

26 HOSSEIN VALAMANESH*
Knocking from the Inside, 1989
Sandstone, granite, wood, ceramic

27 MARIA KUCZYNSKA
No Regrets, 1993
Bronze

28 BRONWYN OLIVER*
Eyrie, 1993
Copper, bronze

29 VICTOR MEERTENS
Rhythms of Construction 1–3, Construction/Thought?Optimism,
1987–92
Bronze

---

* For further information, see the text.

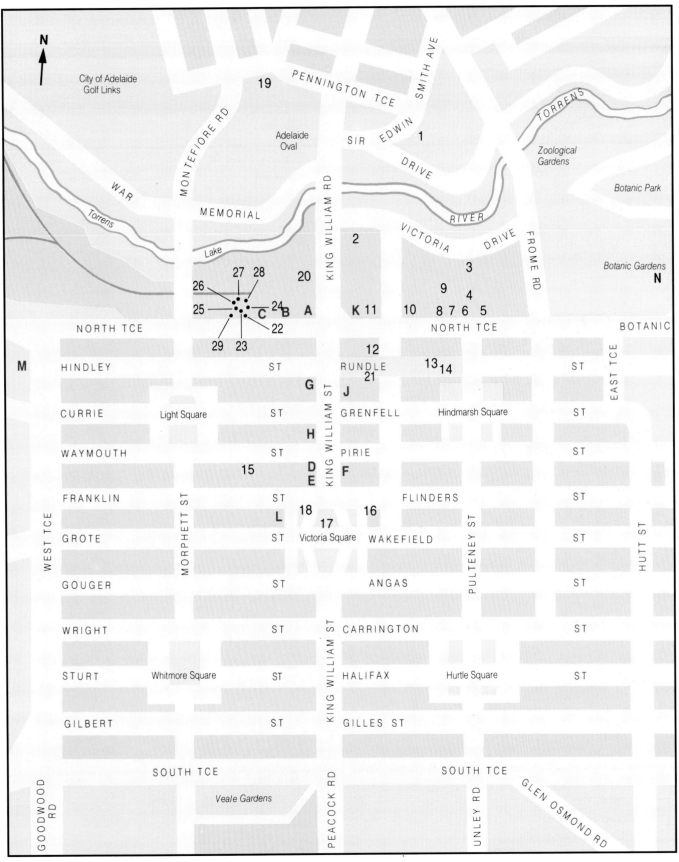

N

City of Adelaide
Golf Links

PENNINGTON TCE

SMITH AVE

19

Adelaide
Oval

MONTEFIORE RD

SIR

EDWIN

1

TORRENS

Zoological
Gardens

WAR

MEMORIAL

Torrens

KING WILLIAM RD

DRIVE

RIVER

Botanic Park

Lake

2

VICTORIA

DRIVE

FROME RD

Botanic Gardens

27 28

3

N

26

9

4

20

25

C 24 B A

K 11

10

8 7 6 5

22

NORTH TCE

NORTH TCE

BOTANIC

29 23

M

12

EAST TCE

HINDLEY

ST

RUNDLE

13 14

ST

G

21

KING WILLIAM ST

J

CURRIE

Light Square

ST

GRENFELL

Hindmarsh Square

ST

H

WAYMOUTH

ST

PIRIE

ST

MORPHETT ST

15

D

F

E

FRANKLIN

ST

FLINDERS

ST

WEST TCE

L

18

16

17

GROTE

ST

Victoria Square

WAKEFIELD

ST

HUTT ST

GOUGER

ST

ANGAS

ST

PULTENEY ST

WRIGHT

ST

CARRINGTON

ST

KING WILLIAM ST

STURT

Whitmore Square

ST

HALIFAX

Hurtle Square

ST

GILBERT

ST

GILLES ST

SOUTH TCE

SOUTH TCE

GOODWOOD RD

PEACOCK RD

Veale Gardens

UNLEY RD

GLEN OSMOND RD

Adelaide: Architecture and sculpture locations

Perth

Architecture

A *Council House*, 1963, HOWLETT AND BAILEY

B *Weld Club*, 1882, J. TALBOT HOBBS

C *Supreme Court*, 1903, J. H. GRAINGER

D *Treasury Buildings* (Central Government Offices), 1874, northern half of west wing by R. R. JEWELL (Government Architect); third storey added in 1896, by G. T. POOLE (also Government Architect)

E *Perth Town Hall*, 1870, R. R. JEWELL (built with free convict labour)

F *Old Perth Boys School* (National Trust Shop), 1852–54, W. A. SANFORD (also built from free labour)

G *The Cloisters*, 1850, J. BRITTAIN

H *His Majesty's Theatre*, 1904, W. WOLFF*

J *Wesley Church*, 1867–70, R. R. JEWELL

K *GPO*, 1915, C. W. ARNOTT

L *Art Gallery of Western Australia*, 1979, C. SIERAKOWSKI

M *Alexander Library Building*, 1986, CAMERON, CHISOLM AND NICOL

N Allendale Square, 1976, CAMERON, CHISOLM AND NICOL

O *London Court*, 1937, B. EVANS*

P *R&I Bank Tower*, 1988, CAMERON, CHISOLM AND NICOL

Q *QV1*, 1989, H. SEIDLER*

Sculpture

1 CLEMENT MEADMORE*
Outdoor Sculpture, 1979–90
Corten steel

2 HENRY MOORE (UK)
Reclining Figure, 1956
Bronze

3 GERHARD MARCKS
Der Rufer (The Caller), 1967
Bronze

4 AKIO MAKIGAWA*
Gate 2, Coalesce, 1987
Granite

5 FRANK WILKINSON
150th Commemorative Fountain: Earth, Fire and Water, 1979 (people's related challenge to these elements for development)
Steel and stone

6 C. P. SOMERS
Captain James Stirling, 1979
Bronze

7 Unknown
Commemorative Plaque Featuring Swans Holding a Crown
Copper, gilt and bronze (on Council House)

8 G. KOSTURKOV
Life, 1983
Stainless steel

9 SIR GEORGE FRAMPTON (UK)
Peter Pan
Bronze

10 MARGARET PRIEST
Untitled bronze statue of a family under a welded construction, 1976
Bronze and steel

11 PIETRO C. PORCELLI
Alexander Forrest, 1902
Bronze

12 HOWARD TAYLOR
Burnt Tree Stumps, 1975
Concrete mould with tile mosaic (outside AMP Building)

13 DAVID JONES
Altair acquile, 1983
Stainless steel (fountain in entrance to SGIO Building)

14 JOAN WALSH-SMITH
Untitled wall piece of horses, 1986
Bronze (on eastern wall of Forrest Building)

15 UNKNOWN
South African War Memorial with four relief panels, 1901
Bronze (Kings Park)

15 F. WILLIAMSON
Queen Victoria, 1902
Stone (Kings Park)

15 BERTRAM MACKENNAL*
Lord Forrest, Explorer Statesman, 1847–1918
Bronze (Kings Park)

15 MARGARET PRIEST
Pioneer Women's Memorial, 1968
Bronze (fountain in lake, Kings Park)

15 ATHANASIOS KALAMARAS
Minmara Gun-Gun (A Place Where the Spirits of Women Rest), 1979
Stone relief wall

Sydney

Architecture

A *Opera House*, 1956–73, J. UTZON*

B *ICI House*, 1959, BATES, SMART AND McCUTCHEON

C *Customs House*, 1885, J. BARNET (note the fish around the clock)

D *Lands Department Building*, 1877–90s, J. BARNET*

E *Education Department Building*, 1913, possibly G. McRAE

Perth: Architecture and sculpture locations

F *Old Treasury* (now Intercontinental Hotel), 1849, M. LEWIS

G *Chief Secretary's Building*, 1878, J. BARNET

H *State Library*, 1839–41; west wing 1906–09, W. L. VERNON

J *Parliament House*, 1816; additions in 1843, W. L. VERNON

K *Sydney Hospital*, 1879–94, T. ROWE

L *Mint Building*, 1816

M *Hyde Park Barracks*, 1817–19, F. GREENWAY*

N *St James Church*, 1820, F. GREENWAY*

O *Supreme Court*, 1820–28 (Greenway dismissed in 1822, completed by another architect in 1828)

P *Art Gallery of New South Wales*, 1885, J. HORBURY HUNT

Q *Anzac Memorial*, 1932–33, B. DELLIT*

R *Sydney Town Hall*, 1868–88; Centennial Hall completed in 1888 by J. WILSON; Tower by T. AND E. BRADBRIDGE*

S *Queen Victoria Building*, 1893–98, G. McRAE*

T *American Express Building*, 1976, JOHN ANDREWS INTERNATIONAL

U *GPO*, 1866–74; Pitt St section 1881–85, J. BARNET

V *Australia Square Tower*, 1967, H. SEIDLER*

W *Chifley Tower*, 1993, KOHN, PEDERSEN FOX/TRAVIS PARTNERS*

Sculpture

1 TOM BASS
Research, 1956–59 (ICI House)
Copper

2 TOM BASS
Stylised copper figures, 1962
Copper (AMP building)

3 JOHN ROBINSON
Bonds of Friendship, 1980
Bronze (in front of Customs House)

4 KOLOZSY
Women's Pioneering Sculpture, 1988
Bronze

5 ROBERT KLIPPEL
Beacon, 1994
Bronze

6 FRANK STELLA (USA)
The Stellas, 1986–87
Steel, wood (in foyer of National Bank)

7 ADRIAN MAURIKS
Bird Totem, 1987
Steel

8 ALEXANDER CALDER (USA)
Crossed Blades, 1967
Painted steel

9 BERTRAM MACKENNAL*
War Memorial, 1928
Bronze

10 BERT FLUGELMAN
Pyramid Tower, 1978*
Stainless steel

11 MARGEL HINDER*
Abstract Copper, 1964
Copper (on facade of Reserve Bank)

12 J. BOEHM
Queen Victoria, 1888
Bronze (note the decoration on cloak)

13 MARGEL HINDER*
Six Day War II, 1973
Steel

14 RICHARD GOODWIN
Mobius Sea, 1986
Stone

15 GEORGE LAMBERT*
Henry Lawson Memorial, 1927–30
Bronze

16 FRANCOIS SICARD
Archibald Fountain, 1927; installed in Hyde Park 1933
Bronze
(Central figure of Apollo represents beauty, light and the arts. The spraying water behind the figure is symbolic of the rays of the sun. The reclining male is a symbol of peace, the figure of Diana with a stag represents harmony, while the remaining figure of Diana fighting the Minotaur is symbolic of the triumph of right.)

17 GERARD HAVEKES
Water, Fire and Earth, 1961
Sandstone
(Three figures are symbolic of the elements. The first is a fisherman looking out to sea; beside him is a woman depicting womanhood, initiation and progress. The final figure is a pioneer.)

18 THOMAS WOOLNER
Captain Cook, 1874–79*
Bronze

19 RAYNER HOFF
Sacrifice, 1931*
Bronze (inside Anzac Memorial)

20 JOHN HUGHES
Queen Victoria
Bronze (originally this sculpture was situated in Dublin)

21 LYNDON DADSWELL*
Shapes on facade of building, 1953
Aluminium

22 BRETT WHITELEY*
Almost Once, 1968–91
Black butt timber, fibreglass

23 AKIO MAKIGAWA*
Night Sea Crossing, 1992
Marble, stainless steel

24 STEPHEN WALKER
The Tank Stream Sculpture, 1981
Bronze

*For further information, see the text.

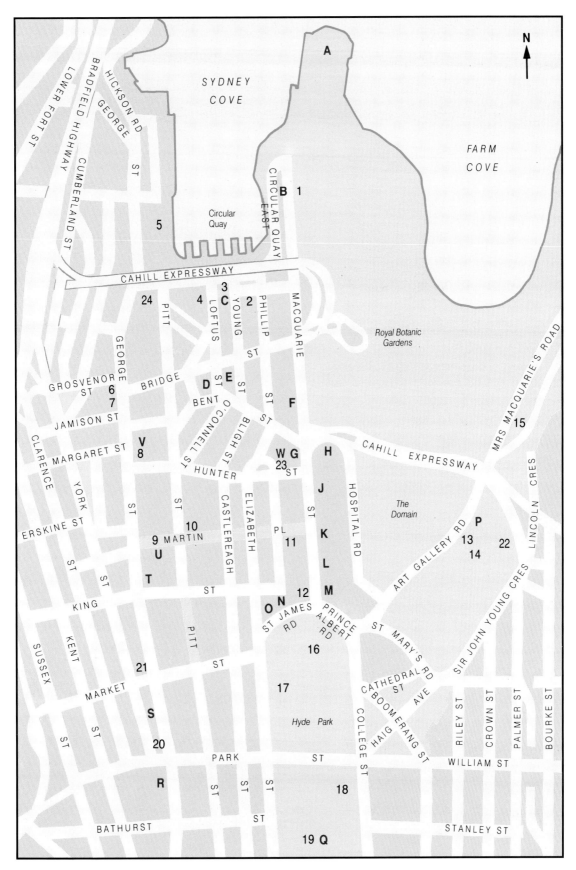

Sydney: *Architecture and sculpture locations*

Brisbane

Architecture

A *Old Government House*, 1860–62, C. TIFFIN

B *Parliament House*, 1865–68, C. TIFFIN

C *Queensland Club*, 1882–84, F. STANLEY

D *Harbours Building*, 1879–81, J. PETRIE

E *Naval Office*, 1900

F *Town Hall*, 1920–30, HALL AND PRENTICE*

G *Bank of NSW*, 1929, HALL AND DEVEREUX

H *Treasury Building*, 1885–89, J. J. CLARK*

J *Queensland Cultural Centre*, 1982, R. GIBSON AND PARTNERS

K *Lands Administration Building*, 1914–22, A. B. BRADY

L *Government Printing Office*, 1874–1910, E. E. SMITH
(note the sculpture of the devil on the building)

M *Macarthur Buildings*, opened 1934, HALL AND COOK

N *Former CML Building*, opened 1931, HENNESSY AND HENNESSY
(note the gargoyles, lions and rich Romanesque decoration)

O *GPO*, 1871–72, F. STANLEY (on Elizabeth Street facade note the superbly stylised relief motifs of the pawpaw and mango trees)

P *Customs House*, 1886–89, J. PETRIE

Q *Queensland National Bank*, 1885–87, F. STANLEY*

R *Anzac Square*, 1930, BUCHANAN AND COWPER

S *Riverside Tower*, 1983–86, H. SEIDLER

Sculpture

1 DAPHNE MAYO*
Frieze: sculptured figures in tympanum, 1930*
Sandstone (Brisbane Town Hall)

2 STEPHEN WALKER
Pioneering Sculpture, 1988
Bronze

3 E. F. KHOLER AND E. TAYLOR
King George V, 1938
Bronze

4 NORMA REDPATH*
Sculptural Column, 1972
Bronze

5 DAPHNE MAYO*
Major-General Sir William Glasgow, 1966
Bronze

6 CATHERINA HAMPSON
Advocacy, 1986
Bronze (Inns of Court)

7 MARY FRASER
Wall sculpture, 1977
Clay and aluminium

8 ANTHONY PRYOR*
Approaching Equilibrium, 1985
Painted steel

8 CLEMENT MEADMORE*
Off Shoot, 1985
Painted aluminium

8 LEONARD AND KATHLEEN SHILLAM
Pelicans, 1985
Bronze

8 RON ROBERTSON-SWANN*
Leviathan Play, 1985
Painted steel

9 LEONARD SHILLAM
Enlightenment, 1959
Aluminium

10 THOMAS BROCK
Queen Victoria Memorial, 1906
Bronze

11 BERTRAM MACKENNAL*
T. J. Ryan, 1925
Bronze

12 MICHAEL SANTRY
Suspended sculpture, 1968
Painted aluminium

13 JOHN DOWIE
Queen Elizabeth II, 1986
Bronze

14 MICHAEL SANTRY
Suspended sculpture, 1987
Painted aluminium

15 NORMAN CARLBERG (USA)
Winter Winds
Steel on marble

16 WILLIAM WEBSTER
Mooney Memorial Fountain, 1879
(Gothic fountain dedicated to John Mooney, a fireman who died while fighting a Brisbane fire)

17 TOM BASS
Relief Panel, 1966
Copper

18 BERTRAM MACKENNAL*
T. J. Byrnes, 1902
Bronze

19 LEONARD SHILLAM
Proclamation figure, 1959
Bronze (St John's Cathedral)

---

*For further information, see the text.

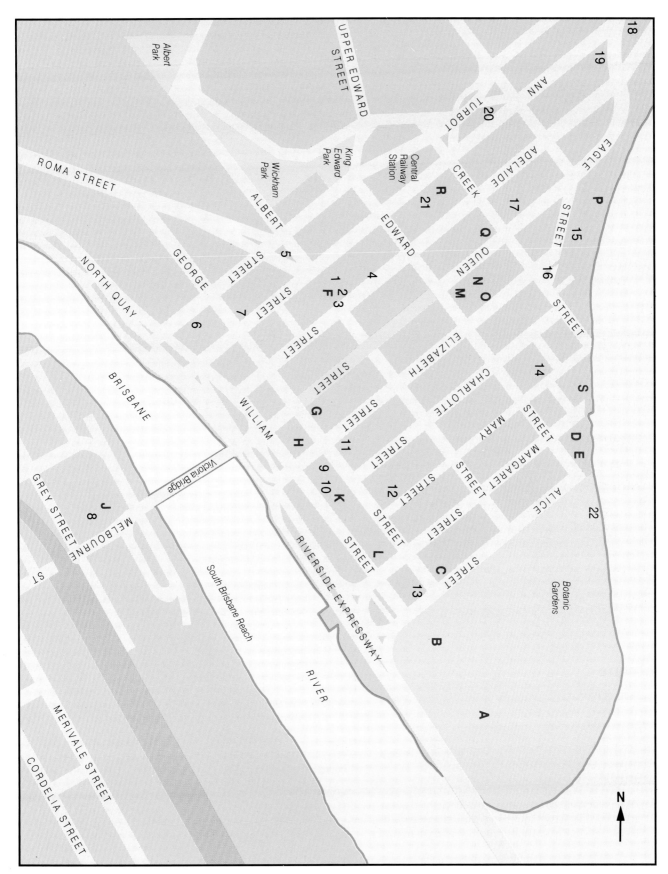

Brisbane: *Architecture and sculpture locations*

19 DAPHNE MAYO*
Stations of the Cross
Plaster

20 ANDOR MESZAROS
Christ Accepting His Cross, 1962
Bronze and wood

21 DAPHNE MAYO*
Relief sculpture, 1932
Sandstone (Women's War Memorial, Anzac Memorial)

22 ROBERT JUNIPER
Plantform, 1989
Painted steel

Hobart

Architecture

A *City Hall*, 1911, R. N. BUTLER

B *Customs House*, 1815, W. WILSON

C *Parliament House*, 1836–41, J. L. ARCHER

D *Savings Bank of Tasmania*, 1858, E. C. ROUNDTREE (note the interior)

E *Colonial Mutual Life Building*, c. 1934–36, HENNESSY AND HENNESSY
(note the gargoyles on the top of the building and the line of decorative faces in between the first and second floors)

F *GPO*, 1905, A. C. WALKER

G *Town Hall*, 1864, H. HUNTER

H *The Royal Hobart Hospital*, 1939, LEIGHTON AND IRWIN

J *The Treasury*, 1823–24, J. L. ARCHER

K *Hydro Building*, 1938–39, A. K. HENDERSON AND PARTNERS

L *Tasmanian Museum and Art Gallery*, 1863, H. HUNTER

Sculpture

1 CHRIS BEECROFT
Minute Man, 1986
Painted steel

2 OLA COHN
Two figures above entrance to Royal Hobart Hospital, 1938
Sandstone
(The male figure is symbolic of science and conveys scientific development over the ages, and the storing of and quest for knowledge. The female figure is symbolic of humanity—the great mother Soul giving understanding, strength, love and care.)

---

*For further information, see the text.

3 LYNDON DADSWELL*
Settlement and Development in Hobart, 1954
Stone mural

3 LYNDON DADSWELL
The Family, 1950s
(figures around the wall of the bank showing 'Creative Arts Community')
Stone

4 TOM BASS
Relief copper and bronze of AMP emblem on wall of AMP building, 1969
Copper and bronze

5 PETER TAYLOR
Piece in foyer of Stock Exchange building, c. 1986
Painted wood

6 IAN McKAY
Bright Prospect, 1979
Painted steel

7 JOHN DAVIS
Untitled, 1970
Aluminium

8 STANLEY HAMMOND
A. G. Ogilvie, Premier of Tasmania, 1934–39
Bronze

9 STEPHEN WALKER
Early Dutch Navigators, 1988
Bronze

10 STEPHEN WALKER
Piece on wall of Criminal Court Building
Bronze

11 ST DAVID'S PARK
Various tombs and monuments in gothic revival and neo-classical styles. The two stone lions on the Davey St corner originally came from the Bank of Van Diemen's Land. The lions were carved in a tent on the footpath by Richard Patterson in 1884.

12 RODNEY BROAD
Australian Coat of Arms, Family Court Building
(note the depiction of the shadow behind the coat of arms)
Bronze

13 STEPHEN WALKER
Australian Coat of Arms on outside of Family Court Building, 1975
Bronze

14 STEPHEN WALKER
Spring Landscape, 1968
Bronze (in garden outside Commonwealth building)

15 STEPHEN WALKER
The Seasons
Bronze (IGIO building)

16 M. RACCI
William Crowther, Premier of Tasmania
Bronze

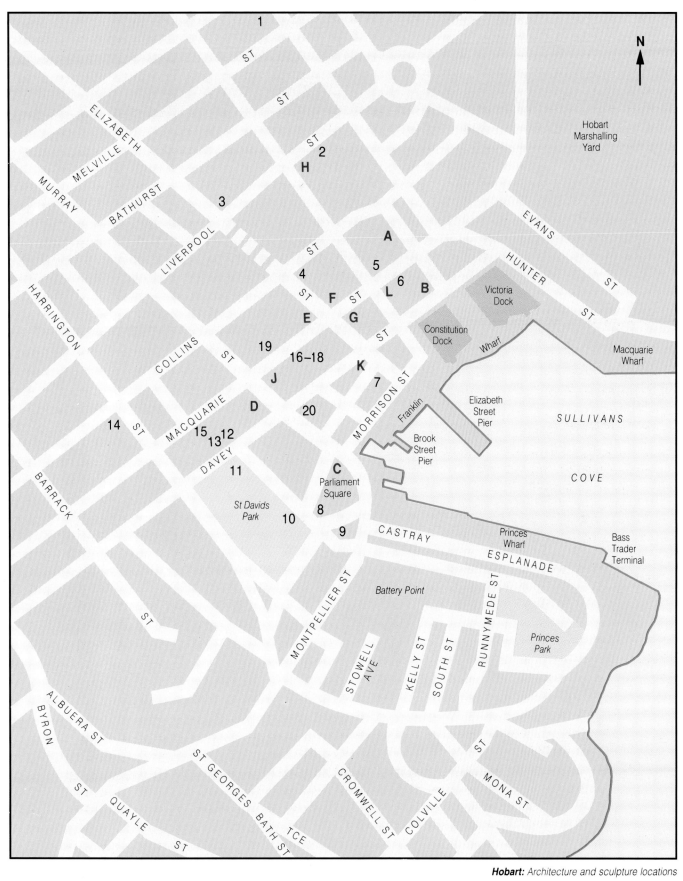

Hobart: *Architecture and sculpture locations*

17 H. NOBLE
John Franklin
Bronze

18 LEONARD JENNINGS
Edward VII The Peacemaker, 1921
Bronze

19 STEPHEN WALKER
Antarctic Piece, 1984
Bronze

20 PETER TAYLOR
Two Figures Exchanging Birds, 1981
Huon pine (in foyer of Executive Building)

Public Art Galleries in Australia

Victoria

Australian Centre for Contemporary Art
Dallas Brooks Drive
SOUTH YARRA 3141
Ph. (03) 654 6422

Benalla Art Gallery
Bridge Street
BENALLA 3672
Ph. (057) 62 3027

Bendigo Art Gallery
View Street
BENDIGO 3550
Ph. (054) 43 4991

City of Ballarat Fine Art Gallery
40 Lydiard Street
BALLARAT 3350
Ph. (053) 31 5622

Geelong Art Gallery
Little Malop Street
GEELONG 3220
Ph. (052) 29 3645

Ian Potter Gallery
University of Melbourne
PARKVILLE 3052
Ph. (03) 344 5148

Latrobe Regional Art Centre
Commercial Road
MORWELL 3840
Ph. (051) 34 1364

McClelland Gallery
McClelland Drive
LANGWARRIN 3910
Ph. (03) 789 1671

Mildura Art Centre
199 Cureton Street
MILDURA 3500
Ph. (050) 23 3733

Monash University Gallery
Monash University
CLAYTON 3168
Ph. (03) 905 4217

Museum of Modern Art at Heide
7 Templestowe Road
BULLEEN 3105
Ph. (03) 850 1500

National Gallery of Victoria
180 St Kilda Road
MELBOURNE 3004
Ph. (03) 685 0222

Shepparton Arts Centre
Welsford Street
SHEPPARTON 3630
Ph. (058) 21 6352

Swan Hill Regional Art Gallery
Horseshoe Bend Road
SWAN HILL 3585
Ph. (050) 32 1403

Waverley City Gallery
170 Jells Road
WAVERLEY 3150
Ph. (03) 562 1609

South Australia

Art Gallery of South Australia
North Terrace
ADELAIDE 5000
Ph. (08) 207 7000

Carrick Hill
590 Fullarton Road
SPRINGFIELD 5062
Ph. (08) 379 3886

Contemporary Art Centre of South Australia
14 Porter Street
PARKSIDE 5063
Ph. (08) 272 2682

Experimental Art Foundation
1 Morphett Street
ADELAIDE 5000
Ph. (08) 211 7507

Flinders University Art Museum
Flinders University
BEDFORD PARK 5042
Ph. (08) 201 2695

Tandanya, National Aboriginal Cultural Institute
253 Grenfell Street
ADELAIDE 5000
Ph. (08) 223 2467

Western Australia

Art Gallery of Western Australia
47 James Street
PERTH 6000
Ph. (09) 328 7233

Geraldton Art Gallery
24 Chapman Road
GERALDTON 6530
Ph. (099) 21 6811

Lawrence Wilson Art Gallery
University of Western Australia
NEDLANDS 6009
Ph. (09) 380 3707

PICA (Perth Institute of Contemporary Art)
51 James Street
PERTH 6000
Ph. (09) 227 6144

ACT

Australian War Memorial
Anzac Parade
CANBERRA 2600
Ph. (062) 243 4211

Canberra Contemporary Art Space
Gorman House
Ainslie Avenue
BRADDON 2601
Ph. (06) 247 0188

National Gallery of Australia
CANBERRA 2600
Ph. (062) 271 2411

New South Wales

Albury Regional Art Centre
546 Dean Street
ALBURY 2640
Ph. (060) 23 8187

Art Gallery of New South Wales
Art Gallery Road
SYDNEY 2000
Ph. (02) 225 1700

Artspace
The Gunnery
Cowper Wharf Road
WOOLLOOMOOLOO 2011
Ph. (02) 368 1899

Lismore Art Gallery
131 Molesworth Street
LISMORE 2480
Ph. (066) 22 2209

Museum of Contemporary Art
The Rocks
SYDNEY 2000
Ph. (02) 252 4033

New England Regional Art Museum
Kentucky Street
ARMIDALE 2350
Ph. (067) 72 5255

Newcastle Region Art Gallery
Laman Street
NEWCASTLE 2300
Ph. (049) 29 3263

Orange Regional Gallery
Civic Square, Byng Street
ORANGE 2800
Ph. (063) 61 5136

S. H. Ervin Gallery
National Trust Centre
Observatory Hill
SYDNEY 2000
Ph. (02) 258 0174

Wollongong City Gallery
85 Burelli Street
WOLLONGONG EAST 2500
Ph. (042) 28 7500

Queensland

City of Ipswich Art Gallery
Cnr Nicholas and Limestone Streets
IPSWICH 4305
Ph. (07) 842 3477

Gladstone Art Gallery and Museum
Bramston Street
GLADSTONE 4680
Ph. (079) 72 2022

Perc Tucker Regional Gallery
Flinders Mall
TOWNSVILLE 4810
Ph. (077) 22 0289

Queensland Art Gallery
South Bank Queensland Cultural Centre
SOUTH BRISBANE 4000
Ph. (07) 840 7333

Rockhampton Art Gallery
Victoria Parade
ROCKHAMPTON 4700
Ph. (079) 27 7129

University Art Museum
Queensland University
ST LUCIA 4067
Ph. (07) 365 3167

Tasmania

Burnie Art Gallery
Wilmot Street
BURNIE 7320
Ph. (004) 31 5033

Devonport Gallery and Art Centre
Stewart Street
DEVONPORT 7310
Ph. (004) 24 8296

Queen Victoria Museum and Art Gallery
Wellington Street
LAUNCESTON 7250
Ph. (003) 311 6777

Tasmanian Museum and Art Gallery
5 Argyle Street
HOBART 7000
Ph. (002) 35 0777

Northern Territory

Araluen Centre for Arts & Entertainment
Larapinta Drive
ALICE SPRINGS 0670
Ph. (089) 52 5022

Northern Territory Museum of Arts and Sciences
Bullocky Point
FANNIE BAY 5790
Ph. (089) 89 8201

24 Hour Art/NT Centre for Contemporary Art
Dimy Lane
PARAP 0820
Ph. (089) 81 5368

Glossary

aesthetics the study of beauty and the appreciation of the arts

alla prima a spontaneous and immediate painting technique where paint is applied directly on to the canvas or board: there is no under-painting

Art Povera the use of odd, natural objects such as twigs, leaves, rocks, and so on in sculpture

avante-garde in this context, innovators in art; ultra-modern

Bloomsbury an artistic and culturally rich inner suburb of London

Bohemian in this context taken to mean a person with artistic talent who lives life in an unconventional way; flamboyant and eccentric

bust sculptured head and shoulders of a person

cupola small dome attached to a roof

facade front of a building or house

fanlight decorative, semicircular window above a door

frieze the decorative section of upper wall below the cornice; the middle section of classical entablature

gable upper triangular area of wall, which carries a pitched roof

juxtapose to place side by side

lintel a horizontal piece of wood or metal which spans a doorway or window

lunette a round or arched space in a dome or ceiling

maquette a miniature copy of a larger, finished piece of sculpture, produced by the sculptor before the finished piece is attempted

Montmartre the artistic and Bohemian centre of Paris

mullion the vertical supports in a window or part between a door and its side windows

neo-classical revival of the style derived from classical Rome and Greece, especially common in architecture

panorama a broad view in all directions

pilaster a flat column which is half buried in a wall

portico a porch supported by columns, open at least at one end

scumbling softening a colour by applying washes of opaque pigment over another colour

stucco a rough plaster finish applied to walls

Synthetic Cubism a form of Cubism in which collage is used, for example bits of fabric, newspaper, imitation wood, and so on, all attached to the work

topography a detailed description or representation on a map of a locality or district

transom the horizontal supports in a window or part between the door and the fanlight

turret a small rounded tower attached to a building

villa a country house; particularly descriptive of Italian homes

void in sculpture and architecture, a hole between two forms

Index